The Meaning of Military Victory

THE Meaning OF Military Victory

ROBERT MANDEL

Viva Books

New Delhi | Mumbai | Chennai | Kolkata | Bangalore | Hyderabad | Kochi

First Indian Edition 2008

VIVA BOOKS PRIVATE LIMITED

- 4737/23 Ansari Road, Daryaganj, New Delhi 110 002
  E-mail: vivadelhi@vivagroupindia.net, Tel. 42242200
- Plot No. 76, Service Industries, Shirvane, Sector 1, Nerul, Navi Mumbai 400 706
  E-mail: vivamumbai@vivagroupindia.net, Tel. 27721273, 27721274
- Jamals Fazal Chambers, 26 Greams Road, Chennai 600 006
  E-mail: vivachennai@vivagroupindia.net, Tel. 28290304, 28294241
- B-103, Jindal Towers, 21/1A/3 Darga Road, Kolkata 700 017
  E-mail: vivakolkata@vivagroupindia.net, Tel. 22836381, 22816713
- 7, Sovereign Park Apartments, 56-58, K. R. Road, Basavanagudi, Bangalore 560 004
  E-mail: vivabangalore@vivagroupindia.net, Tel. 26607409, 26607410
- 101-102 Mughal Marc Apartments, 3-4-637 to 641, Narayanguda, Hyderabad 500 029
  E-mail: vivahyderabad@vivagroupindia.net, Tel. 27564481, 27564482
- Beevi Towers, First Floor, SRM Road, Kaloor, Kochi 682 018, Kerala
  E-mail: vivakochi@vivagroupindia.net, Tel: 0484-2403055, 2403056

www.vivagroupindia.com

Published by arrangement with

Lynne Rienner Publishers, Inc.
1800 30th Street, Suite 314
Boulder, CO 80301
USA

ISBN-10: 81-309-0808-5
ISBN-13: 978-81-309-0808-3

Published by Vinod Vasishtha for Viva Books Private Limited, 4737/23, Ansari Road, Daryaganj, New Delhi-110 002. Printed and bound by Anand Sons, Delhi - 110 092

Contents

Figures

Preface

My desire to write this book stemmed from the widespread controversies in the aftermath of recent wars about whether victory was achieved, what victory means, and whether the sacrifice for victory was warranted. I became intrigued with the intellectual puzzles surrounding meaningful triumph in modern warfare, and without any polemical preconceptions about the utility of war or the attainability of victory in the current global security environment, I set out on this fascinating quest. My hope is that the results of my investigation will not only shed significant new light on the topic, but also help those in positions of responsibility to grapple successfully with a complex set of emerging threats.

The book reflects a fresh, integrative look at victory, probing the meaning of the concept and analyzing the pitfalls and opportunities surrounding the pursuit of war-winning and peace-winning strategies. My goal is to refine our understanding of postwar triumph so as to maximize success and minimize humiliating and costly failure. I focus on international warfare (including wars involving nonstate actors) because international violence appears to embody the greatest risks in the pursuit of victory. Though I include discussion of the vital historical context, as well as examples of victory from a variety of time periods, I concentrate on the post–Cold War application of notions of victory because of the need to gain insight relevant to current and emerging security threats. My analysis tilts toward the United States and the West because of their global power dominance.

This work is designed to speak to both international relations scholars and national security policymakers about the opportunities and limits surrounding victory in warfare. I believe that bridging the gap between academic and government security studies is absolutely crucial: first, to increase sensitivity on both sides to the differing perspectives involved, and second, to allow each group to benefit directly from the findings of the other. I hope that this book serves to further that end.

* * *

As with my previous books, this study reflects years of pondering. During those years, I have had conversations with many colleagues in both academic and policy settings who have significantly contributed to my thinking, and I wish to thank them all, as well as the anonymous reviewers of my manuscript. Deserving special mention here is Dominic Johnson, whose investigation of victory and defeat along very different lines fostered a fantastic opportunity for the fruitful mutual exchange of ideas. A wonderful student research assistant, Durban Swartz, helped me to crystallize some of the complex arguments presented in the pages that follow.

This book is dedicated to those policymakers who endeavor to the best of their abilities to pursue victory in wars aimed at protecting their citizenry and enhancing global stability. Although at times their pursuit may be misguided, and peaceful avenues to resolving disputes may be preferable, the nobility of this goal in the minds of those who strive to accomplish it should not be underestimated.

—Robert Mandel

1

Introduction: Military Victory and Strategic Victory

Over the ages, the central thrust in waging war has been clear—as General Douglas MacArthur put it so succinctly, "in war there is no substitute for victory."[1] Victory has the capacity to "influence the destiny of nations, shaping alliance behavior, perceptions of credibility and resolve, post-conflict expectations, and notions of revenge."[2] Yet across time, circumstance, and culture, victory has had dissimilar and often unclear and contradictory meanings for winners and losers.[3] This first chapter reviews the definitional morass surrounding victory, splits the concept into two parts, and identifies the elements of strategic victory.

Regardless of the margin of victory, especially after the end of the Cold War it has been rare for military triumphs in battle to yield substantial postwar payoffs. From the viewpoint of soldiers, fighting in a war inevitably entails intense physical and psychological devastation, whereby those in the military suffer the loss of loved ones and jolting disruption to their family life. So it is no surprise that a common hope among those who put their lives on the line is to end such violence on terms that make the bloody effort worth the huge sacrifices. When such terms are not clearly articulated or achieved, a depressing sense of futility can ensue. From the viewpoint of political leaders, an inadequate understanding of the complexities surrounding victory can result in decisionmaking paralysis, embarrassment, and loss of internal and external support, escalating postwar violence, pyrrhic triumphs, and ultimately foreign policy failure.[4] Due to the increasing interconnectedness of foreign and domestic policy, difficulties surrounding victory in external war can sometimes even affect internal security. Both sympathetic and unsympathetic onlookers hold these leaders accountable to demonstrate that the benefits of military battle dramatically outweigh the costs. Often the absence of decisive victory after war has ultimately led to removal of heads of state from office.

Uniqueness of This Line of Inquiry

A broad survey of holes in the existing literature highlights how ripe the topic of victory is for investigation. Existing theory on war termination, despite renewed interest in recent years, is still decidedly underdeveloped. Most discussions of victory are case-specific, emphasizing the historical issues surrounding the outcome in a particular conflict or narrow set of conflicts rather than providing a broad conceptual treatment of the topic. Academic analyses of warfare have focused much more heavily on the causes of war or the prevention of war than on the outcome and aftermath of war; and military treatises have emphasized specific strategies and tactics for fighting wars rather than war termination challenges. Indeed, "perhaps the least understood, and certainly the least studied, aspect of wars is how they end"; and as a result "the most difficult problem caused by contemporary warfare, all in all, is the difficulty of achieving a stable, secure ending to it."[5] Although many in one way or another "have sought to identify the elements of victory," considerable ambiguity has characterized this quest.[6] In the wake of the heated debate about the outcome of the 2003 Iraq War, most recent discussion centers more on techniques of postwar reconstruction and nation building than on the more immediate prior questions concerning the changing meaning, misperception, and management challenges surrounding victory itself.

What makes this book different is not just that it addresses a key gap in the literature on war and takes a broad conceptual look at the topic of victory. Indeed, this study is highly unusual in that rather than simply blithely providing an overarching definition of victory, it first splits the notion between military and strategic victory; rather than looking at victory challenges in a vacuum, it contrasts modern victory and premodern victory and identifies state-level deficiencies in the West and system-level deficiencies in the global "rules of the game" that impede the achievement of meaningful victory; rather than simply discussing the abstract virtues of victory notions, it examines exasperating misconceptions surrounding victory and specific conditions under which strategic victory is likely to follow military victory; rather than just analyzing current conventional warfare, it explores ongoing and future unconventional warfare; and rather than just enumerating limitations and drawbacks to prevailing ideas about victory, it actually suggests some specific ways of overcoming these obstacles.

This book's analysis of victory has direct implications for other important international security issues. The questions raised encompass such intertwined topics as the nature of modern warfare and battlefield strategies, civil-military relations, the value of weapons technology, the clarity of international communication, the prerequisites for international legitimacy, the role of force in international relations, the effectiveness of deterrence, the changing nature of emerging threats, the tradeoff between morality and stability, the role of democracy in restraining coercive activity, and the emergence of global security norms. The study also raises broader questions about when military initiatives of any kind have the greatest chance of being successful in today's daunting anarchic global setting.

Looking at victory now seems particularly important because of the sharp disagreements surrounding the proper goals or payoffs of war and the ways of assessing whether these goals or payoffs have been achieved. As with every field of human endeavor, being successful is most likely if complete clarity exists about the meaning of success; without a clear strategy with clear goals in a war, "there is no good way to gauge progress."[7] Particularly for the soldier on the battlefield, understanding what is meant by mission success is vital: as retired US Army colonel Bill Taylor pleads, "give us a definition of victory, what would it look like when we get there, and we can do it."[8] Armed with widely varying notions of victory, scholars and policymakers talk past each other and seem unable to establish common understandings even in interpreting the outcomes of recent violent conflicts. Indeed, it is most common for the concept of victory to be bandied about quite loosely, with a tacit assumption that everyone understands what it means and yet without any precise definition at all.

At the present time, given the dismal post–Cold War pattern of war outcomes, security policymakers are struggling to discover how to achieve political payoffs following military success on the battlefield. In so many predicaments of late, military victory seems to have been squandered in the aftermath of war. In many cases, triumph in violent conflict has appeared in the long run not to achieve any fundamental positive changes, or, worse, to cause an already unstable situation to deteriorate further. The net result has been that both one's domestic public and international onlookers begin to exhibit skepticism about whether a war effort was really worth it. This growing disaffection surrounding the war effort tends to intensify even further if a military victor has found itself shackled with onerous postwar obligations in the vanquished state, unable to extract itself easily or quickly from what may appear to be endless turmoil without significant payoff.

Prevailing global conditions have fostered a security predicament whereby major powers like the United States do not always have clear guidelines about how to judge the success or failure of a particular war or intervention. Given such confusion, it becomes difficult to judge fairly when sacrifice is warranted. Their reduced post–Cold War sense of obligation to address foreign problems has often caused these states to retreat to a position where they attempt to maintain global stability and to keep "truants" in line while minimizing their risk or commitment to engage in the kinds of unabashedly protracted and bloody confrontations necessary to achieve decisive and lasting victory. The aspiration of this book is to help put an end to the agonizingly frustrating pattern of postwar futility.

The Definitional Morass

Conflicting understandings abound of victory, and as is usual with international security terminology, traditional dictionary definitions (involving defeating enemies or succeeding in struggles) are relatively useless to resolve the differences. Similarly, political leaders' public statements about victory are vague and often exhibit a kind of Orwellian doublespeak: as Zbigniew Brzezinski notes, "We talk about liberation when it's an occupation; we talk about peace when it's war; we talk about sovereignty when it's limited authority."[9] The emergence of advanced war-fighting technologies, unorthodox forms of conflict, and intangible war objectives has fostered considerable confusion about how to assess modern victory. Uncertainty even surrounds what exactly is being protected, due to ambiguities about core national security interests impeding the identification of tangible victory yardsticks.[10]

Multiple avenues exist for judging success in the aftermath of war. Informally, military establishments talk about such metrics as "the aggression is defeated," "the enemy's war-making potential is eliminated or greatly reduced," or "the status quo ante is restored." One report more ambitiously necessitates deviation from past warlike attitudes: "Peace requires rejection of the earlier path that led to the conflict requiring intervention; after war and after military operations other than war, the military's role is to point the combatant groups away from their original path and toward more peaceful pursuits."[11] Lord Maurice Hankey has tried to summarize the elements of victory by arguing that "the first aim in war is to win, the second is to prevent defeat, the third is to shorten it, and the fourth and the most important, which must never be lost to sight, is to make a just and durable peace."[12] Some analysts suggest more specific measures: decreased insurgent strength, combat incidents, casualties among one's own soldiers, and assassination of postwar government officials; or increased successful contacts with the enemy, actionable intelligence tips from the defeated society population, and bounties offered by insurgents to kill government officials.[13] Still other victory wrinkles include whether violent fighting continues or stops; whether both belligerents remain or one is exterminated or expelled; whether one side withdraws or does not; whether the belligerents themselves resolve issues or third parties are involved; whether the defeated state citizenry accept or resist the new reality; and whether one side capitulates to the other or both negotiate a settlement.[14]

Ambiguity, Fluctuation, and Inappropriateness of Identified End State

In addressing definitional challenges, many scholars and policymakers consider victory to be achieving a predetermined fixed end state. The desired end state notion argues that victory occurs if the war outcome is more or less in correspondence with a state's previously articulated policy aims and outcomes that precipitated its entry into warfare. This approach views victory as a relationship between war aims and war outcomes, with successful outcomes of fighting necessitating satisfactory attainment of one's own war aims and, preferably, frustration of opponents' war aims.[15] An underlying assumption here is that "people seldom if ever take up arms...without intending some preferred outcome."[16] Exemplifying this approach is World War II, judged a success in the European front because of achievement of the aim of stopping the Nazis and replacing the German regime.

Virtually all governments and military establishments initiate war with some sort of predetermined objective end state identified, but frequently this is ambiguously stated at the outset; and because the course of a war may require modification of this end state and dynamic alteration of strategic war-fighting concepts in response to changing battle-space conditions, problems may emerge if the objectives either remain too static or shift too fundamentally in the course of a war.[17] Part of the underlying problem here is that victory is not always a product of premeditated strategic choice: war termination often lacks order and coherence, with the possibility of different parties ending their participation at different times; and wars rarely follow a course anticipated by the participants, as "states rarely finish wars for the same reasons they start them."[18] With an end state focus, unfortunately "military forces will rarely receive political objectives that contain the clarity they desire." General Maxwell Taylor remarks, "It is common practice for officials to define foreign policy goals in the broad generalities of peace, prosperity, cooperation, and good will—unimpeachable as ideals, but of little use in determining the specific objective we are likely to pursue and the time, place, and intensity of our efforts."[19]

Beyond ambiguity and fluctuation, measuring victory in terms of achieving war aims raises questions about their appropriateness. What if national security policymakers identify a wrong-headed end state, making its accomplishment meaningless or irrelevant to attaining their actual underlying desires in the aftermath of war? Historical cases abound where the identified war aims of victors have appeared, with the benefit of hindsight, to be misguided. For example, in the aftermath of the 1991 Gulf War, the United States appeared to satisfy many of its strategic objectives, as immediately after a decisive military victory the United States enjoyed a huge boost in international prestige, Saddam Hussein was punished, and other tyrannical despots watched all this with horror; however, these may not have been the right objectives, as they did not include regime change. Given the turmoil that quickly emerged within Iraq, regime change perhaps could have prevented the need for another war twelve years later. In such cases, should victory be judged by what the victor said it wanted to achieve, or by what the victor *should have* said it wanted to achieve?

Within the United States, political and military officials have disagreed especially after the Cold War about how to define victory:

> The deployments of the 1980s and 1990s reveal a contrast between US diplomatic strategies and military doctrine. The diplomatic strategies often began with a strategic end state of "restoring stability," at least to a point where vital US interests are no longer threatened. The enemy's defeat became a secondary issue, partially because diplomatic strategies generally rest on cooperation and consultation more than imposing a state's will.
>
> In contrast, US military doctrine held to its traditional focus on the enemy, including enemy-held objectives and enemy-utilized centers of gravity. Mission accomplishment and end state was defined in terms of defeating the enemy, leaving broader aspects of "end state" to officials at the strategic level. Most importantly, military leaders saw their respective missions as imposing US will and forcing the enemy to abandon unacceptable courses of action, rather than the strategic goal of creating stable circumstances not dependent on US forces. The net result was a shifting set of conditions for strategic objectives, leaving both military and diplomatic planners uncertain as to how to plan transition from military to diplomatic action.[20]

Moreover, in this context "the 'end-state' sought by military action was seldom clearly-defined and was often modified at mid-course."[21]

Conflicting Cost-Benefit Metrics

In contrast to utilizing fixed end-state identification to gauge victory, others emphasize attaining a fluid positive cost-benefit ratio. These analysts focus on whether war generally has been worth the effort, justifying the lives lost and money spent.[22] The NATO involvement in Kosovo in 1999 exemplifies this more flexible approach.

However, this ratio involves several potentially contradictory elements. These include whether the costs and benefits of continuing to fight are lower than the costs and benefits of ceasing to fight (determining the degree to which it is worth laying down arms and ending the pursuit of victory); whether one's postwar benefits exceed one's costs of fighting a war (determining the degree to which a net gain or loss exists for each party to the conflict); whether one's state is better off after the war than it was before the war (determining the degree to which absolute material gain exists, usually best in a non–zero-sum conflict), including whether one ends up better than what "an objective observer" might have expected; whether one's gains and losses are more advantageous than those of the adversary, including whether one prevents the other side from achieving its goals (determining the degree to which relative comparative gain exists, usually best in a zero-sum conflict); whether one's accomplishments through the use of force match one's political aims behind the use of force (determining the degree to which a desired end state has been achieved); and whether one's gains from war are greater than what could have been accomplished without war (determining the degree to which, given the opportunity costs, the war was worth fighting).[23] Figure 1.1 summarizes the complex cost-benefit calculations surrounding victory.

It is not at all clear which of these cost-benefit metrics are most critical. For example, is it more important that one wins decisively over an opponent, with the victor gaining a far greater positive payoff than the loser, or that one improves a country's predicament substantially over what it was before a war? Whereas selecting among or weighting possible cost-benefit yardsticks usually is a relatively straightforward task, in judging victory there appear to be few if any

Figure 1.1 Victory Cost-Benefit Calculus

DECIDING WHEN A WAR SHOULD END
Determining Expected Utility of Terminating War

Assessing magnitude, ongoing trends, and future probability of costs and benefits pertaining to continuing to fight versus ceasing to fight

ASSESSING SUCCESS OR FAILURE OF WAR
Determining Tangible Payoffs from Undertaking War

Assessing magnitude and ongoing trends in the gap between one's own postwar benefits versus one's own war costs

Assessing magnitude and ongoing trends in the gap between one's own postwar outcomes versus one's own prewar conditions

Assessing magnitude and ongoing trends in the gap between one's own postwar outcomes versus the enemy's postwar outcomes

Assessing magnitude and ongoing trends in the gap between one's own postwar outcomes versus one's own war aims

Assessing magnitude and ongoing trends in the gap between one's own postwar outcomes versus one's probable outcomes using approaches other than war objective criteria for ranking their importance or choosing some over others.

For the United States, special obstacles exist to balanced wartime cost-benefit analysis. In what some call "the new American way of war," spurred on by the quest to maintain domestic support for war efforts, the heavy tilt has seemed to be on cost minimization, avoiding extensive carnage or long-term commitment:

> Spurred by dramatic advances in information technology, the US military has adopted a new style of warfare that eschews the bloody slogging matches of old. It seeks a quick victory with minimal casualties on both sides. Its hallmarks are speed, maneuver, flexibility, and surprise. It is heavily reliant on precision firepower, special forces, and psychological operations.[24]

Indeed, leaders' wartime overattentiveness to such costs may skew weighing of broader costs and benefits:

> A strong aversion to casualties is rooted in American history and culture. Americans value the individual much more than they do the state, and they have always sought—and with considerable success it might be added—to substitute technology for blood in battle. But only recently has aversion become, at least in the minds of those making war and peace decisions, a phobia—i.e., an aversion so strong as to elevate the safety of American troops above the missions they are assigned to accomplish.[25]

The result of this skewing can be labeling a war outcome as a victory simply because its costs are low, even if benefits are close to nonexistent.

Inherent Subjectivity of Victory

Whether the focus is on a fixed end state or a fluid cost-benefit ratio, complicating matters is the seemingly inescapable *subjectivity* of victory, wherein objective criteria such as material gains and losses and tangibly satisfying stated aims seem to be playing less of a role.[26] Instead, perceptual bias and manipulation appear to dominate interpretation of military triumphs.[27] Indeed, "all students of history must be struck by the ambivalence, irony, or transience of most military victories, however spectacular and 'decisive' they appear at the time."[28] Under scrutiny, the clarity surrounding victory can vanish quickly:

> On the face of it, evaluating the winner and loser in quarrels between countries might seem to be a straightforward question: who made the greater gains in the final outcome? However, in international relations, military victory, or indeed the gain of any tangible prize at all, is neither *necessary nor sufficient* for people to think a leader has won. Not *necessary* because perceived victory can be obtained despite net losses; not *sufficient* because even substantial gains do not guarantee that people will view events as a success. Sometimes, of course, victory and perceived victory are synonymous, as in 1945. Quite often, however, one side can exploit geography, technology, and strategy to defeat an opponent militarily, yet still emerge as the perceived loser, with all the tribulations that this status involves.[29]

It is thus quite difficult within an anarchic and dynamic international security environment for most recent wars to generate widespread consensus that they ended unambiguously in either victory or defeat.

Two central roots of the differing victory interpretations are (1) the question of time span, revolving around how long after the end of major battlefield combat should one look to see if postwar payoffs have been achieved; and (2) the question of perspective, revolving around whose viewpoint should one attend to the most to determine whether victory is at hand. Most of the differences in war outcome interpretation, both at the time of the war and long afterward, stem from discrepancies in choices surrounding time span duration and viewing perspective reliance.

Looking first at the time span issue, little agreement exists about whether to emphasize short-term or long-term assessments of the outcome of warfare. For example, it is possible to question whether it is appropriate to label the outcome of World War I as victory against Germany since World War II had to be fought against the same country some twenty years later. Thus policymakers considering the victory time span issue may find that it varies significantly across situations and may need to balance the danger of using so short a perspective that contained threats may reemerge soon afterward against the danger of using so long a perspective that no war could possibly be seen as truly accomplishing its objectives.

Turning to the disagreement about whose view matters in determining victory, during no historical period has everyone pursuing victory in warfare possessed a common understanding of what it means. Some analysts feel that the perceptions of the country leaders involved in the war are all that matters; others contend that the attitudes of the domestic population, within both the winning and losing states, play a role in assessing victory; and still others assert that the views of foreign onlookers and the international community as a whole may be central. Some observers focus on just the defeated party's perspective, arguing that the war is over and victory is at hand only when the loser decides to submit to the winner's demands, thus recognizing and accepting military defeat; others contend that this focus is foolish because the winning state can easily raise its demands once it realizes its advantage, and they often more generally assert that the winner in battle can hegemonically impose its view of the outcome on outsiders.[30] Looking back over "the history of the twentieth century suffices to remind us that many ways exist to win a war, various ways are not equivalent, and final victory does not necessarily belong to the side that dictates the conditions of peace."[31]

With differences in time span and viewing perspective, certain general perceptual patterns about victory rise to the surface. States may differ markedly from nonstate groups in their views of victory: "unlike traditional adversaries, these non-state entities seek victory by avoiding defeat," as "simply surviving is an indicator of success."[32] As a result, disruptive nonstate forces in the international system can as easily label military defeat as political victory—with credibility in the eyes of regional onlookers—as they can label terrorists as freedom fighters. Similarly, when comparing perspectives on victory across culture, more powerful and dominant cultures may see victory as a way of offensively establishing hegemony and control, whereas weaker and more peripheral cultures may see victory as a way of defensively maintaining sovereignty and warding off external interference. This cultural difference may often cause strong states to anticipate a significantly larger postwar payoff from victory than weak states.

The time span and viewing perspective differences also have led to opposing victory interpretations in recent international clashes, exemplified even by looking at the success of just one country—the United States—during the post–Cold War period. Colin Gray argues, "with the exception of the Somalia debacle of 1993–94, the United States enjoyed a decade of all but unalloyed strategic success; from the Gulf War in 1991, through Bosnia in 1995, to Kosovo in 1999, concluding (after a fashion) with Afghanistan in 2001–02, the United States achieved fair facsimiles of victory."[33] In contrast, Jeffrey Record contends, "the paradox of American power at the start of the

21st century" is "the superpower's staggering prowess at winning wars and its equally remarkable ineptitude at securing the peace," reflecting at least in part "civilian decision-makers' failure to accord war termination adequate priority" and "the professional military's disdain for so-called operations other than war, especially those entailing peacemaking and nation-building responsibilities."[34]

Decline in the Occurrence of Clear-Cut Victory

Paralleling these conceptual difficulties in assessing victory related to the end state, cost-benefit assessment, and embedded subjectivity, there has been an observable operational decline in the proportion of wars in which there is a clear-cut winner or loser when taking into account not only triumph on the battlefield but also achievement of stated ambitions.[35] Although there may be "no permanent trend toward deterioration of the success rate of war initiators" in interstate conflict, it appears that "wars do not end the way they used to," with fewer terminating in clean decisive victory for one side over the other.[36] When considering the endings of both interstate and intrastate wars, one analyst concludes, "as outcomes go, victory and defeat may be going the way of dueling and slavery."[37] Even World War II may have ended a bit "raggedly," as it is difficult to determine exactly when and where the war was truly over on all fronts.[38] Impeding proper responses to this decline in clear-cut victory has been the reluctance of some analysts to acknowledge it: "The tendency to treat war as a zero-sum game persists in the literature on military statecraft," with "the idea that 'every war has a winner' deeply embedded in the literature on military force."[39]

One consequence of this declining definitiveness in war outcomes has been a lowered stability payoff from war, as, for example, "almost half of the international wars since World War II have been followed by renewed fighting between at least one pair of belligerents."[40] This lower stability can emerge in part from the differences between a winning state reaping the fruits of victory and the conflict region attaining stable peace. One can easily imagine a circumstance whereby a victor gains a lot from a war but the region of conflict becomes less stable as a result, with benefits to the war winner not helping—or even detracting from—the stability of the conflict zone. For example, Great Britain considered itself triumphant in the 1982 Falkland Islands war, yet Argentina was left in political shambles and had trouble getting back on its feet afterward.

Splitting Up the Concept of Victory

As a result of these conceptual and operational obstacles, a temptation exists to throw in the sponge, arguing that there is just no way to clarify the concept of victory sufficiently to make it an analytically useful lens for evaluating war outcomes. However, despite the seductive appeal of abandoning this fuzzy, contentious, and emotionally charged notion, this book instead chooses to persevere and clarify its meaning. The concept of victory has been just too central over time to scholars, heads of state, and soldiers in comprehending patterns of violent confrontation to throw it on the intellectual scrap heap and then substitute alternative terminology.

Right from the outset, the concept of victory needs to be divided into two highly interconnected yet distinct time phases. Specifically, "war is won, or lost, in two phases—military outcomes on the field of battle, and the battle to win the peace through reconstruction and reconciliation afterward; what is won on the battlefield can be lost entirely thereafter if the countries attacked are not turned into better and safer places."[41] The first phase—called here "war-winning"—occurs when a state attempts to bring a war to a successful military conclusion, affecting the mode of battle in terms of how one fights and whether one continues or ceases to fight. The second phase—called here "peace-winning" (alternatively termed stabilization, reconstruction, postconflict transition, or Phase IV operations)—occurs when a state attempts to reap the payoffs of war, affecting the mode of postcombat activities in terms of how one manages the transition afterward and whether one stays in or leaves the area where the fighting occurred. Clearly involved in this second phase is the extent to which triumph in battle can yield durable postwar stability. Many (including the United States Department of Defense) have begun calling overall success after this second phase "strategic victory."

In most warfare, practitioners have paid much more attention to the first phase than the second, with implicit downplaying of military victory simply being a means to pursue political ends:

> History shows that gaining military victory is not in itself equivalent to gaining the object of policy. But as most of the thinking about war has been done by men of the military profession there has been a very natural tendency to lose sight of the basic national object, and identify it with the military aim. In consequence, whenever war has broken out, policy has too often been governed by the military aim—and this has been regarded as an end in itself, instead of as merely a means to the end.[42]

Indeed, a classic error in warfare is "to mistake military victory for political victory" and to ignore the reality that "victory is not assured when the shooting stops."[43] In order to be counted victorious, a leader has to progress beyond military triumph to preserve the political control needed to secure an advantageous and enduring peace settlement.[44] In the end, "soldiers and statesmen must never lose sight of the fact that wars are fought to achieve political aims" and that "battlefield victories are an insufficient ingredient of a lasting peace."[45] Concentrating exclusively on military means and military success seems particularly problematic in today's world, where many of the major security threats—including disease, resource scarcity, and natural disasters—are not readily susceptible to military solutions.

Historical examples abound in which military victory has been followed by strategic failure:

> For example, Napoleon won a long series of stunning military victories but was unable or unwilling to undertake the alteration of Prussian, Austrian, or Russian societies that would have consolidated his triumphs. Similarly, in World War I the Western Allies won a clear military victory, but did not have the will to turn it into strategic victory by altering the elements of German society and culture that spawned armed aggression. In World War II, by contrast, military victory was transformed into strategic victory.[46]

Most analysts now agree that "military victories do not themselves determine the outcomes of wars; they only provide political opportunities for the victors—and even those opportunities are likely to be limited by circumstances beyond their control."[47] Indeed, success in the battlefield needs "to help shape the international or regional political environment" in ways favorable to the initiator's strategic interests."[48] Strategic victory requires considerable patience, as "while the military contest may have a finite ending, the political, social, and psychological issues may not be resolved even years after the formal end of hostilities."[49]

The United States has experienced special problems in dealing with the second strategic victory phase. American postconflict peace-winning strategies have often exhibited "poor planning, problems with relevant military force structure, and difficulties with a handover from military to civilian responsibility," a pattern that appears to ignore that "national objectives can often be accomplished only after the fighting has ceased."[50] Part of the difficulty stems from

> a persistent bifurcation in American strategic thinking—though by no means unique to Americans—in which military professionals concentrate on winning battles and campaigns, while policymakers focus on the diplomatic struggles that precede and influence, or are influenced by, the actual fighting; this bifurcation is partly a matter of preference and partly a by-product of the American tradition of subordinating military command to civilian leadership, which creates two separate spheres of responsibility, one for diplomacy and one for combat.[51]

As a result, some analysts even conclude that currently "US leaders have little if any idea how to 'attain victory' or 'restore stability' when planning military operations."[52] Simple formulas, such as "winning the peace involves aligning the 'hearts and minds' of a people with American political objectives, thus creating a politically and economically stable nation friendly to US interests," do not resolve these strategic victory shortcomings.[53]

Defining Strategic Victory

Widespread neglect of strategic victory has generated considerable ambiguity about what it really means, even among government security officials. Because of the little rigorous exploration of all the elements involved in defining strategic victory, a pressing need exists to scope it out comprehensively and place it in a practical interpretive security framework. For without clear metrics for strategic victory, facilitating the ability to judge whether any particular conflict has achieved this outcome, war seems unlikely to fulfill its postwar payoff potential.

Before dealing with strategic victory, however, military victory itself needs brief clarification. A longstanding "prime canon of military doctrine" is that "the destruction of the enemy's main forces on the battlefield constituted the only true aim in war."[54] Military victory, which in its most basic sense involves winning in combat, requires achieving predetermined battle campaign objectives, including (1) defeating aggression on terms favorable to oneself and one's allies, as quickly and efficiently as possible; (2) reducing substantially the enemy's future war-making potential; (3) setting the conditions whereby the victim of aggression is able to defend itself effectively against future threats; and (4) doing so with absolute minimum collateral damage to civilians and their infrastructures. Military victory may entail overpowering the enemy's military capacity, leaving it unable to resist one's demands, and inflicting sufficiently high costs on an enemy that it is willing to negotiate an end to hostilities on the terms one desires. Often such triumph occurs through wearing down enemies to the point where they are not able to launch any further resistance and then will accept military defeat. For any single battlefield clash, military victory entails the complete withdrawal or retreat, if not laying down arms or surrender, of enemy troops, thwarting their objectives while accomplishing one's own. For a series of battlefield clashes, military victory would entail a consistent pattern over time of enemy withdrawal, retreat, laying down arms, or surrender. It is certainly considerably easier to determine whether military victory has occurred on the battlefield than whether strategic victory has occurred after the battlefield combat is over.

Well beyond prevailing in combat on the battlefield, strategic victory entails accomplishing the short-term and long-term national, regional, and global goals for which the war was fought. To determine achievement of these goals, strategic victory is composed of interrelated informational, military, political, economic, social, and diplomatic elements. Although some or all of these elements may be applicable during internal wars, international crises, and small-scale foreign military operations, or alternatively applicable during a variety of historical periods, this definition explicitly targets international warfare during the post–Cold War global security setting, tuned particularly for the West. Each of these six elements, summarized in Figure 1.2, implicitly represents a continuum ranging from absence of strategic victory on one end to presence of strategic victory on the other.

This definition of strategic victory does not entail complete success in every element; nonetheless, because the elements are interconnected, attaining certain minimum thresholds in all seems necessary. Although a temptation may exist to scrap individual elements in cases where the costs of achieving all of them seem too high or strain domestic credibility and support, the dangers of leaving some unaddressed—and suffering cascading postwar problems as a result—outweigh these concerns. Whereas military victory in war may occur quickly at a discrete point in time, the informational, political, economic, social, and diplomatic elements are usually more drawn out, with differing achievement timetables. In sum, "peacebuilding is complex, expensive, and slow," and its goals—including security, socioeconomic development, political institution building, and reconciliation—"are like interdependent pillars; if one is weak, the whole

Figure 1.2 Defining Strategic Victory

SCALES MEASURING STRATEGIC VICTORY
FOLLOWING MILITARY VICTORY ON THE BATTLEFIELD

Information Control: the extent to which the victor maintains adequate *intelligence* about the internal and external sources of postwar disruption and its enemy's willingness to quit fighting, and protects its own information systems while manipulating or disrupting those of its enemy.

Military Deterrence: the extent to which the victor provides *military security* in the defeated state by deterring any internally or internationally belligerent parties from engaging in violent disruptive behavior due to their anticipation of subsequent punishment from the victor.

Political Self-Determination: the extent to which the victor establishes *political stability* in the defeated state by developing a duly-elected government, involving locals taking responsibility for administration, with policies favorable to the victor's core national interests.

Economic Reconstruction: the extent to which the victor solidifies assured *access to needed resources* in the defeated state and successfully engages in postwar rebuilding of the defeated state's economic infrastructure, integrating it into the regional and global economy.

Social Justice: the extent to which the victor justly *manages internal turmoil* within the defeated state, particularly volatile ethnic/religious/ nationalistic violence, transforming it in the direction of reliance on civil discourse to resolve internal and external disagreements.

Diplomatic Respect: the extent to which the victor possesses *external legitimacy,* involving reliable approval and tangible support for the war outcome from the victor's domestic public, foreign allies, international organizations, and other influential observers.

structure may collapse."[55] To determine whether strategic victory is present, one must decide (1) how long after the war, and in whose perception, judgments should be rendered, and (2) what threshold of success is minimally acceptable for each element.

The Informational Element

The informational objectives of strategic victory encompass four intertwined components maximizing the military victor's postwar control: (1) maintaining adequate intelligence on one's enemy and its internal and external supporters that might interfere with winning the peace; (2) monitoring any signals directly from one's enemy about its willingness to negotiate and/or stop fighting; (3) manipulating information received by the enemy so as to maximize the chances of its capitulation or acceptance of terms favorable to the victor; and (4) protecting one's own information, communication, and transportation systems. Thus, both offensive and defensive issues are vital to information control.

More than ever before, postwar mop-up operations require speedy and reliable data on targets, for operating blind—even when possessing overwhelming force advantages—is a sure path to failure. One thrust of this postwar intelligence effort would emphasize identifying any sources of potential disruption or insurgency that might reignite violence and instability within the defeated society. A second intelligence thrust requires hypervigilance to any signals from one's former adversaries about their willingness to negotiate and to begin to enter into constructive arrangements with the military victor that increase the chances of favorable outcomes and the prospects for stability in the area.

Influencing the information received by the enemy is also critical to strategic victory. This effort involves psychological operations (PSYOPS), spreading propaganda favorable to one's side so as to manipulate one's foe. The US Defense Department defines psychological operations as "planned operations to convey selected information and indicators to foreign audiences to influence their emotions, motives, objective reasoning and, ultimately, the behavior of foreign governments, organizations, groups or individuals."[56] After a war, in order "to gain and maintain the initiative in persuading the populace of the defeated state," a military victor "should have planned for immediate, massive 'informational assistance' in the transition phase, just as it planned for large-scale humanitarian assistance."[57] Part of this effort may involve a victor on the battlefield beginning "to revitalize its information efforts in a focused and effective way that takes advantage of tools like satellite broadcasting and the Internet while working directly in country."[58]

In parallel fashion, protecting one's own information systems while penetrating those of the enemy is vital for success. Information disruption, "often cited as the *leitmotif* of early 21st century conflict,"[59] involves corrupting, blocking, overwhelming, controlling, distorting, and leaking vital information; the techniques used include inserting false data or harmful programs, stealing valuable data or programs, eradicating data or programs, manipulating system performance, or denying system access.[60] A common notion is that "victory in information warfare depends on knowing something that your adversaries do not and using this advantage to confound, coerce, or kill them; lose the secrecy, and you lose your advantage."[61] The incentives to influence one's enemies' defense information systems in the aftermath of warfare are identical to those for protecting one's own systems: "as everyone becomes increasingly dependent on automated information systems, the value of maintaining and securing them rises; conversely, the value to an adversary of gaining access to the system, denying service and corrupting its contents, also rises."[62] One analyst quips, "if you want to shut down the free world, the way you would do it is not to send missiles over the Atlantic Ocean—you shut down their information systems and the free world will come to a screeching halt."[63] However, given backfire possibilities and modern strategic victory's aspirations (discussed later) to rehabilitate rather than devastate defeated states, any postwar use of information disruption against an enemy would need to be short-term rather than long-term and be carefully tuned so as to influence but yet not incapacitate the target.

The Military Element

The military objectives of strategic victory encompass providing postwar security in the defeated state by signaling deterrence to any belligerents, keeping them from engaging in disruptive behavior. An ideal postwar outcome might be when a vanquished state has "no significant armed opposition," "violence is ended," and external "military forces are no longer needed to provide security."[64] For accomplishing military victory to be worthwhile, particularly within an anarchic international system, triumph against one foe needs to help to restrain that foe, its supporters, and other foes in the future from engaging in internally or internationally disruptive behavior. As Thomas Schelling notes, what states wish from their military forces is "the art of coercion, of intimidation and deterrence," reflecting "the influence that resides in latent force...the bargaining power that comes from its capacity to hurt, not just the direct consequence of military action."[65] Put in more concrete terms, for strategic success the world must learn from the war that the military victor, when severely antagonized, is to be feared.

Providing security through deterrence is an essential postwar military goal to address the security vacuum that often emerges in the wake of warfare:

> Post-conflict situations, almost by definition, have at their core a security vacuum that is often the proximate cause for external intervention. Indigenous security institutions are either unable to provide security or are operating outside generally accepted norms. Security, which encompasses the provision of collective and individual security to the citizenry and to the assistors, is the foundation on which progress in the other issue areas rests. Refugees and internally displaced persons will wait until they feel safe to go home; former combatants will wait until they feel safe to lay down their arms and reintegrate into civilian life or a legitimate, restructured military organization; farmers and merchants will wait until they feel that fields, roads, and markets are safe before engaging in food production and business activity; and parents will wait until they feel safe to send their children to school, tend to their families, and seek economic opportunities.[66]

In order to reap the military deterrent fruit of triumph on the battlefield, it is important to convince through credible threat of punishment those who are capable of undertaking violent disruption that such actions would prove futile. In today's interdependent world, such an approach might persuade those who could engage in unruly behavior that "aggression would cut them off from the global economy and thus condemn them to potentially disastrous decline and isolation," causing their leaders to "recognize that any military victory would be pyrrhic."[67] This postwar deterrence effort needs to confront the major challenge that during the 1990s, "only half of the attempts to stabilize a postconflict situation and prevent a return to large-scale violence have been successful; the potential for a return to violence is so strong that, once international military forces have intervened to improve or stabilize a security situation, they are extremely difficult to extract."[68]

One question that arises about this military dimension of strategic victory is whether it matters how much sacrifice it takes to deter belligerents and achieve postwar security in the defeated state. The military victor's costs, in terms of its own assets, from a postwar military deterrence thrust could range from being very small, due to more than a little intelligence and luck, to very large, including much human loss of life and property destruction. Although ideally a military victor should suffer minimal postwar costs, lest its public opinion be inflamed, low cost is nonetheless decidedly not an absolute prerequisite for strategic victory. Similarly, attaining strategic victory does not specify any ceiling on the postwar costs shouldered by the defeated society population, in terms of casualties or property damage. Nonetheless, it is prudent during the aftermath of war to select carefully which particular weapons systems and offensive and defensive battle tactics are likely to have the greatest deterrent impact on potentially disruptive forces in and around the conflict zone, while simultaneously having the smallest chances of creating the kind of damage that would endanger the military victor's human and capital investment in the defeated state or enrage this state's citizenry in a manner that would cause further security problems.

The post–Cold War security environment poses special challenges for deterrence, as even President George W. Bush in his 2002 national security strategy doctrine admitted that "rogue" states cannot be contained or deterred.[69] Yet this "peace through strength" metric for strategic victory seems to apply well to today's major powers:

> The surest way to avoid suffering the provocations that could lead to war, as has been recognized since Roman times, lies in seizing this opportunity to rebuild the full power and credibility of American deterrence. The world must learn again that the United States, when severely antagonized, is to be feared; that it grinds its mortal enemies to powder, as it did sixty years ago; that the widespread view in extreme Islamic circles that it is cowardly, decadent, and easily intimidated by the thought of casualties is false.[70]

Although this view is certainly an extreme formulation colored by the hysteria following the September 11, 2001, attacks on the United States, it reflects the genuine need to translate military success in one war into more general restraint by potentially unruly countries in dealing with likely future tensions. Recent conventional military capability enhancements—involving intelligence sensors, defense suppression systems, and precision guidance systems—can increase the success of postwar efforts to deter violent behavior; for example, this development "adds a new and powerful dimension to the ability of the United States to deter war; while it is certainly not as powerful as nuclear weapons, it is more credible as a deterrent in some applications, particularly in regional conflicts that are vital to US national interests."[71]

The Political Element

The political objectives of strategic victory encompass achieving postwar political stability in the defeated state, with that country developing a duly-elected government—involving locals taking responsibility for administration—exhibiting policies favorable to the military victor's core national interests. In order for postwar payoffs to occur in a coherent manner, a military victor needs to have—from the outset of a war—a well-developed understanding of its political war aims, the linkages between these war aims and its core national interests, and the ways in which these war aims can be achieved through political self-determination in the vanquished state. Indeed, such an understanding can, within the military victor's state, "have a great deal to do with the willingness of the society to pay the human costs of war" and, within the defeated state, help to prevent the political transformation from going in unanticipated and undesired directions.[72]

To identify political war aims, the military victor needs a sound understanding of its preferred postwar governance structure within the vanquished state. Under the assumption that "states are not fungible, easily replaceable, or dispensable, there have to be powerful grounds for overthrowing any regime effectively governing a state, and a clear idea of how to replace it."[73] Considerable advanced planning is essential to lay the groundwork for establishing a self-determined duly-elected political regime favorable to the military victor's interests, particularly if the defeated state has had no prior experience with this kind of rule.

For strategic victory, a key ingredient making a military victor's political involvement conducive to establishing a stable defeated state regime is for locals within the defeated state to assume a major portion of the responsibility for the postwar government transition. The regime transformation could then proceed more smoothly, as it would not exclusively depend on the military victor's initiatives and would represent more of a collaborative effort. This local participation serves not only to relieve the military victor of onerous responsibilities to manage the postwar governance structure but also to increase the chances that the postwar regime will be tuned to the interests of the indigenous population. As a consequence, local involvement increases the chances that the emerging postwar regime will effectively confront postwar political challenges.

To identify core national interests, the military victor needs explicit comprehension of the geopolitical value of the target and of the fundamental political beliefs at stake, such as the protection and promotion of freedom. Western domestic populations' political intolerance of high war costs "when perceived core national interests are not at stake" underscores the need to link defeated state regime transformation to the military victor's core national interests.[74] The spread of democracy across the globe makes this articulation of core interests—and links to war aims—especially critical to justify the drive to attain postwar political objectives. In a highly porous and interconnected global environment, structural incentives exist to be honest and open about these core interests and war aims, as deceitful or disingenuous rationales may be quickly exposed. Limiting Western states' ability in recent wars to reap positive postwar political payoffs, and to provide stable political security, has been their difficulties in pinpointing core national interests or identifying appropriate means to protect these interests: "In the absence of such clarity, even the best armed forces in the world could, in the future, be sent to defeat or—worst yet—to die for trivial or peripheral purposes."[75]

The Economic Element

The economic objectives of strategic victory encompass solidifying assured postwar access to needed resources in the defeated state and successfully engaging in postwar rebuilding of the defeated state's economic infrastructure, integrating it into the regional and global economy. Whereas many economic analyses focus on monetary reparations flowing out of a defeated state in the aftermath of war, the "real test for the success" is whether the defeated society can "be rebuilt after the war" through the military victor's help.[76]

Assured access to the resources of the defeated state does not mean that the military victor plunders whatever is available there, but instead simply guarantees that the military victor will be able to purchase and trade for vital commodities or natural resources possessed by the defeated state. Resource access is often at the center of ongoing international disputes, and this has been particularly true for the West after the end of the Cold War:

> Other objectives—of a more self-interested, tangible character—have come to dominate the American strategic agenda. Among these objectives, none has so profoundly influenced American military policy as the determination to ensure US access to overseas supplies of vital resources. As the American economy grows and US industries come to rely more on imported supplies of critical

> materials, the protection of global resource flows is becoming an increasingly prominent feature of American security policy.[77]

In the aftermath of war, the military victor could also use the defeated state for vital bases, transit routes, or supply lines. Though the postwar trade relationship between winner and loser may very well end up skewed in favor of the winner, this outcome would not normally be the result of coercion. For strategic victory, then, a balance is needed in the area of resource access: a military victor should not face fewer economic opportunities after a war than before a war within a vanquished state. At the same time, the military victor's dependence on the defeated state's economic assets should not be to the degree that this becomes the primary or exclusive means to rectify its own economic failings.

Economic reconstruction of the defeated state means getting the economy to the point where it can eventually function without the influx of outside aid from the military victor. Often this involves rebuilding destroyed buildings and transportation and communication systems, as well as having the military victor help open up some businesses. Indeed, one possible gauge of whether this postwar reconstruction is successful is if foreign multinational corporations are willing to invest in the defeated country after a war ends, as such investment would be based on the country's perceived levels of economic stability, functioning business infrastructure, and future growth potential. In undertaking such reconstruction, however, there needs to be adequate discrimination between cosmetic and meaningful economic resuscitation initiatives, for victors' postwar economic reconstruction efforts within vanquished states have been "often associated with politically expedient but often superficial assistance that does not tackle the root causes of conflict."[78] Furthermore, it seems important to avoid the creation of long-term dependence by the loser on the winner for accomplishing this economic transformation.

An underlying assumption here is that without such postwar economic reconstruction, military victory would be quite a hollow experience. Winning in battle against a country whose economy is left dysfunctional would yield little of tangible benefit to the military victor and increase the likelihood of dissatisfaction among the residents of the defeated state. Moreover, in today's world the international criticism levied against a war winner that failed subsequently to aid a decimated defeated party, even if the losers had themselves been absolutely ruthless during warfare, would be sizable.

The Social Element

The social objectives of strategic victory encompass reducing postwar turmoil within the defeated state, particularly ethnic, religious, or nationalistic discord, and moving the country toward a reliance on civil discourse to resolve domestic and international disagreements. To be effective in the long term, the management of this social turmoil needs to align with widely accepted principles of justice. These principles need to take into account the perspectives of both the winner and the loser in battle.

To establish a stable and just civil society in the aftermath of war, a military victor needs to find ways within a defeated state to minimize volatile indigenous passions that trigger postwar friction. At the same time, it appears useful to fan the flames of internal antagonism toward existing violent disruptive forces in such a way that the vanquished society will appreciate, or temporarily desire, the military victor's external help in managing this internal disorder. As with political self-determination, safeguards need to exist that prevent the defeated society's social transformation from going in unanticipated and undesired directions; and as with economic reconstruction, they need to exist to prevent long-term dependence by the loser on the winner for this social transformation. Considerable societal monitoring by the military victor can help implement these safeguards.

As part of this effort to minimize turmoil and promote progressive social transformation, the winner in battle should attempt to avoid alienating the majority of the defeated state's population, in particular avoiding the inflammation of any preexisting antagonism toward the military victor, so as to reduce the psychological and social repair work needed after the war. As one analyst sagely suggests, "the essence of prudence in victory is the ability to skim off the cream of victory while causing the smallest possible increase in enmity on the part of the defeated."[79] In this regard, developing considerable cultural sensitivity, so as to lower the chances of triggering a rise in virulent nationalism and resistance against the war winner, seems essential.[80] The military victor particularly needs to avoid an image of widespread ethnocentrism and ignorance, such as what has occurred during the 2003 Iraq War, where "US soldiers and statesmen generally lack understanding of the Arab worldview," triggering close-minded anti-Western sentiments among many Arabs.[81] In its postwar security operations, a military victor should attempt to hit only vital military targets and to avoid religious shrines and other socially significant national landmarks, and to ensure the provision of humanitarian assistance to innocents affected by social turmoil. In other words, the conduct of postwar security operations needs to help facilitate postwar social rehabilitation.

If a military victor is careless in this regard, such as "where security measures are haphazardly or unevenly applied, and significant segments of the defeated state's population are antagonized by the foreign imposition of an exploitative exchange of values," then as soon as members of the defeated society have a chance, they will thwart the progressive social policies of the military victor.[82] This predicament opens the door to new divisive rifts in the defeated society. In addition, such inattentiveness can decrease the effectiveness of the military victor's postwar social justice initiatives.

The Diplomatic Element

The diplomatic objectives of strategic victory are to attain postwar external legitimacy so that reliable approval and tangible support for the war outcome are voiced by the military victor's domestic public, foreign allies, international organizations, and other important observers. Specifically, what is needed in this area of international respect is significant internal and external government and public opinion enthusiasm for the war winner's mission and success, preferably combined with global antagonism toward the defeated enemy, its supporters, and insurgencies attempting violently to disrupt postwar stability. To enhance this external support, the military victor needs to be able to influence and stabilize domestic and international public opinion.

Given the global spread of democracy, a state experiencing military success in battle would be imprudent to launch postwar initiatives that lack significant domestic and international support. If, for example, a state achieved military victory and accomplished all the postwar payoffs specified by the mission but the reactions from the domestic public, allies, and other foreign onlookers were entirely disapproving, then any claim by national leaders of strategic victory would be suspect. This diplomatic element thus requires that the military victor achieve outside understanding of, and support for, its pursuit of postwar payoffs.

Even for states experienced in managing the perceived legitimacy of their actions, obtaining outside support in the aftermath of war is often a real challenge, as "the military battle for security...often conflicts with the information battle for legitimacy."[83] Moreover, the winner is often striving to attain legitimacy in the eyes of multiple parties with conflicting interests and desires: for example, in the 2003 Iraq War, "the battle for legitimacy is compounded because the US forces are fighting to gain or maintain legitimacy in the eyes of three different constituencies: the international community, the American people, and the Iraqi people."[84] To create or maintain outside support for one's war effort, some methods to minimize the defeated society's alienation are parallel to those mentioned earlier: for example, it is possible to win the hearts and minds of a defeated state's populace by avoiding damage to civilian infrastructure from offensive military strikes or by providing relief and other benefits to civilians whose support infrastructure has been disrupted by the military victor's security operations.

Although international image may initially seem to be simply a cosmetic, superficial, and volatile phenomenon that alone cannot produce a discernible impact on strategic victory, such is far from the case. As war winds down, "if the mass publics conclude that the costs of fighting exceed the possible gains from victory, and the state cannot alter this calculus through either coercion or inducements, then the mass publics will withdraw their support for the war," significantly handicapping a military victor's chances for success.[85] Moreover, "the international community has a strong effect on belligerents' decisions about war and peace," and as a result in the aftermath of war "states worry about international audience costs."[86]

Concluding Thoughts

From a purely theoretical perspective, the portrait of strategic victory is relatively clear. Such victory entails the victor exercising full information control and military deterrence against foes; attaining stable political self-determination, economic reconstruction, and social justice within the vanquished state; and enjoying unbridled internal and external diplomatic respect. This conceptual picture may seem so self-evident that one might wonder why it is not universally in place today.

Unfortunately, as subsequent chapters will more fully reveal, in practice this ideal model of strategic victory is very difficult to realize within the current anarchic global security environment. Indeed, the impediments are so significant that it is quite difficult to find a recent case providing a textbook example to emulate. Furthermore, within a given state's security bureaucracy, different factions typically employ different metrics of success depending on their position, role, constituency, and interests, making consensus on these metrics within a country difficult. Internationally, the differences in perspective as to how to measure strategic victory are even greater, fueled by wide differences in political ideology and cultural values. Thus, taking the notion of strategic victory and having it guide war policy in today's world is a decidedly uphill battle, but one certainly worthy of the effort.

In evaluating strategic victory in the context of today's diverse set of threats, a widespread misguided tendency exists to focus only on the most visible and tangible of war outcome measures, and to try to develop deterministic formulas to apply them to actual conflicts. Indeed, many quantitative analyses of war termination appear content to rely on the most readily available, easily measurable indicators to determine whether each outcome is victory, defeat, or stalemate, ignoring in the process the particular historical and situational context as well as the distinctive intentions, goals, expectations, and desires of the leaders involved. In contrast, this study suggests that a mix of the tangible and intangible yardsticks for victory provides the best understanding. Therefore, determining whether strategic victory is present is not a simple binary "yes-no" issue: despite the common preference for precise closure and fixed algorithms in assessing such an outcome, an admixture of fluid measures appears more appropriate to capture its essence.

Close scrutiny reveals that after military victory, each element of strategic victory entails the victor delicately balancing competing postwar pressures, preventing the application of a "full-steam-ahead" pursuit of any one without a careful consideration of what is being sacrificed in the process. These balances encompass the following tradeoffs: for information control, disrupting the enemy's information systems versus improving the defeated state's capacity to function effectively; for military deterrence, imposing security versus protecting freedom; for political self-determination, ensuring favorable policies versus allowing defeated state leaders to make their own choices; for economic reconstruction, maintaining economic access versus rebuilding the economy in a manner best for the defeated state; for social justice, injecting progressive social transformation versus honoring the defeated society's long-standing cultural traditions; and, finally, for diplomatic respect, compromising core interests versus pursuing internal and external approval. Choosing how to address these balances obviously necessitates considerable skill and understanding of tradeoffs surrounding how to win the peace.

Notes

1. Douglas MacArthur, "Farewell Speech" (West Point, NY: United States Military Academy, May 12, 1962), http://www.localvoter.com/speech_dm1.asp.

2. Dominic Johnson and Dominic Tierney, *Failing to Win: Perceptions of Victory and Defeat in International Politics* (Cambridge, MA: Harvard University Press, forthcoming), chapter 1.

3. Stephen D. Biddle, *Military Power: Explaining Victory and Defeat in Modern Battle* (Princeton, NJ: Princeton University Press, 2004), chapter 1; and Victor Davis Hanson, *Why the West Has Won: Carnage and Culture from Solamis to Vietnam* (London: Faber and Faber, 2001).

4. Thomas C. Schelling, *Arms and Influence* (New Haven, CT: Yale University Press, 1966), p. 12.

5. Stuart Albert and Edward C. Luck, eds., *On the Endings of Wars* (Port Washington, NY: Kennikat Press, 1980), p. 3; and James Turner Johnson, *Morality and Contemporary Warfare* (New Haven, CT: Yale University Press, 1999), p. 191.

6. John I. Alger, *The Quest for Victory: The History of the Principles of War* (Westport, CT: Greenwood Press, 1982), p. 173.

7. Andrew F. Krepinevich Jr., "How to Win in Iraq," *Foreign Affairs* 84 (September/October 2005), p. 87.

8. John Diedrich, "War Far from Over on Anniversary of Bush Announcement," *Journal-Sentinel,* April 30, 2004.

9. Zbigniew Brzezinski, *PBS Online News Hour,* "Transfer of Power in Iraq," June 28, 2004, http://www.pbs.org/newshour/bb/middle_east/jan-june04/sovereignty_6-28.html.

10. Robert Mandel, "What Are We Protecting?" *Armed Forces & Society* 22 (Spring 1996), pp. 335–355; and Center for Strategic and International Studies and Association of the United States Army, *Building Better Foundations: Security in Post-Conflict Reconstruction* (Washington, DC: Center for Strategic and International Studies and Association of the United States Army, 2002), p. 2.

11. Manfred K. Rotermund, *The Fog of Peace: Finding the End-State of Hostilities* (Carlisle Barracks, PA: US Army War College Strategic Studies Institute, 1999), pp. 1–2.

12. Maurice Hankey, *Politics, Trials, and Errors* (Oxford: Pen-in-Hand, 1950), pp. 26–27, as quoted in Richard Hobbs, *The Myth of Victory: What Is Victory in War?* (Boulder, CO: Westview Press, 1979), p. 5.

13. Krepinevich, "How to Win in Iraq," pp. 100–103.

14. Paul R. Pillar, *Negotiating Peace: War Termination as a Bargaining Process* (Princeton, NJ: Princeton University Press, 1983), p. 14.

15. Berenice A. Carroll, "How Wars End: An Analysis of Some Current Hypotheses," *Journal of Peace Research* 6 (1969), p. 305; William T. R. Fox, "The Causes of Peace and Conditions of War," *Annals of the American Academy of Political and Social Science* 392 (November 1970), p. 2; Dominic D. P. Johnson and Dominic Tierney, "Essence of Victory: Winning and Losing International Crises," *Security Studies* 13 (Winter 2003/2004), p. 352; and Raymond G. O'Connor, "Victory in Modern War," *Journal of Peace Research* 6 (1969), p. 376.

16. Michael Howard, "When Are Wars Decisive?" *Survival* 41 (Spring 1999), p. 126.

17. On predetermined objective end states see, for example, Carl Osgood, "Bush Administration's Strategic Policy Creates a Conundrum for US Military," *Executive Intelligence Review* 32 (May 20, 2005), http://www.larouchepub.com/other/2005/3220war_games.html.

18. G. John Ikenberry, *After Victory: Institutions, Strategic Restraint, and the Rebuilding of Order after Major Wars* (Princeton, NJ: Princeton University Press, 2001), p. 257; Fred Charles Ikle, *Every War Must End* (New York: Columbia University Press, 1991); and Albert and Luck, pp. 3, 4–5.

19. Quoted in William Flavin, "Planning for Conflict Termination and Post-Conflict Success," *Parameters* 32 (Autumn 2003), pp. 97–98.

20. David J. Bame, "The Exit Strategy Myth and the End State Reality" (Washington, DC: unpublished US State Department paper, 2001), pp. 42–43.

21. Andrew J. Bacevich, "'Splendid Little War': America's Persian Gulf Adventure Ten Years On," in Andrew J. Bacevich and Ephraim Inbar, eds., *The Gulf War of 1991 Reconsidered* (Portland, OR: Frank Cass, 2003), p. 154.

22. Lieutenant Colonel Joseph L. Osterman, *Then and Now: A Strategic Primer for Post-Conflict Activities* (Carlisle Barracks, PA: US Army War College Strategy Research Project, 2000), p. 1.

23. B. H. Liddell Hart, *Strategy* (New York: Penguin, 1991), p. 357; and Johnson and Tierney, "Essence of Victory," p. 352; Carroll, "How Wars End," p. 305; and Monica Duffy Toft, "End of Victory? Civil War Termination in Historical Perspective" (paper presented at the annual national meeting of the International Studies Association, Honolulu, March 2005), p. 6.

24. Max Boot, "The New American Way of War," *Foreign Affairs* 82 (July/August 2003), p. 42.

25. Jeffrey Record, "Collapsed Countries, Casualty Dread, and the New American Way of War," *Parameters* (Summer 2002), p. 12.

26. Dominic Tierney and Dominic Johnson, "Winning and Losing the War on Terror" (paper presented at the annual meeting of the International Studies Association, Honolulu, March 2005), pp. 36–37.

27. Johnson and Tierney, "Essence of Victory," p. 350.

28. Brian Bond, *The Pursuit of Victory: From Napoleon to Saddam Hussein* (New York: Oxford University Press, 1996), p. 1.

29. Johnson and Tierney, *Failing to Win*, chapter 1.

30. H. C. Calahan, *What Makes a War End?* (New York: Vanguard Press, 1944), pp. 18–19; Berenice A. Carroll, "Victory and Defeat: The Mystique of Dominance," in Albert and Luck, *On the Endings of Wars*, pp. 51, 69–70; and H. E. Goemans, *War and Punishment: The Causes of War Termination and the First World War* (Princeton, NJ: Princeton University Press, 2000), pp. 4–7.

31. Raymond Aron, *Peace and War: A Theory of International Relations* (Garden City, NY: Doubleday, 1966), p. 577.

32. Steven Metz and Raymond A. Millen, *Future War/Future Battlespace: The Strategic Role of American Landpower* (Carlisle Barracks, PA: US Army War College Strategic Studies Institute, 2003), pp. viii, 12.

33. Colin S. Gray, *Defining and Achieving Decisive Victory* (Carlisle Barracks, PA: US Army War College Strategic Studies Institute, 2002), p. 4.

34. Jeffrey Record, *Dark Victory: America's Second War against Iraq* (Annapolis, MD: Naval Institute Press, 2004), pp. 118, 153.

35. Page Fortna, "Where Have All the Victories Gone? War Outcomes in Historical Perspective" (paper presented at the annual meeting of the International Studies Association, Honolulu, March 2005), p. 32.

36. Kevin Wang and James Lee Ray, "Beginners and Winners: The Fate of Initiators of Interstate Wars Involving Great Powers since 1495," *International Studies Quarterly* 38 (March 1994), p. 150.

37. Toft, "End of Victory?" p. 2.

38. A. J. P. Taylor, *How Wars End* (London: Hamish Hamilton, 1985), p. 103.

39. David A. Baldwin, "The Sanctions Debate and the Logic of Choice," *International Security* 24 (Winter 1999/2000), p. 94.

40. Virginia Page Fortna, *Peace Time: Cease-Fire Agreements and the Durability of Peace* (Princeton, NJ: Princeton University Press, 2004), p. 1.

41. Robert C. Orr, "After the War, Bring in a Civilian Force," *International Herald Tribune*, April 3, 2003, p. 8.

42. Liddell Hart, *Strategy*, p. 338.

43. Hanson W. Baldwin, *Great Mistakes of the War* (New York: Harper and Brothers, 1950), pp. 107–108; and Metz and Millen, *Future War/Future Battlespace*, p. 22.

44. Bond, *The Pursuit of Victory*, pp. 201–202.

45. Thomas G. Mahnken, "A Squandered Opportunity? The Decision to End the Gulf War," in Bacevich and Inbar, *The Gulf War of 1991 Reconsidered*, pp. 122, 123.

46. Metz and Millen, *Future War/Future Battlespace*, pp. 22–23.

47. Howard, "When Are Wars Decisive?" p. 130.

48. Michael P. Noonan and John Hillen, "The New Protracted Conflict: The Promise of Decisive Action," *Orbis* 46 (Spring 2002), p. 236.

49. Albert and Luck, *On the Endings of Wars*, pp. 3, 5.

50. Conrad C. Crane and W. Andrew Terrill, *Reconstructing Iraq: Insights, Challenges, and Missions for Military Forces in a Post-Conflict Scenario* (Carlisle Barracks, PA: US Army War College Strategic Studies Institute, 2003), pp. v, 1.

51. Antulio J. Echevarria II, *Toward an American Way of War* (Carlisle Barracks, PA: US Army War College Strategic Studies Institute, 2004), p. 7.

52. Bame, "The Exit Strategy Myth and the End State Reality," p. 44.

53. Justin Gage, William Martin, Tim Mitchell, and Pat Wingate, "Winning the Peace in Iraq: Confronting America's Informational and Doctrinal Handicaps" (Norfolk, VA: Joint Forces Staff College, September 5, 2003), p. 1, http://www.jfsc.ndu.edu/current_students/documents_policies/documents/jca_cca_awsp/Winning_the_Peace_in_Iraq.doc.

54. Liddell Hart, *Strategy,* p. 339.

55. Dan Smith, *The Penguin Atlas of War and Peace* (New York: Penguin Books, 2003), p. 107.

56. Joint Publication 1-02, *Department of Defense Dictionary of Military and Associated Terms* (Washington, DC: Government Printing Office, 1994).

57. Gage, Martin, Mitchell, and Wingate, "Winning the Peace in Iraq," p. 11.

58. Anthony H. Cordesman, *The "Post Conflict" Lessons of Iraq and Afghanistan* (Washington, DC: Center for Strategic and International Studies), 2004, p. v.

59. Martin C. Libicki, "Information War, Information Peace," *Journal of International Affairs* 51 (Spring 1998), pp. 411–412.

60. Richard O. Hundley and Robert H. Anderson, "Emerging Challenge: Security and Safety in Cyberspace," in John Arquilla and David Ronfeldt, eds., *In Athena's Camp: Preparing for Conflict in the Information Age* (Santa Monica, CA: RAND Corporation, 1997), p. 231.

61. Bruce D. Berkowitz, "War Logs On: Girding America for Computer Combat," *Foreign Affairs* 79 (May/June 2000), pp. 8–12.

62. Libicki, "Information War, Information Peace," pp. 416–417.

63. Joe Havely, "Why States Go to Cyber-War," February 16, 2000, http://news.bbc.co.uk/1/hi/sci/tech/642867.stm.

64. Lieutenant Colonel James M. Castle and Lieutenant Colonel Alfred C. Faber Jr., *Anarchy in the Streets: Restoring Public Security in Complex Contingencies* (Carlisle Barracks, PA: US Army War College Strategy Research Project, 1998), p. 3; and Anthony H. Cordesman, *Iraq and Conflict Termination: The Road to Guerrilla War?* (Washington, DC: Center for Strategic and International Studies, 2003), p. 23.

65. Schelling, *Arms and Influence*, p. 34.

66. Center for Strategic and International Studies and Association of the United States Army, *Play to Win: Final Report of the Bi-Partisan Commission on Post-Conflict Reconstruction* (Washington, DC: Center for Strategic and International Studies and Association of the United States Army, 2003), p. 13.

67. Metz and Millen, *Future War/Future Battlespace*, p. 6.

68. Center for Strategic and International Studies and Association of the United States Army, *Building Better Foundations*, p. 2.

69. James Fallows, "Blind into Baghdad," *Atlantic Monthly* 293 (January/February 2004), p. 56. See also Robert Mandel, *The Changing Face of National Security: A Conceptual Analysis* (Westport, CT: Greenwood Press, 1994), p. 24.

70. Conrad Black, "What Victory Means," *National Interest* (Winter 2001/2002), p. 156.

71. William J. Perry, "Desert Storm and Deterrence in the Future," in Joseph S. Nye Jr. and Roger K. Smith, eds., *After the Storm: Lessons from the Gulf War* (Lanham, MD: Madison Books, 1992), p. 241.

72. Scott Sigmund Gartner and Gary M. Segura, "War, Casualties, and Public Opinion," *Journal of Conflict Resolution* 42 (June 1998), p. 298.

73. Paul W. Schroeder, "The Risks of Victory," *National Interest* (Winter 2001/2002), p. 31.

74. Piers Robinson, *The CNN Effect: The Myth of News, Foreign Policy, and Intervention* (New York: Routledge, 2002), p. 40.

75. Alvin Toffler and Heidi Toffler, *War and Anti-War* (New York: Warner Books, 1993), p. 215.

76. Minxin Pei and Sara Kasper, *Lessons from the Past: The American Record on Nation Building* (Washington: Carnegie Endowment for International Peace Policy Brief No. 24, May 2003), p. 1.

77. Michael T. Klare, *Resource Wars: The New Landscape of Global Conflict* (New York: Henry Holt and Company, 2001): pp. 5–7; see also Robert Mandel, *Conflict Over the World's Resources* (Westport, CT: Greenwood Press, 1988).

78. Matthias Stiefel, "Rebuilding after War: Lessons from WSP" (Geneva, Switzerland: War-Torn Societies Project, 1999), http://wsp.dataweb.ch/wsp_publication/rebu-05.htm.

79. Nissan Oren, "Prudence in Victory," in Nissan Oren, ed., *Termination of Wars: Processes, Procedures, and Aftermaths* (Jerusalem: Magnes Press, 1982), p. 150.

80. Peter Liberman, *Does Conquest Pay? The Exploitation of Occupied Industrial Societies* (Princeton, NJ: Princeton University Press, 1996), pp. 19, 31.

81. Gage, Martin, Mitchell, and Wingate, "Winning the Peace in Iraq," pp. 1–2.

82. Jay L. Kaplan, "Victor and Vanquished: Their Postwar Relations," in Albert and Luck, *On the Endings of Wars*, p. 83.

83. Gage, Martin, Mitchell, and Wingate, "Winning the Peace in Iraq," p. 4.

84. Ibid.

85. Allan C. Stam III, *Win, Lose, or Draw: Domestic Politics and the Crucible of War* (Ann Arbor: University of Michigan Press, 1996), p. 59.

86. Fortna, *Peace Time*, p. 213.

2

Modern Victory in Historical Context

To understand the concept of strategic victory in today's global security setting requires a knowledge of history. Looking back across time, there appears to be a significant difference between premodern war and modern war. Even though categories of war are continually merging and transforming, these two general war classifications stand out in the full victory continuum, ranging from total annihilation on one end to just a slight alteration in an opponent's policies on the other.[1] With the goal of isolating modern victory's peculiarities, this chapter discusses informational, military, political, economic, social, and diplomatic dimensions—paralleling the strategic victory elements discussed in Chapter 1—of the divide between premodern and modern triumph.

Premodern Total War Versus Modern Limited War

Temporal differences in victory notions cluster around the total war/limited war distinction. Total war occurred more in ancient times, whereas limited war is more of a modern phenomenon. However, exceptions to this pattern certainly exist: despite the recent popularity of limited war, it occurred in previous eras (such as during the eighteenth century), and total war has more than once reared its head during modern times (such as World War II and the 1980–1988 Iraq-Iran War). It is impossible to identify a precise date that splits premodern from modern warfare; instead, distinctive modes of military thinking separate them.

Many ways exist to distinguish between premodern total and modern limited war, but this study explains the distinction in terms of *contrasting motives, strategy and tactics,* and *expected outcomes surrounding warfare.* The motivational split relates to whether the belligerents involved are rigidly pursuing decisive strategic triumph entailing the elimination of an enemy as a political entity, or alternatively more flexibly open to political compromise, allowing the continued existence of a rehabilitated enemy state. The difference in strategy and tactics relates to whether the belligerents use everything at their disposal to fight a war or alternatively hold back some capabilities: this involves the extent to which all military technology is utilized, with the possibility of retaining weapons of mass destruction such as nuclear weapons; "the degree of popular involvement in the conduct of the war," with the possibility of keeping large sectors of the civilian population insulated from such involvement; and, most generally, the proportion of a belligerent's total "material resources mobilized, consumed, and destroyed in war."[2] The expected outcome divide relates to the zero-sum or non–zero-sum nature of war outcomes, reflected by the degree to which one belligerent expects to succeed in enhancing its military and political position directly at the other's expense.[3]

Premodern total war victory involves "complete defeat of the enemy," in which the winner "is able to resolve the conflicts by *completely* eradicating" the opposition by winning it over, removing it, or causing it to surrender.[4] Specifically, total war's goal is "to remove completely the enemy government or even to extinguish any trace of the enemy as a separate nation."[5] Often the justification for total war victory is passionate and emotional belief in the virtue of one's cause and the demonic nature of one's foe.[6] In addition to a commanding military advantage, total war victory assumes the presence of absolute political control: "The statesman must be in a position to end hostilities at an opportune moment; persuade the beaten enemy to accept the verdict of battle; and reach a settlement which is not only acceptable to the warring parties, but also to other interested parties who may otherwise interfere to overthrow the settlement and perhaps even combine against the victor."[7]

Exemplifying this rather ruthless mode of victory, terminating violent conflicts "symbolized by the images of 'blood and iron' the West now allegedly abhors," are wars that occurred well prior to the emergence of the modern nation-state system.[8] As Brian Bond writes, "In classical warfare, battles seldom lasted for longer than a single day and were frequently 'decisive' in the sense that one side was defeated on the field, harried and slaughtered while retreating, and deprived of any capacity to offer further resistance."[9] This decidedly primitive approach is perhaps best illustrated by the Roman strategy to eradicate Carthage during the Third Punic War (149–146 B.C.), showing that at least in the short-term, annihilation and brutality can lead to total control, albeit at great cost:

> A Carthaginian peace can only be maintained at great cost to both the victor and the vanquished. In the victor state, these costs are likely to breed dissatisfaction and factiousness that weaken its security posture. In the vanquished state, these costs are likely to breed a spirit of resistance and revenge that will further strain the resources and resolve of the victor.[10]

Many centuries later, the Napoleonic style of military campaign—"obtained by the destruction of the enemy in a decisive battle"—continued this strategy.[11] It is, of course, possible to have total war without total victory: as Bruce Walker writes, "total war means undertaking every action available and all the strength of the nation to win a conflict," whereas "total victory means that the conclusion of the conflict utterly confirms the will of the victors."[12]

In contrast, limited modern war victory emphasizes "more subtle applications of military force" in which limited war—"armed conflict short of general war...involving the overt engagement of the military forces of two or more nations"—becomes primarily a diplomatic instrument whereby military forces are used more for signaling than for fighting, and decisive military outcomes are neither necessary nor even desirable.[13] Looking back through the history of war, more conflicts have involved participants with limited political aims than with total victory ambitions.[14] It is, however, apparent that victory in limited war is trickier to demarcate—and often to achieve—than in total war:

> A limited war is more likely to result in a standoff or stalemate between two warring states since the level of destruction itself has to be carefully controlled. Clausewitz' dictum of targeting the will of the nation and destruction of its military power, therefore, can be fulfilled only partially. This is also a reason for some countries seeking to conduct an asymmetric war by using the weapon of terror. The problem is that as war starts to move down the intensity spectrum, victory and defeat shift more into political and psychological dimensions. And, between a bigger country and a smaller country, a standoff in a limited war is likely to create the image of the smaller country having won.[15]

The concept of limited war explicitly entails the use of limited motives and means and the expectation of limited (and uncertain) outcomes, whereby war participants prefer compromise or minimal gains to going beyond a certain level of cost.[16] Under limited war precepts, "the goal of force may be not annihilation or attrition but calibrated 'elimination of the enemy's resistance' by the careful and proportional use of counterviolence."[17]

Of course, such a war may not always remain limited. Indeed, "there are not guarantees that limited objectives will stay limited once the anticipated costs of achieving them plummet," and belligerents who learn they are stronger than they previously estimated may expand their war aims.[18] All in all, the potential to misperceive or misinterpret both the motivations and outcomes surrounding limited war is quite high.

Especially since the mid-nineteenth century, it has become quite difficult to fight and win traditional total war: military commanders have found it increasingly tough "to win victories which were 'decisive,' in the sense that they annihilated the enemy's main army or battle fleet to the extent of making further organized resistance impossible," because of "the revolution in fire-power, the rapid spread of railways and the telegraph, and perhaps most significant of all, the ability of industrialized nation states to raise and maintain huge conscript armies and echelons of reserves," all of which suggest that wars would be decided more by attrition than by decisive battles.[19] Quincy Wright posits that "since 1920, the concept and practice of war have changed radically."[20] Other scholars move the date to more recently, after 1945, when "the traditional belief in the possibility of 'victory' in warfare has been most seriously undermined by the existence of nuclear weapons in control of more than one power," with such weapons decreasing the chances of truly decisive military outcomes.[21]

Aside from the spread of advanced war-fighting technologies, other elements have conspired against the recent viability of traditional total war victory. In the era of democracy, "wars may have been harder to begin but have also been very much harder to bring to an end," as the norms of civil discourse and tolerance for disagreement embedded in democracy make it hard to conceive of annihilating a threatening society, while simultaneously increasing sensitivity to the international community's adverse reaction to such a move.[22] In addition, the spread of interdependence and globalization has impeded fighting and winning total war because one would rarely desire the utter destruction of a country from which you receive vital needs.

The American public has traditionally preferred the clarity of traditional total war but in recent decades has had to cope with the gray shadings of limited modern war:

> Americans prefer a "strategy of annihilation"—unconditional surrender, total defeat of the enemy, complete victory for our side. This is how Americans fought their "big" wars: the Civil War, WWI, and WWII. But Americans, particularly since 1945, have fought in many limited wars: from Greece and Turkey, through Korea, through the Dominican Republic, Vietnam, into Grenada, El Salvador, Panama, the Persian Gulf, Somalia, and finally ending up in the Balkans and Iraq.[23]

Particularly during the 2003 Iraq War, the limited nature of the objectives has been troublesome to many Americans, doggedly "sticking to their victory-at-all-costs tradition":

> George Bush is engaged in one of the most difficult tasks of any American president: maintaining domestic support for a limited war. History teaches that Americans are prepared to accept and inflict massive casualties in pursuit of victory (witness the campaign against Japan in the Second World War). But as both the Vietnam quagmire and the first Gulf War suggest, they are much more nervous about backing a government perceived to be pursuing half-hearted aims.[24]

The greatest military power in the world has had considerable difficulty achieving strategic victory in limited war, and yet onlookers (including national leaders) persist in inappropriately assuming that vast superiority in military capabilities should result in the ability to obtain any postwar payoffs desired.

Contrast Between Premodern and Modern Victory

Looking specifically at informational, military, political, economic, social, and diplomatic dimensions of the victors' conduct in vanquished states highlights the sharp contrast between victory in premodern and modern warfare, summarized in Figure 2.1. By looking at the differences within each dimension, we can isolate the special contemporary international security meaning of the strategic victory

Figure 2.1 Premodern vs. Modern Victory

PREMODERN TOTAL WAR SUCCESS	MODERN LIMITED WAR SUCCESS
Informational Dimension	
Coerce formal surrender	Influence cessation of hostilities
Military Dimension	
Destroy and subjugate enemy	Neutralize and deter enemy
Political Dimension	
Impose foreign-dominated government	Allow self-determined government
Economic Dimension	
Exploit economic resources	Develop economic reconstruction
Social Dimension	
Enforce hierarchical social order	Promote progressive social transformation
Diplomatic Dimension	
Accomplish war aims on one's own	Invite third-party conflict involvement

elements. In each case, victors appear to have gradually moved away from the quest for obliteration or total dominance of one's foes and toward the desire to maintain positive influence over these adversaries; as a result, detecting strategic victory has become a lot more subtle. Moreover, most premodern wars had a clearer end state, lower reliance on attaining a fluid positive cost-benefit ratio, and more decisive unambiguous endings than most modern wars.

Victory as Coercing Formal Surrender Versus Influencing Cessation of Hostilities

Looking first at the informational ramifications of victory, we see a key difference between a *de jure* formal signing of a surrender agreement, wherein one coerces the enemy to capitulate and accept defeat, and a *de facto* informal cessation of hostilities, wherein one influences the enemy through sensitive and vigilant monitoring and manipulation of communication to increase its willingness to negotiate or quit the fighting. The first, a more traditional position, provides a simple and clear-cut notion of victory, with the desired positive outcome having the victor coercively dictate terms to the vanquished through a formal surrender agreement: formal surrender occurs "when a military engagement or war is terminated by an agreement under which active hostilities cease and control over the loser's remaining military capability is vested in the winner; in such cases one side achieves a monopoly of armed strength and the other is reduced to defenselessness, thus accomplishing the classic objective of total victory."[25] Carl von Clausewitz refers to this state of affairs as an opposing leader communicating an "open avowal" of military defeat by "the relinquishment of his intentions."[26] Clear benefits from this coerced formal capitulation include (1) "the act of surrender is important in persuading a people to fulfill their obligations under occupation"; (2) there is no need to focus on detecting when one's adversary is ready to cease its fighting; and (3) formal surrender is an effective political/psychological sell to the public and the media.[27] However, this decidedly premodern notion of victory is indeed a rarity in modern times, in terms of both the signing of and the compliance to such agreements after interstate conflicts: of 311 wars from 1480 to 1970, only 137—all before World War I—concluded with a peace treaty.[28] Although "equating victory with the defeat and surrender of the enemy may have been and may still be consistent with conventional usage," "the modern world experience reveals that such a decisive conclusion to armed conflict is the exception rather than the rule."[29]

In contrast, the second modern position gauges victory more modestly as influencing the enemy to accept informally a cessation of hostilities as a result of sensitively and vigilantly monitoring and manipulating—using the latest protected high-quality intelligence and information technologies—its willingness to negotiate or withdraw. This less definitive outcome can include short-term use of information warfare's abilities to disrupt military command-and-control systems, wreak havoc with coordinated military action, alter government policies and popular support for them, and keep soldiers from receiving proper directives. The resulting provisional (and sometimes temporary) cessation of hostilities often occurs through armistices, cease-fire lines, suppression of insurrections, or acquiescence to territorial changes.[30]

There are a number of ways in which a provisional laying down of arms in response to war initiation can be considered victory, including if the war initiator's objectives are satisfied by a stable cessation of the fighting (such as in the 1950–1953 Korean War), if the war initiator has convincingly signaled to its enemy that no further disruptive activity will be tolerated, or (of course) if the war initiator has destroyed the enemy's capacity to undertake further military aggression. Bucking much prevailing wisdom, this modern approach to war outcomes contends that formal surrender is decidedly not necessary for either military or strategic victory. In many of today's conflicts, including the war on terror and low-intensity confrontations, there is no expectation on the part of a war initiator that its opponent will ever surrender, rather only that its threat will be successfully contained or negated. Interestingly, one reason that the United States has not as yet formally declared the kind of victory in Iraq and Afghanistan that would permit its withdrawal is that under the Geneva Conventions, a formal declaration would require the United States to release all prisoners of war, many of whom are still being interrogated to gain intelligence for counterterrorism purposes.[31]

Victory as Destroying and Subjugating the Enemy Versus Neutralizing and Deterring It

A central military difference between premodern and modern warfare revolves around whether winning a war necessitates eradicating the power of enemy military forces and subjugating them under one's control, usually through a long and intrusive foreign military occupation, or alternatively neutralizing and deterring from future aggression largely intact enemy forces, usually through a relatively short and ancillary foreign occupation. Traditionalists embracing the first notion see the enemy's military forces as a severe threat and thus seek to minimize risk and remove that threat by annihilating, exiling, incarcerating, or dominating these forces through a lengthy postwar foreign military occupation that thwarts any uprising. As von Clausewitz classically contends, "the aim of war in conception must always be the overthrow of the enemy"; "whatever may be the central point of the enemy's power against which we are to direct our operations, still the conquest and destruction of his army is the surest commencement, and in all cases the most essential."[32] This approach may involve revenge or retribution, and in earlier historical periods usually meant the acquisition of territory, with sustained occupation by victorious soldiers and even annexation into the empire following military victory. Traditionally military victors perceived such foreign occupation of territory as permanent, not temporary, and viewed removal of enemy leaders as just the first step, not the last, in achieving victory. Regardless of whether the method is destruction or subjugation, "in total war victory comes to be defined in almost purely military terms," with internal legitimacy within the vanquished state being inversely proportional to the amount of external coercion employed by the victor.[33] However, for this primitive approach's logic to work, the occupier must choose to "follow a destructive military victory that has eviscerated prewar political, economic, and social institutions," where such a victory "demonstrates that the preoccupation regime can no longer deliver vital needs to the population," and thus "the population is more likely to accept the occupation as a necessary evil."[34]

Alternatively, modern strategists look at victory as neutralizing and deterring the enemy's armed forces, with a strong emphasis on preventing future aggression by one's foes and their sympathizers through threat of punishment rather than actual annihilation. A positive war outcome means that these adversaries would—without significant casualties on the victor's side—quickly and smoothly operate in the manner the victor desires, including the possibility of comprising a police force designed to restore order within the vanquished society. This approach requires that the victor possess sophisticated communication and monitoring capabilities to keep order; the premise is that a victor ought to occupy militarily a vanquished state only until a base level of compliance of enemy forces occurs, with the underlying assumption that this compliance will emerge very rapidly. With this orientation, coercive conquest is inherently self-defeating—and long-term foreign occupation of a defeated state superfluous—in terms of payoffs for the victor: postwar management of defeated societies in today's world often faces obstacles of inhospitable physical terrain and hostile traditions and culture, creating a fierce and primitive local resistance to outside authority. Although "nation building is not the central goal of occupations," and instead "the primary objective of military occupation is to secure the interests of the occupying power and prevent the occupied territory from becoming a source of instability," if this more modern approach entails short-term occupation by a victor of a vanquished state, then the ultimate long-term goal is the restoration rather than the destruction of the defeated state's own capacity to enforce internal order.[35]

Victory as Imposing Foreign-Dominated Government Versus Allowing Self-Determined Government

Turning to the political dimension, a victor may either insist on complete external coercive political control over a new government in the defeated state or, alternatively, permit a self-determined government favorably inclined to the victor's preferences but yet conforming to the local wishes of the citizenry. The first camp—the more traditional view—sees dominance of the enemy's political system, transforming it in the long-run, as the key to victory; for example, von Clausewitz's very definition of war is "an act of violence intended to compel our opponent to fulfill our will."[36] The many superpower-encouraged wars of national liberation fought within the Third World during the Cold War, designed to implant puppet governments in these states, largely conform to this approach. Such victor-imposed regimes are more successful if those vanquished "accept the fact of defeat and realise there is no chance of reversing the verdict in the foreseeable future."[37] However, keeping another state firmly under one's political thumb can be quite costly, and a danger exists that the victor may find itself trapped in "an inescapable and open-ended military occupation and rule of the defeated side."[38]

In comparison, peaceful—usually democratic—self-determination of governance by a vanquished society is a more modern approach to postwar success. In this view, a positive war outcome could be a "return to normalization" in a defeated state where "extraordinary outside intervention is no longer needed" and "the processes of governance and economic activity largely function on a self-determined and self-sustaining basis."[39] Many analysts argue that "the ideal form of political transition in [postwar] nation building appears to be the quick transfer of power to legitimately elected local leaders."[40] In this view, for victory to occur, the defeated people "must become reconciled to their defeat by being treated, sooner or later, as partners in operating the new international order."[41] The key here is the ability of locals to develop both a capacity and a willingness to manage their own problems: for example, in the aftermath of the 2003 Iraq War when responding to a question about when US forces could declare success, Deputy Secretary of Defense Paul Wolfowitz replied, "when it becomes an Iraqi fight and the Iraqis are prepared to take on the fight."[42] Here a much more limited desired political end state is involved than with traditional premodern warfare: "Any victory that does not result in the dissolution of the enemy state and its replacement by a totally new state or its incorporation into an existing state is in some degree limited, for it is an implicit recognition of the residual authority of indigenous political expressions, of the costs of overcoming local loyalties, and of the potential utility to the victor of existing structures and attitudes."[43] There may, of course, be irreconcilable differences between the desires of the winner in battle and the local population about postwar political rule.

Victory as Exploiting Economic Resources Versus Developing Economic Reconstruction

The economic dimension of victory revolves around whether the winner wants (1) to monopolize, use for its own purposes, and ultimately drain the vanquished state's resources, or (2) to accomplish reconstruction of the defeated state's business infrastructure for that country's benefit. The more traditional notion sees unbridled exploitation of the defeated enemy's resources as part of the spoils of war (indeed, a shortage of raw materials may have caused the war in the first place). In cases where the motivation for a war was resource shortages and the desire to acquire new sources of raw materials, success in warfare would logically entail the victor using for its own purposes the vanquished state's resources: as major powers' population and technology grow, so do their resource demands, and these states have historically defined success in war as expanding their resource base because domestic sources could not readily satisfy these demands.[44] The payoff here is all the tribute and plunder one can extract and bring back after defeating an enemy. The European powers' colonization during the age of exploration of much of the Third World had this kind of victory metric. The immediate benefits of this approach are indeed immense, but the long-run chances of resentment and retaliation are also high.

In stark contrast, adherents of the second approach believe that "the conquest of territory for economic gain has become an anachronism"[45] and see postwar rebuilding of the devastated defeated state's economic infrastructure, while still maintaining the victor's access to vital resources in the defeated state, as critical to victory. Rather than exploiting resources from the vanquished state, this mode often has the winner pour resources back into the defeated country (of course, the victor's contractors benefit from the otherwise apparently altruistic rebuilding programs). Often driving this reverse flow of funds are concerns more political and social than purely economic. An explicit expression of need from the vanquished state for external economic assistance can help enhance stability in this regard. The US implementation of the Marshall Plan after World War II exemplified this approach.

Victory as Enforcing Hierarchical Social Order Versus Promoting Progressive Social Transformation

Considering the social dimension, disagreement exists about whether the goal of war is to achieve stable hierarchical order within the vanquished society or to strive for progressive social transformation. Traditionalists feel that restoring internal hierarchical order is the most essential component of victory: for example, centuries ago conquerors stressed obedience, unity, and order, not freedom or individual rights. As Wright notes, "Monarchs in the 15th, 16th, and 17th centuries used war to compel small feuding principalities to accept a common rule, and after establishing their authority in the following centuries, they created nations by the power which military control gave them over civil administration, national economy, and public opinion."[46] According to this view, enforcing certain patterns of social conformity is the central social goal of the victor, but these patterns may or may not be just in the context of the culture in which they are applied.

A more modern view is that a vanquished society's progressive social transformation may be a crucial measure of victory. This transformation may involve treating postwar psychological scarring and grief; developing voluntary community associations; improving internal communication and transportation systems; promoting human rights; ending inhumane torture, rape, slavery, and prostitution; opposing structural inequalities; addressing refugees' and displaced peoples' needs; reducing societal polarization into extremist factions; pushing civil society norms; and, most generally, restoring dignity, trust, and faith within the vanquished society.[47] The goal is to establish social structures that functionally serve the interests of the people. The postwar modernization efforts in the wake of the US war against terrorism in Afghanistan in 2001–2002 exemplify this quest for progressive social transformation.

Victory as Accomplishing War Aims on One's Own Versus Inviting Third-Party Conflict Intervention

Finally, moving to the diplomatic area, a victor may either try to win a war and manage its aftermath on its own or invite third-party involvement. Traditionalists—the former group—believe that it is essential for postwar compliance for the victor to have won and established postwar stability by dint of its own efforts. This view rejects war participants engaging in "mindless coalition-building" or expending any energy at all on analyzing whether the outside world approves of its foreign military action.[48] Thus the high status accruing to the victor would be a direct result not of finely-tuned diplomatic efforts but of highly visible tangible results it had accomplished by "going it alone." In this way, there would be no uncertain issues such as trust in one's coalition partners or in third parties to dilute the participant's benefits. However, particularly in an interdependent global setting, going solo in warfare can be highly risky, and so this mode could easily backfire.

Modern postwar involvement of third parties rests on the premise that it enhances both the legitimacy and stability of any outcome. The most common third parties are powerful states, allies, or regional and international organizations. Making postwar occupation of a vanquished state multilateral can increase the acceptability of the status quo both to other states and the occupied population, even though providing the losing society security and improving living conditions may be far more important to stable victory than whether the intervention is unilateral or multilateral.[49] Sometimes third parties write war-ending accords; sometimes international bodies such as the United Nations monitor and certify election results for defeated states' newly constituted regimes; and sometimes third-party intervention even prior to the end of the fighting can be effective—"wars between relatively small states are often settled through great power intervention or international conflict resolution efforts before they can be resolved militarily."[50] However, controversy surrounds the value of unilateral versus multilateral efforts: the claim that "unilateral efforts are more likely to cause [postwar] nation building to fail" conflicts with the contention that after a war "peace lasts no longer when an outsider has gotten involved…than when no third state has tried to help make peace," at least in part because the level of commitment by the third-party intervener may be quite low.[51] Since World War II, external pressures have often caused the termination of hostilities, including if the pressure results from substantial interest by a great power; however, the victor may lose control of postwar operations in such cases.[52] Although third-party involvement often makes wars longer than when they involve only the initiator and the target, in some cases such intervention can hasten war termination.[53] Finally, although postwar third-party involvement can increase outside support, it can also complicate payoffs: as the number of participants increases, the benefits of victory become more widely distributed, reducing any individual state's gains from victory.[54]

Concluding Thoughts

Placing strategic victory in historical context raises a number of important questions. Does a rigid unilateral "might make right" approach make sense, or is a more flexible orientation encouraging external international approval essential? Is success to be evaluated in terms of obliterating or totally dominating an enemy, or alternatively in terms of fostering reorientation, self-determined government, economic reconstruction, and social transformation? Is coercive top-down order the goal, or is it legitimate bottom-up support? Is formal capitulation required, or does a provisional laying down of arms suffice? Should victors measure triumph in terms of what they can get from the conquered territory, such as through extracting spoils, or should they measure success in terms of being able to get the defeated state back on its feet and fully functioning again?

Although on the surface modern victory appears far superior to premodern victory, in reality both are mixed blessings. The premodern approach has a greater chance of ensuring short-term stability but at the same time lacks the tools for fostering long-term productive cooperation between the victor and the vanquished or reintegrating the defeated state back into the international community. In contrast, the modern emphasis on rebuilding, revitalizing, and modernizing defeated societies is helpful for long-run stability, but it does not address the stubborn persistence of long-standing violent frictions within these societies. Furthermore, pursuing victory in modern limited war may even result—due to its usual protracted length and indeterminate outcome—in more suffering and loss of human life than pursuing victory in premodern total war. Thus, despite the evolution of warfare, modern strategists can learn a great deal about strategic victory by examining past postwar military successes.

Reflecting on the simplicity and clarity of premodern warfare, with its more easily measured war aims and notions of victory, makes the complexity and ambiguity of modern warfare look far less attractive. Nonetheless, this study chooses to focus on the modern meaning of strategic victory. In the current international security environment, characterized by high levels of interdependence, communication, and transparency, the premodern ideas about victory in their pure form may not yield the most crucial payoffs for the victor. However, modern limited war victory does indeed make achievement and management of strategic victory clearly a lot more challenging: attaining political self-determination, economic reconstruction, social justice, and diplomatic respect in today's world is much more difficult than just winning in combat on the battlefield. As the next chapter's discussion of morality illustrates, modern victory makes the victor's choices a lot tougher as well. Attempting to defeat an enemy that one intends to rehabilitate afterward is a bit like walking a tightrope, with inherent contradictions and constraints in the mode both of achieving victory and of restoring the defeated society.

Notes

1. Michael Evans, "From Kadesh to Kandahar: Military Theory and the Future of War," *Naval War College Review* 41 (Summer 2003), p. 139; and Monica Duffy Toft, "End of Victory? Civil War Termination in Historical Perspective" (paper presented at the annual national meeting of the International Studies Association, Honolulu, March 2005), p. 6.

2. Michael Howard, "When Are Wars Decisive?" *Survival* 41 (Spring 1999), p. 130; and Paul Kecskemeti, *Strategic Surrender: The Politics of Victory and Defeat* (Stanford, CA: Stanford University Press, 1958), pp. 17–18.

3. Ibid.

4. Michael P. Noonan and John Hillen, "The New Protracted Conflict: The Promise of Decisive Action," *Orbis* 46 (Spring 2002), p. 231; and Matthew Kee Yeow Chye, "Victory in Low-Intensity Conflicts" (2000), http://www.mindef.gov.sg/safti/pointer/back/journals/2000/Vol26_4/4.htm.

5. Richard Hobbs, *The Myth of Victory: What Is Victory in War?* (Boulder, CO: Westview Press, 1979), p. 59.

6. John W. Dower, *War Without Mercy* (New York: Pantheon Press), pp. 3–4.

7. Brian Bond, *The Pursuit of Victory: From Napoleon to Saddam Hussein* (New York: Oxford University Press, 1996), p. 5.

8. Evans, "From Kadesh to Kandahar, p. 136.

9. Bond, *The Pursuit of Victory*, p. 2.

10. Jay L. Kaplan, "Victor and Vanquished: Their Postwar Relations," in Stuart Albert and Edward C. Luck, eds., *On the Endings of Wars* (Port Washington, NY: Kennikat Press, 1980), p. 83.

11. Bond, *The Pursuit of Victory*, p. 3.

12. Bruce Walker, "Not Just Total War—Total Victory," May 20, 2002, http://www.enterstageright.com/archive/articles/0502/0502totalvictory.htm.

13. *Department of Defense Dictionary of Military and Associated Terms* (Washington, DC: United States Department of Defense Joint Publication 1-02, April 12, 2001, amended May 9, 2005), p. 307; Noonan and Hillen, "The New Protracted Conflict," p. 231; and Robert Endicott Osgood, *Limited War: The Challenge to American Strategy* (Chicago: University of Chicago Press, 1967).

14. Toft, "End of Victory?" pp. 5–6; and Hobbs, *The Myth of Victory*, p. 502.

15. Jasjit Singh, "Dynamics of Limited War," *Strategic Analysis* 24 (October 2000), http://www.ciaonet.org/olj/sa/sa_oct00sij01.html.

16. Charles J. Wolf, "The Logic of Failure: A Vietnam 'Lesson,'" *Journal of Conflict Resolution* 16 (September 1972), p. 397.

17. Evans, "From Kadesh to Kandahar," pp. 141, 143.

18. Quote from Toft, "End of Victory?" p. 10; see also H. E. Goemans, *War and Punishment: The Causes of War Termination and the First World War* (Princeton, NJ: Princeton University Press, 2000), p. 29.

19. Bond, *The Pursuit of Victory*, pp. 4–5.

20. Quincy Wright, "How Hostilities Have Ended: Peace Treaties and Alternatives," *Annals of the American Academy of Political and Social Science* 392 (November 1970), p. 54.

21. Bond, *The Pursuit of Victory*, p. 174.

22. Howard, "When Are Wars Decisive?" p. 130.

23. John Czarnecki, "Welcome to the World of Limited War," http://www.d-n-i.net/fcs/comments/c271.htm.

24. "Still All Signed Up," *Economist* 366 (March 29, 2003), pp. 29–30.

25. Kecskemeti, *Strategic Surrender*, p. 5.

26. Carl von Clausewitz, *On War* (New York: Penguin Books, 1982), p. 313.

27. Justin Gage, William Martin, Tim Mitchell, and Pat Wingate, "Winning the Peace in Iraq: Confronting America's Informational and Doctrinal Handicaps" (Norfolk, VA: Joint Forces Staff College, September 5, 2003), p. 9.

28. Berenice A. Carroll, "How Wars End: An Analysis of Some Current Hypotheses," *Journal of Peace Research* 6 (1969), pp. 296, 305; Raymond G. O'Connor, "Victory in Modern War," *Journal of Peace Research* 6 (1969), p. 376; and Quincy Wright, "How Hostilities Have Ended: Peace Treaties and Alternatives," *Annals of the American Academy of Political and Social Science* 392 (November 1970), p. 52.

29. O'Connor, "Victory in Modern War," p. 376.

30. Wright, "How Hostilities Have Ended," p. 61.

31. Thom Shanker, "No Victory for the Winner," *New York Times,* May 4, 2003, p. 2.

32. Von Clausewitz, *On War*, pp. 388–390.

33. Kaplan, "Victor and Vanquished," p. 78.

34. David M. Edelstein, "Occupational Hazards: Why Military Occupations Succeed or Fail," *International Security* 29 (Summer 2004), pp. 59–60.

35. Ibid., p. 50.

36. Von Clausewitz, *On War*, p. 101.

37. Howard, "When Are Wars Decisive?" p. 132.

38. Jeffrey Record, "Exit Strategy Delusions," *Parameters* 31 (Winter 2001-2002), p. 23.

39. Center for Strategic and International Studies and Association of the United States Army, *Post-Conflict Resolution Task Framework* (Washington, DC: Center for Strategic and International Studies and Association of the United States Army, 2002), p. 2.

40. Minxin Pei, "Lessons of the Past," in Carnegie Endowment for International Peace, *From Victory to Success: Afterwar Policy in Iraq* (New York: Carnegie Endowment for International Peace, 2003), p. 53.

41. Howard, "When Are Wars Decisive?" p. 132.

42. Deborah Zabarenko, "Pentagon's Wolfowitz Says Iraq Is No US Quagmire," June 22, 2004, http://wireservice.wired.com/wired/story.asp?section=Breaking&storyId=882443&tw=wn_wire_story.

43. Kaplan, "Victor and Vanquished," p. 77.

44. Robert Mandel, *Conflict Over the World's Resources* (Westport, CT: Greenwood Press, 1988), pp. 11–12; Nazli Choucri and Robert C. North, *Nations in Conflict: National Growth and International Violence* (San Francisco: W. H. Freeman, 1975); Robert C. North, "Toward a Framework for the Analysis of Scarcity and Conflict," *International Studies Quarterly* 21 (1977), pp. 569–591; and Richard J. Barnet, *The Lean Years: Politics in the Age of Scarcity* (New York: Simon and Schuster, 1980), chapter 8.

45. Klaus M. Knorr, *The Power of Nations: The Political Economy of International Relations* (New York: Basic Books, 1975), pp. 124–125.

46. Quincy Wright, *A Study of War,* abridged edition (Chicago: University of Chicago Press, 1964), p. 77.

47. Matthias Stiefel, "Rebuilding after War: Lessons from WSP" (Geneva, Switzerland: War-Torn Societies Project, 1999), http://wsp.dataweb.ch/wsp_publication/rebu-05.htm.

48. Conrad Black, "What Victory Means," *National Interest* (Winter 2001/2002), p. 156.

49. Edelstein, "Occupational Hazards," pp. 69–73.

50. Paul R. Pillar, *Negotiating Peace: War Termination as a Bargaining Process* (Princeton, NJ: Princeton University Press, 1983), p. 15; Christopher Preble, "After Victory: Toward a New Military Posture in the Persian Gulf," *Policy Analysis* 477 (June 10, 2003), pp. 10–11; and Albert and Luck, *On the Endings of Wars*, p. 3.

51. Pei, "Lessons of the Past," p. 52; and Virginia Page Fortna, *Peace Time: Cease-Fire Agreements and the Durability of Peace* (Princeton, NJ: Princeton University Press, 2004), p. 186.

52. Lincoln P. Bloomfield, "Why Wars End: CASCON's Answers from History," *Millennium: Journal of International Studies* 26 (1997), pp. 709–726.

53. Kevin Wang and James Lee Ray, "Beginners and Winners: The Fate of Initiators of Interstate Wars Involving Great Powers since 1495," *International Studies Quarterly* 38 (March 1994), p. 151; and Goemans, *War and Punishment*, p. 321.

54. Allan C. Stam III, *Win, Lose, or Draw: Domestic Politics and the Crucible of War* (Ann Arbor: University of Michigan Press, 1996), p. 55.

3

Morality and Victory

Perhaps the most neglected facet of strategic victory is the issue of morality. Virtually everyone has accepted that wartime combat necessitates a set of moral strictures different from those during peacetime, and a lot of effort has gone into articulating, codifying, and enforcing these in practice. In stark contrast, little discussion has specifically focused on morality during the peace-winning phase of conflict following victory on the battlefield. With respect to strategic victory, this chapter identifies fundamental morality dilemmas; underlying moral principles, democratic beliefs, and international law; differing perspectives on morality; moral hazards and responsibilities; and conditions under which moral dilemmas are most intense.

The common postwar aspiration of establishing "a just and lasting peace" necessitates explicit reflection about the moral facet of strategic victory.[1] Considering this normative issue is crucial because postwar stability can in part be a function of the perceived and actual morality or immorality of the victor's behavior toward the vanquished. A case in point is the debilitating turmoil in the aftermath of the 2003 Iraq War surrounding alleged mistreatment by the United States of Iraqi prisoners.

However, in this context major ambiguities exist surrounding the ability to distinguish between genuine morality and perceived or projected morality. Rather than complete adherence to strict moral standards, a victor could exhibit token, cosmetic, and selective attentiveness to these concerns, or alternatively private disregard for them, with a concerted emphasis on manipulating the international image of its postwar behavior to conceal its true aims. A cynic might argue that compared to true moral action, this disingenuous behavior could yield just as high postwar payoffs from victory, at least in the short run. In order for winners to apply postwar moral strictures in a meaningful way in their pursuit of strategic victory, these ambiguities need to be addressed and resolved.

The Fundamental Morality-Victory Dilemmas

Looking across the broad sweep of human history, traditionally protection of human life has not been the highest sovereign state national security goal.[2] Protection of territory and of regime has usually taken precedence over such humanitarian concerns, with many rulers explicitly deeming the lives of their citizenry—whether soldiers or civilians—to be expendable. The long-term pattern surrounding armed conflicts demonstrates convincingly that most commonly "we turn away from moral issues to issues we can address in battle."[3] However, the advent of more representative forms of government, in which leaders have become more accountable to the people, has gradually posed increasing challenges to this long-standing priority system.

Key moral questions surround the aftermath of warfare.[4] Are noncombatants spared hardships? Are economic assets preserved? Are populations displaced? Are atrocities committed? Are prisoners treated well? Are the rules of war observed? Along these lines, in an ideal world it is possible to conceive of a just peace as one that vindicates the human rights of all parties to the conflict.[5] Yet significant tensions exist in the aftermath of war between justice and stability, fairness and efficiency, and legitimacy and coercion (the choice between forcing a vanquished society to transform and waiting for it to choose on its own to transform). Most fundamentally, a central dilemma surrounds the question of whether imposing postwar morality interferes with the winner's ability to reap fully the postwar payoffs from its military triumph in warfare.

Considerable logic supports the contention that strategic victory entails moral treatment of the vanquished. With such treatment, both the leaders and the people of the defeated country can see the postwar predicament as an opportunity for national survival and national growth, and the anticipated magnanimity of the victor could even speed the surrender of adversaries (or their cessation of hostilities) due to their expectation of fair treatment.[6] One example of this beneficial moral treatment of the vanquished is George Washington's humane treatment of prisoners of war during the American Revolutionary War.[7] Through this general orientation, even disgruntled members of a defeated society could see a desirable "light at the end of the tunnel." Thus, perceiving the victor as ethical could in a practical way enhance postwar stability.

However, this argument is not without controversy. Some analysts believe that morality and victory are in a zero-sum relationship—the more security policymakers take into account moral considerations, the more limited their victory will be. In this view, exhibiting morality in the aftermath of war is equivalent to signaling a form of weakness—involving hesitation, restraint, and lack of resolve—to the enemy that will ultimately prove to be debilitating. Specifically, a victor's morality may be exploited by the most unruly elements of a defeated society, as exemplified by some behavior during the 2003 Iraq War:

> As Saddam Hussein's operatives and the Iraqi military take asymmetrical warfare to the extreme, Baghdad is using US adherence to the rules of the Geneva Convention in Iraq almost as a weapon in its arsenal. Iraqi fighters are trying to force unpalatable decisions on US commanders far less willing to kill or threaten civilians than the Iraqi military itself.... Iraqi soldiers have waved white flags to lure an enemy into an ambush, something that's clearly proscribed under the Geneva Convention, which also bans firing from behind human shields of women and children—another Iraqi tactic. Likewise, storing munitions in hospitals and setting up mortar and machine-gun positions on the roofs of schools and mosques isn't considered acceptable by any conventional measure of wartime engagement.[8]

In other words, countries battling the United States—or more broadly Western military coalitions—may try to exploit these advanced industrial societies' respect for the international rules of war, as "their goal is to gain political leverage by portraying US forces as insensitive to LOAC [laws of armed conflict] and human rights."[9] According to this view, a defeated foe has no right to expect postwar morality from the victor.

Instead, this group of skeptical commentators may advocate stern imposition of the harshest kind of postwar penalties for even suspected misbehavior on the part of the defeated population, incorporating a high potential for human rights violations in terms of both intrusive monitoring and due process for the accused, in order to send a clear message that complete compliance with the new regime is absolutely mandatory. In this view, if the victor is perceived as somewhat immoral in terms of overly swift and severe punishment, all the better, for such a perception would cause members of the vanquished society to have that much greater of an incentive to stay in line.

A parallel criticism rejects the need to focus on morality after military victory on the grounds that it pragmatically interferes with the ability to achieve mission success. These observers may emphasize in their thinking the presence of a world devoid of universally recognized moral absolutes, making it exceeding difficult to distinguish cleanly between good and evil, between threat and nonthreat, or between unjustified offensive aggression and justified defensive protection on the international level. The contentious differences in moral standards often cause these critics to lose confidence that moral considerations ought to play a prominent role in war termination efforts. Instead, they believe that expediency and efficiency ought to dictate the management of victory, so that the victor can achieve the maximum benefit with the minimum cost after the travails of battle are over.

For still other cynics, coming from a very different set of assumptions, no postwar strategic victory—no matter how conducted—can be moral. To these observers, any such triumph inescapably involves the imposition of the will of the victor on the vanquished simply on the basis of superior force, a rationale they find morally unacceptable under all circumstances. Why should one belief system prevail over another simply because a state ascribing to it has superior coercive capabilities? Those supporting this critical view may find negotiated postwar settlements, in which both sides respected and attended to each other's preferences, to contain a far higher potential for moral acceptability than military triumph on the battlefield.

However, this view seems to ignore that in many cases the purpose of the conflict is to rectify a tangibly morally objectionable predicament. Several major wars of the past, including the Crimean War, World War I, World War II, and the Falklands War, have involved leaders motivated at least in part by the normative pursuit of justice.[10] Indeed, a moral obligation may exist for one or more outside parties to come in and terminate unacceptable conditions within a given state under some circumstances: for example, if people are being oppressed by an unjust government (especially when mass genocide is occurring), then basic principles of human rights may demand that foreign coercive intervention seek victory in terms of ousting the existing regime (some analysts make this argument concerning the turmoil in Rwanda in the mid-1990s and more recently concerning the violence in Sudan); or if a small country is experiencing an unwarranted military invasion from an imperialist outside power, then principles of sovereignty and self-determination of peoples may similarly demand that foreign coercive intervention seek victory in terms of repelling the invader (such as when Iraq invaded Kuwait in 1990). It is quite common for a war initiator to portray its entry into conflict as being based on high-minded adherence to ethical principles protecting innocent civilians. Thus, from a strictly moral perspective, ignoring narrow national self-interest, in many troublesome international predicaments the seeming immorality of military victory must be weighed against the probable immorality of complete inaction.

Moreover, the modern strategic victory thrust may make these postwar morality objections decidedly untenable, for to achieve diplomatic respect the defeated society has to believe that it has received fair postwar treatment—even when it is inefficient or costly—from the victor. Any effort by a victor to attain political self-determination, economic reconstruction, social justice, and diplomatic respect would necessitate vigilance about the morality of its actions, or at least vigilance about the appearance of morality of these actions. If, as most analysts believe, moral sanctions are to play any role during warfare, then out of principles of fairness "post-war behavior also must come under moral scrutiny."[11]

Moral Principles

A brief review of some of the moral principles relevant to the victor's postwar behavior seems in order. Principles deriving from moral philosophy can be powerful grounds for restraining the behavior of soldiers following overseas military confrontations. Even though these principles are largely intangible and devoid of enforcement, and even though many states disagree on both the nature and meaning of these principles, they can still contribute to the perceived legitimacy of coercive security actions at home and abroad.

Just war theory's criteria surrounding the employment of force during warfare help form the basis of criteria surrounding the employment of force in the aftermath of warfare. According to these criteria, if a state goes to war, it needs to concern itself in its conduct during the conflict with proportionality of means and noncombatant protection: during combat the state must employ no greater use of force than is absolutely necessary, and it must do as little damage as possible to noncombatants. The first principle serves to minimize casualties among allied and enemy soldiers by prohibiting gratuitous or unnecessary harm to fighting forces; the second principle minimizes casualties among allied and enemy civilians, with a growing international consensus since roughly 1900 that seeks "to protect from the ravages of war whole classes of people not directly involved in the prosecution of war."[12] The most important formal moral thrust to restrain the destructiveness of war "has taken place in the modern period" because of "the realization of war's increasingly devastating capabilities and the use of armed power during war to attack civilian noncombatants."[13] The basis in just war theory for the protection of human life—of soldier and civilian and friend and foe alike—is that "the rules of 'fighting well' are simply a series of recognitions of men and women who have moral standing independent of and resistant to the exigencies of war," with a legitimate act of war being "one that does not violate the rights of the people against whom it is directed."[14] The greatest moral sanctions would be against intentional rather than accidental occurrences of unnecessary harm during and after warfare.

Translating these wartime moral principles into the postwar context is not easy, as considerable confusion surrounds the question of how the moral standards for postwar behavior ought to differ from those applied to wartime behavior. A common implicit assumption is that postwar moral standards ought to be higher and tighter than those operating during war, yet at the same time somewhat lower and looser than those during peacetime. In the aftermath of war, when members of the defeated society can no longer be easily divided between combatants and noncombatants, what kind of uses of force by the victor are and are not permissible? How would the moral imperative to minimize casualties apply to disgruntled insurgent groups within the vanquished country who do not accept the reality or legitimacy of the war outcome?

Democratic Beliefs

The principles of democracy inherently embody respect for the sanctity of human life, and as this form of government has spread around the world so has this fundamental human rights value. Although few states live up to the lofty ideals of pure democracy, and though democratic regimes may be just as likely as nondemocratic regimes to kill noncombatants purposefully as part of wartime political-military strategies, there is little doubt that this form of government associates at some level with concern about human suffering.[15] To achieve strategic victory, democracies need to maintain popular support, and to maintain popular support—as well as to maximize external legitimacy—democratic governments must to some extent exhibit sensitivity to avoidance of unnecessary human carnage or atrocities during and after wartime.[16]

When military victors are liberal democratic regimes, they seem especially likely to be susceptible to a postwar moral code:

> In the wake of the September 11th terrorist attacks in the United States which killed about 3,000 innocent civilians, President George W. Bush argued that only barbarians target civilians, whereas civilized people—presumably those residing in Western liberal democracies—respect human rights and avoid hurting noncombatants.... Theoretically, the liberal beliefs and democratic institutions of such states suggest that they should be careful not to kill many civilians in war. Liberal norms, for example, prohibit the harming of innocent individuals, even enemy civilians in wartime. Democratic institutions, on the other hand, force leaders to be mindful of public opinion in making foreign policy choices. Just as fighting a costly war—or even worse, a losing one—is a policy likely to result in a leader's repudiation at the ballot box, killing large numbers of civilians in combat operations is liable to provoke public censure, possibly leading to loss of elected office for the officials responsible. Finally, liberal democracies are presumably the type of regime most sensitive to international ethical norms prohibiting intentional or disproportionate harm to noncombatants, since democracies themselves abide by similar norms domestically and advocate and propagate them internationally.[17]

In Western culture, "the ideas of noncombatancy and of noncombatant protection run deep in moral tradition," with the distinction between the soldier and the civilian traditionally based on who does and does not bear the moral guilt for waging and participating in the war.[18] The tenets of liberal internationalism thus open the door to ethical restraint in the aftermath of warfare.

The United States in particular has repeatedly at the very least paid lip service to the postwar relevance of moral principles. The US government has traditionally claimed that "respect for human life and consequent casualty consciousness are fundamental to what makes a nation civilized"; that, given its position as a superpower, "the sanctity of human life in time of war or peace certainly ought to be" the country's "foremost example to the world of how to act"; and that "it is therefore a moral issue that leadership must be casualty conscious in prosecuting war, for technology has turned acceptable wastage rates of the past into today's indictments of horrifying military incompetence."[19] The country thus desires to exemplify and expound to the world a set of civilized and humane norms both during and after warfare. There is some evidence that this moral concern has occasionally led to actual restraint: for example, during the 1999 Kosovo conflict, "US officials are reported to have decided against deploying their electronic arsenal because of fears that the impact on civilian life would have led to charges of war crimes under the Geneva Convention."[20] Regardless of whether the actual postwar behavior of the United States always conforms to these high standards of conduct, its frequent reference to these standards acknowledges at least their symbolic importance.

Furthermore, democracy induces a special restrained calculus in postwar military commitments:

> In a democracy, policymakers contemplating the deployment of troops into a situation that is, or might become, hostile, should sensibly evaluate three considerations insofar as they desire support for the action from the public. First, they must consider the value the public places on the venture, and they may try to use whatever persuasive skills they possess to enhance this value—that is, to sell the project to the public. Second, they must consider the likely costs of the venture, particularly in American battle deaths. And third, they must evaluate the potential of the political opposition to exploit the situation should battle deaths surpass those considered tolerable by the public.[21]

Indeed, modern democracies may fail to achieve their goals in warfare because they are unable "to find a domestically acceptable tradeoff between brutality and sacrifice"—unable to forge a winning balance between expedient and moral tolerance for the costs of war—with educated citizens abhorring the brutality of limited overseas coercive engagements but at the same time refusing to sustain the level of casualties resulting from fighting in other ways.[22] Thus the restrained fighting calculus induced by democracy, increasing the odds of internal and external legitimacy, may not always lead to the most effective military operation or to truly decisive victory. Moreover, despite its virtues, there is no evidence whatsoever that the global spread of democracy reduces or prevents terrorism.[23]

International Law

An ideal outcome of these moral principles and democratic beliefs would be codified laws protecting the rights of a defeated society's citizenry after war, parallel to the laws protecting their rights during wartime. Existing "laws of war" amount to "a body of rules that the world's nations have collectively crafted over 137 years of conventions in Geneva and The Hague—but enforced with only sporadic success":

> The idea that certain fixed laws should apply even amid the violence and anarchy of war isn't new. The saying may have it that all's fair in war, but restrictions on battlefield conduct have always been recognized. The Hebrew Bible forbade soldiers from, among other things, destroying fruit-bearing trees in hostile lands, and chivalric codes existed in the Middle Ages.[24]

Even under the current global anarchy, communication through processes such as the proliferation of informal intergovernmental networks may be increasing the possibility of "convergence, compliance with international agreements, and improved cooperation among nations on a wide range of regulatory and judicial issues," including laws governing the treatment of a defeated society—protecting civil rights and civil liberties—in the aftermath of war.[25] Thus, international law may at least be in the process of providing a concrete starting point for the concerns surrounding human suffering in the aftermath of war, with a particular emphasis on protecting noncombatants from adverse effects.

Differing Perspectives on Postwar Morality

After warfare, morality for the victor, morality for the vanquished, and morality for foreign onlookers may reflect very different concerns. Although in many of today's international confrontations it looks to some observers as if only one of the sides has a genuine concern about morality, amplifying the perceived asymmetry of will to fight, in reality all participants in war usually have some moral codes, albeit dramatically different ones. The different standards for judging morality create a fundamental challenge for victors: by necessity they would be operating on the basis of their own sense of perceived justice or injustice in the aftermath of war, a perception that may or may not correspond with reality, the perception of the defeated society, or the perception of international onlookers.[26] There is little doubt that the primary moral responsibility falls on the victorious state, for it possesses the postwar power over the defeated society and has the larger range of choice available in its decisions. However, the tensions among the three differing perspectives require some degree of reconciliation for military victory to yield its maximum postwar payoffs.

The Victor's Perspectives on Postwar Morality

The most basic moral quandary for a militarily victorious state is whether to apply brute force or pursue legitimacy to establish order in the vanquished society. Should the victor implement a series of policies designed to promote "enlightenment" within the defeated state and wait for the indigenous population to "see the light" voluntarily, or should the victor simply impose its will to foster dramatic transformation in a presumably positive direction? What kinds of means should the victor use in pursuing its postwar ends? How patient or impatient should the victor be in waiting to see the desired changes in the vanquished state? Victors may be torn in their moral choice between their desire to see tangible evidence of the fruits of victory in the short run and their desire for regional stability in the long run.

In the aftermath of war, a militarily victorious state also faces crucial moral choices with regard to its own domestic population. How many casualties of its own soldiers should it tolerate in establishing postwar order in the vanquished state? How long should it persist in peace-winning efforts if little forward progress is evident? Looking at the casualty issue, moral and domestic political pressures push in the same direction—to tolerate as few casualties as possible—but the pragmatic needs for continued sacrifice, involving loss of life, generated by existing turmoil in the defeated society may push in the opposite direction. This issue is especially important because domestic popular support for a successful overseas military intervention may easily erode if too many soldiers come home in body bags, regardless of the value of such efforts in restoring order in war-torn societies. Turning to the persistence issue, a victor in battle needs to balance its commitment to attaining its postwar payoffs in the defeated state against its moral responsibility not to squander its domestic resources in what could be a futile effort.

The Vanquished State's Perspectives on Postwar Morality

Though clearly less of a focus for monitoring by the international community, members of the defeated state also face important moral choices, in this case about whether resistance or compliance is warranted. If there is to be resistance, what kinds of means of subversive action—both violent and nonviolent—are acceptable? What kinds of ends make the sacrifices of those involved in the resistance, and those around them affected by resistance activities, worth the effort? If there is to be compliance, to what extent and in what ways should members of the vanquished society aid the victors? Leaders of defeated states face especially challenging decisions here, as they must weigh the intensity of their objection to the victor's behavior against the probability of retribution against their citizenry. Although the victors may severely constrain the range of moral choice among defeated society citizens, it is never nonexistent.

In connection with the resistance-compliance issue, a vanquished society may confront moral questions about whether the infliction of death—to others or to oneself—is an honorable way to pursue one's aims in the aftermath of war. The West has experienced shock and disbelief in the aftermath of recent wars due to the relatively high frequency of suicide bombings killing innocent people and destroying nonstrategic property, and it has generally assumed these actions have been taken by those who "circumvent morality"; for example, such shock and disbelief have certainly been the response of the West when truly desperate zealous terrorists attempt to kill as many innocent civilians as possible and "intentionally cross the lines that define the conventions of war that have been developed, in accordance with basic morality, to try to limit and regulate conflict."[27] In contrast, however, it may be that many of those involved in this violence—including extremist ideologues and religious fanatics—have highly principled ideals about the morality of their actions, including moral justifications for killing innocent bystanders such as spreading religious beliefs or compelling the retreat of modern democracy, and indeed it may be precisely these justifications that makes them so willing to die for their cause regardless of the level of opposing military force.[28] Such extreme violent action is not confined to non-Western sources, as for example an American terrorist fighting for freedom wreaked havoc in England during the Revolutionary War.[29] Just because behavior contradicts civilized norms does not automatically mean it is immoral or irrational.[30]

Outside States' Perspectives on Postwar Morality

During the aftermath of war, vigilant outside parties face a moral choice about whether to support or oppose the postwar behavior of the military victor in the vanquished state. It is common for these observers to develop judgments about the victor's morality that clash with the victor's positive self-image. Onlooker "expectations concerning the post-war morality of a victorious nation are usually based on the apparent morality of that nation's pre-war (and wartime) behavior."[31] Regardless of the victor's justifications for its actions, foreign observers—including the victor's own allies—watch closely to see how the winner treats members of the defeated society, monitoring both the winner's behavior and the loser's reactions. Part of the motivation for this scrutiny is that some of the defeated state's ethnic or religious groups may exist in sizable numbers among these observing states' own citizenry.

Moral Hazards of Victory

Attempting to achieve postwar strategic victory in any context is fraught with moral hazards. But perhaps the greatest danger is attitudinal rather than behavioral—the emergence of a "dubious sense of superiority" that can accompany such victory, allowing a narrow focus on the accumulation and maintenance of power as an end in itself.[32] Underlying this self-absorbed pride is the tendency of many victorious states to see themselves as completely virtuous, totally oriented toward overcoming evil, and thus impervious to moral deficiencies. Specifically, after the combat ceases, "in the 20th century it became a habit of the victors of war to claim that God and morality were on their side and that they were incapable of committing war crimes."[33] Exemplifying this tendency was the American tendency in the early 1950s to characterize its foe as "godless communists." This kind of "black-and-white" thinking, incorporating a moral self-image and a diabolical enemy image, is a real impediment to genuine moral sensitivity during war termination.[34] Moreover, with special though not exclusive reference to the United States, the sense of superiority can translate into an unwarranted belief that everyone should embrace one's own values: in the aftermath of war, "the US cannot succeed through a mix of arrogance and ethnocentrism," for it "is not the political, economic, and social model for every culture and every political system."[35]

Bolstering this inflated sense of postwar superiority for a winner is the polemical propagandistic language (such as the "all-out war for a total victory over international terrorism" rhetoric following the September 11, 2001, terrorist attack on the United States[36]) accompanying war efforts:

> In modern war, extreme language is often used in propaganda dealing with the problem of quitting or continuing to fight. Propagandists tend to speak as if the question ought to be decided on moral or political grounds, independently of the military situation. Hence the occasional vogue of such slogans as "No surrender in any circumstances," or "Better death than dishonor," in belligerent societies doomed to defeat.[37]

This attitude makes compromise, sensitivity to other moral perspectives, and honest self-reflection unlikely.

It is possible in this age of high-tech warfare that the victor's possession of advanced weapons systems can worsen the dangers surrounding this inflated sense of postwar superiority. Technology can distance users from the horrors of war, desensitize them to its true human costs, and remove their prudent sense of political and diplomatic restraint during wartime; it can also automate command-and-control systems in a way that makes human judgment hard to interject. For the United States, addiction to such technology could promote a dangerous sense of no-cost global dominance:

> High-tech military capabilities—to strike with accuracy and impunity, to anticipate and parry attack—reduce the uncertainty formerly inherent in the use of force. Technology largely obviates the need for sacrifice. It seemingly permits the United States to pursue global policies without subjecting the home front to the unwelcome dislocations of large-scale armed conflict—political protest or economic instability, for example. In short, technology enables the United States to use its military power to sustain American hegemony without the necessity of fighting messy old-fashioned wars.[38]

From a moral standpoint, the absence of direct confrontation with human suffering of the enemy can reduce the probability of principled self-discipline in actions during and after a war.

When victors feel superior, swallow the hyperbole of war propaganda, and use advanced weapons technology, the postwar potential for morally inexcusable excesses escalates. Among the most obvious and tangible postwar problems for the victorious state are excesses in violence against property, looting and plundering national treasures, brutalization of enemy civilians (including rape of women), and stamping out of innocuous local traditions. Whatever tolerance existed for these excesses during war—and existing international law indicates that tolerance should be minimal—the tolerance after the combat is over needs to be even lower, as "to stop fighting is to be done with military objectives and morally dubious means of attaining them.[39] Nonetheless, the emotional euphoria or exhaustion following military victory in a hard-fought war makes these excesses difficult to stop.

Moral Responsibilities Accompanying Victory

In light of these moral dangers surrounding victory, winners in war have an obligation to shoulder certain postwar moral responsibilities. Perhaps foremost of these responsibilities is the need to make a concerted effort to fulfill promises made to the population in the losing state. For example, in the aftermath of the 2003 War in Iraq, "many Iraqis still live in fear and do not enjoy what coalition officials anticipated, the exhilaration of liberation," and as a result feel a sense of moral betrayal.[40] Those emphasizing postwar moral responsibilities for the victor clearly embrace modern victory values: "nations must recognize the sensitive nature of postwar operations and train their troops to participate in these operations—including facilitating, when appropriate, an honorable surrender, rebuilding infrastructure, reestablishing societal institutions, restoring the environment, providing for *post bellum* justice and the rule of law, and building a spirit of reconciliation and cooperation with former enemies."[41]

More specifically, the range of possible victor postwar responsibilities includes being open to expressing regret, conciliation, humility, and possibly contrition; providing immediate security for both occupying forces and the defeated society; safeguarding the lives of innocent noncombatants; restoring the damaged physical environment; being willing to work together with the vanquished people to rebuild the defeated society; preparing soldiers for their reentry into society; prosecuting war crimes justly; returning sovereignty to the defeated state; and reflecting on the decision to use force in war.[42] The difficult quest for postwar justice in the defeated state thus spans several types of issues, including in the victor's imposition of settlement terms, military occupation, setting up of a provisional government, reintegration of displaced peoples, cleanup of toxic residue and unexploded munitions from war, involvement in economic aid, and treatment of war crimes, political prisoners, and members of the vanquished armed forces. The victor is responsible for adhering to principles of justice in restoring military security, establishing political self-determination, completing economic reconstruction, and implementing social transformation.

In order to execute successfully these postwar moral responsibilities, victors on the battlefield need to get civilians working together with military forces, as well as locals working together with occupying forces.[43] Victors also may need to give up control of certain dimensions of postwar justice management to international bodies that are in a better position to manage some of these issues.[44] Instituting such just improvements may prove difficult for any victor, as changes need to be compatible both with the winner's desires and the loser's preexisting cultural values.

In the aftermath of war, the victor's sense of moral responsibility and restraint may be put to the test in a rather quick and dramatic fashion. After the combat is over, lawlessness, corruption, and crime often break out, and the occupying power has to decide how to manage this chaos. The moral issues center on whether, in addition to traditional military deterrence, the victor can put into place credible justice mechanisms and sensitive reconciliation procedures to deal with past and ongoing grievances and atrocities. Some of the situations encountered involve very complex moral judgments requiring tradeoffs of moral costs and benefits: for example, when confronting postwar turmoil, tightening rules of engagement can lessen the chances of inadvertently killing innocent bystanders and thereby increase the victor's legitimacy with the defeated population, but such a move might also decrease overall security.[45] Thus, throughout history even many well-intentioned victors have failed to live up to their own enlightened rhetoric, or to outsiders' high expectations, at least in part because these winners have failed to anticipate the scope and intensity of postwar moral dilemmas.

When Are the Moral Dilemmas of Victory Most Intense?

The moral dilemmas surrounding strategic victory seem greatest when the moral values of the victor and the vanquished clash dramatically with each other. It is one thing for two countries to have different cultural traditions, yet quite another for them to have directly conflicting moral values (such as between many modern Western and traditional Islamic societies). The notion of a social contract between the ruler and the ruled can differ markedly across societies, and this difference can directly affect the degree to which citizens of the vanquished state are willing to give up certain basic human rights to facilitate order in the society under reconstruction. Prosecuting war crimes after a war can be rendered impossible—or possible only with naked cultural imperialism—if basic moral conceptions about what constitutes a crime differ markedly. Determining the ethically proper processes for moving toward political self-determination, economic reconstruction, and social transformation can similarly hit roadblocks. Although recent globalization trends have increased the standardization of these moral values, recent international warfare patterns indicate that conflicts between those with sharply differing senses of morality are highly likely within the foreseeable future. Finding existing commonalities among these values or, more boldly, forging new agreements based on common moral codes, appears to be an uphill battle in the context of the current anarchic global security environment.

Ironically, premodern total war victory notions may possess considerably greater moral clarity than do modern limited war victory notions, causing moral dilemmas to be more intense in the latter than in the former. From the premodern total war perspective, victors should have absolutely no moral responsibilities to the vanquished, as the defeated state is deemed worthy of utter annihilation in an unambiguous battle between good and evil. In modern limited war, in contrast, victors possess considerably greater moral concerns because of their desire to rehabilitate the vanquished society so that it can again function and become a part of the international community. In other words, modern limited war's "use of armed force in a surgical manner—the rapier rather than the broadsword—would require that military thinking and action be politically sophisticated, legally disciplined, and ethically correct."[46] Of course, in this modern war framework a victor's desire to rehabilitate a defeated society is not entirely dominated by moral concerns devoid of self-interest: pragmatic worries can also play a crucial role here, including the long-term security of the region, domestic legitimacy and support, international legitimacy widening the range of acceptable interventions, and avoidance of global constraints such as economic sanctions and diplomatic censure. Regardless, the modern limited war approach introduces significantly greater fuzziness in determining what means justify what ends, leading to considerable caution and even hesitation surrounding moral decisions involved in the pursuit of strategic victory.

In a parallel fashion, the notion of moral honor in the armed forces associates more easily with the premodern total war notion of unconditional surrender of an adversary than with the modern limited war notion of temporary cessation of hostilities.[47] Whether soldiers fighting in war live or die, their pride in their sacrifice—and belief that the cause was morally virtuous—can be heavily tainted by whether their side prevailed with a definitive positive outcome. Historical patterns demonstrate convincingly that quick and decisive postwar victories silence moral outrage, whether from military personnel involved in the mission, domestic civilians, or foreign observers.[48] This tendency serves to intensify the moral dilemmas surrounding the often nondefinitive conclusions of modern wars.

Concluding Thoughts

There is an inherent tension between the global spread of morality, democracy, and law and the global condition of anarchy—without overarching common security values—that characterizes today's world. The drive to achieve postwar strategic victory is directly caught up in this tension: the values associated with morality, democracy, and law, reinforced by high levels of globalization and interdependence, induce a caring about civilized behavior and protection of human life; but the anarchic system structure promotes a kind of "might-makes-right" exercise of power that concerns itself with nothing more than whether someone else is strong enough to stop you or punish you for what you are doing. This second, more chaotic perspective is especially exacerbated by the proliferation of disruptive nonstate forces challenging national sovereignty, the rapid diffusion of weapons technology across porous national borders, and the acceleration of violent low-intensity conflicts across the globe.[49] It is, of course, apparent that war does not represent fulfillment of the moral ideals either for an enlightened civilized global society as a whole or for the military establishment itself.

Given this international context, how likely are military victors in today's wars to be sensitive to postwar moral strictures? In many hard-fought conflicts where core interests are at stake, a certain reluctance—even on the part of Western states—would exist to placing postwar moral limitations on what means could be used to accomplish one's objectives, especially if these limitations appear to the victors to reduce the likelihood of maintaining defeated state security, keeping one's soldiers in the combat zone alive and well, or most generally achieving postwar payoffs. The narrowest notion of postwar obligation would thus reflect a rather complete unwillingness to be straightjacketed by moral principles in the aftermath of warfare. Nonetheless, countering this understandable reluctance to impose strict postwar morality rules is the realization that (1) moral principles are more likely simply to change rather than to eliminate postwar management options; (2) constrained options may often be more likely to achieve long-run effectiveness in the defeated state than unconstrained options; and (3) diplomatic respect, involving internal and external legitimacy, is an absolutely crucial element of modern strategic victory.

In the wake of military victory, then, thinking about the moral justifications and limits of one's own side's actions, as well as about the moral justifications and limits of one's enemy's behavior, appears vital to be able to reap postwar payoffs from military success. This chapter's discussion of morality thus directly influences the kinds of policy recommendations proffered in the concluding chapter. Through a moral lens, a victor's sense of postwar moral fulfillment can come more from seeing a decimated society successfully rehabilitated than from seeing a thriving enemy society demolished. Although victors on the battlefield need to take into account differing moral viewpoints and weigh the importance of moral imperatives against that of the postwar safety and security of those they are protecting, particularly when facing absolutely ruthless opponents, they should never completely ignore moral considerations. Moral restraint in the aftermath of violent conflict may never prevent the occurrence of all brutal acts taking advantage of a vulnerable defeated population, but it clearly deserves to be a vital part of the postwar strategic victory calculus.

Notes

1. Louis V. Iasiello, "*Jus Post Bellum*: The Moral Responsibilities of Victors in War," *Naval War College Review* 42 (Summer/Autumn 2004), p. 33.

2. Robert Mandel, "What Are We Protecting?" *Armed Forces & Society* 22 (Spring 1996), pp. 335–355.

3. Jack Perry, "America Can Win, Yet Suffer Defeat: Military Action Won't Put on the Road to a Better World," March 26, 2003, http://ciponline.org/nationalsecurity/articles/032603perry.htm.

4. Robert E. Williams and Dan Caldwell, "*Jus Post Bellum*: Just War Theory and the Principles of Just Peace," unpublished paper, 2005, p. 19.

5. Ibid., p. 24.

6. Clark Claus Abt, "The Termination of General War" (PhD dissertation, Massachusetts Institute of Technology, 1965), pp. 257–258.

7. David Hackett Fischer, *Washington's Crossing* (New York: Oxford University Press, 2004), p. 255.

8. Alex Salkever, "Time to Rewrite the Rules of War?" *Business Week Online*, April 1, 2003, http://www.asia.businessweek.com/technology/content/apr2003/tc2003041_2114_tc047.htm.

9. Colonel Charles J. Dunlap Jr., "Law and Military Interventions: Preserving Humanitarian Values in 21st Century Conflicts" (paper presented at the Harvard University John F. Kennedy School of Government Carr Center for Human Rights Policy Humanitarian Challenges in Military Intervention conference, New York, November 29, 2001), p. 5.

10. David A. Welch, *Justice and the Genesis of War* (Cambridge: Cambridge University Press, 1993).

11. Michael J. Schuck, "When the Shooting Stops: Missing Elements in Just War Theory," *Christian Century*, October 26, 1994, pp. 982–984.

12. James Turner Johnson, *Morality and Contemporary Warfare* (New Haven, CT: Yale University Press, 1999), p. 5.

13. Ibid., pp. 5, 36.

14. Micheal Walzer, *Just and Unjust Wars: A Moral Argument with Historical Illustrations* (New York: Basic Books, 1977), p. 135.

15. Alexander B. Downes, "Targeting Civilians in War: Does Regime Type Matter?" (paper presented at the annual meeting of the International Studies Association, Portland, OR, February 26–March 1, 2003), p. 3.

16. Scott Sigmund Gartner and Gary M. Segura, "War, Casualties, and Public Opinion," *Journal of Conflict Resolution* 42 (June 1998), p. 279.

17. Downes, "Targeting Civilians in War," p. 2.

18. Johnson, *Morality and Contemporary Warfare*, p. 125. See also Pauline M. Kaurin, "Innocence Lost: The Future of the Combatant/Noncombatant Distinction" (unpublished paper, Joint Services Conference on Professional Ethics, 2002), http://www.usafa.af.mil/jscope/JSCOPE02/Kaurin02.html.

19. Eric A. Ash, "Casualty-Aversion Doctrine?" http://www.airpower.maxwell.af.mil/airchronicles/apj/apj00/sum00/ed-sum00.htm.

20. Joe Havely, "Why States Go to Cyber-War," February 16, 2000, http://news.bbc.co.uk/1/hi/sci/tech/642867.stm.

21. John Mueller, "Public Opinion as a Constraint on US Foreign Policy: Assessing the Perceived Value of American and Foreign Lives" (paper presented at the annual meeting of the International Studies Association, Los Angeles, March 14–18, 2000), p. 2.

22. Gil Merom, *How Democracies Lose Small Wars: State, Society, and the Failures of France in Algeria, Israel in Lebanon, and the United States in Vietnam* (New York: Cambridge University Press, 2003), pp. 19–21, 230–231.

23. F. Gregory Gause III, "Can Democracy Stop Terrorism?" *Foreign Affairs* 84 (September/October 2005), pp. 62–76.

24. David Greenberg, "Fighting Fair: The Laws of War and How They Grew," January 17, 2002, http://slate.msn.com/id/2060816/.

25. Anne-Marie Slaughter, *A New World Order* (Princeton, NJ: Princeton University Press, 2004), pp. 261, 270–271.

26. Welch, *Justice and the Genesis of War*, p. 19.

27. Benjamin Netanyahu, "Three Key Principles in the War against Terrorism," March 19, 2002, http://www.amigospais-guaracabuya.org/oagim016.php.

28. Robert A. Pape, *Dying to Win: The Strategic Logic of Suicide Terrorism* (New York: Random House, 2005).

29. Jessica Warner, *John the Painter: Terrorist of the American Revolution* (New York: Thunder's Mouth Press, 2004).

30. Robert Mandel, *Irrationality in International Confrontation* (Westport, CT: Greenwood Press, 1987).

31. Abt, "The Termination of General War," p. 257.

32. J. Glenn Gray, "Ending with Honor," in Stuart Albert and Edward C. Luck, eds., *On the Endings of Wars* (Port Washington, NY: Kennikat Press, 1980), p. 151.

33. Raju G. T. Thomas, "NATO's Victory, Morality, and Justice: Reflections on the First Anniversary of the Bombing of Yugoslavia," 2000, http://www.worldwidewamm.org/newsletters/2000/special/yugoseries/natosv ictory.html.

34. Ralph K. White, *Nobody Wanted War: Misperception in Vietnam and Other Wars* (Garden City, NY: Doubleday, 1970), chapter viii.

35. Anthony H. Cordesman, *The "Post Conflict" Lessons of Iraq and Afghanistan* (Washington, DC: Center for Strategic and International Studies, 2004), p. iii.

36. Paul W. Schroeder, "The Risks of Victory," *National Interest* (Winter 2001/2002), p. 26.

37. Paul Kecskemeti, *Strategic Surrender: The Politics of Victory and Defeat* (Stanford, CA: Stanford University Press, 1958), p. 15.

38. Andrew J. Bacevich, "Neglected Trinity: Kosovo and the Crisis in US Civil-Military Relations," in Andrew J. Bacevich and Eliot A. Cohen, eds., *War Over Kosovo* (New York: Columbia University Press, 2001), p. 180.

39. Williams and Caldwell, "*Jus Post Bellum*," p. 20.
40. Iasiello, "*Jus Post Bellum*," p. 33.
41. Ibid., p. 39.
42. Ibid., pp. 40–51.
43. Ibid., p. 43.
44. Ibid., p. 48.
45. Justin Gage, William Martin, Tim Mitchell, and Pat Wingate, "Winning the Peace in Iraq: Confronting America's Informational and Doctrinal Handicaps" (Norfolk, VA: Joint Forces Staff College, September 5, 2003), p. 6.
46. Michael Evans, "From Kadesh to Kandahar: Military Theory and the Future of War," *Naval War College Review* 41 (Summer 2003), p. 143.
47. Gray, "Ending with Honor," p. 152.
48. "Victory Changes Everything," *Times of India,* March 23, 2003, http://www.swaminomics.org/articles/20030323_victory_changes.htm.
49. Robert Mandel, *The Changing Face of National Security: A Conceptual Analysis* (Westport, CT: Greenwood Press, 1994), chapter 1.

4

Misconceptions Surrounding Victory

Controversies about victory's meaning, amplified by its historical changes and moral dilemmas, have spawned key misconceptions. This chapter discusses military victors' postwar informational, military, political, economic, social, and diplomatic fallacies (paralleling the strategic victory elements), summarized in Figure 4.1. Both the rapidly evolving complexity and the emotionalism surrounding the aftermath of war can heighten optimistic perceptual distortions surrounding victory.

Three principal bodies of psychological theory help to explain these fallacies: (1) *selective attention*—ignoring incoming information that contradicts preexisting images; (2) *wishful thinking*—focusing just on positive outcomes where desires take precedence over expectations; and (3) *cognitive bolstering*—seeking out further evidence to enhance the credibility of preexisting beliefs.[1] In the context of strategic victory, selective attention deemphasizes obstacles to postwar success; wishful thinking exaggerates the speed, magnitude, duration, and seamlessness of this success; and cognitive bolstering attempts to find proof that progress toward achieving these payoffs is going smoothly. Thus victors' optimistic perceptual distortions may emerge because either they do not focus on postwar peace-winning challenges (selective attention) or they do focus on such challenges but color their interpretation of them (wishful thinking and cognitive bolstering).

Although optimistic assumptions by victors have long been evident, the identified set of postwar distortions among leaders of winning states applies particularly to modern war triumphs in the

Figure 4.1 Fallacies Surrounding Victory

INFORMATIONAL FALLACIES

The victor is likely to *overestimate* the value of technology in managing postwar problems, assuming that this can facilitate control of the defeated society.

The victor is likely to *overestimate* its intelligence ability to get an accurate postwar picture of the defeated society, assuming an ability to interpret correctly opportunities and obstacles.

MILITARY FALLACIES

The victor is likely to *overestimate* the postwar payoff of military capabilities, assuming that superiority in military force can guarantee compliance and deterrence.

The victor is likely to *overestimate* the postwar flexibility of the armed forces to pursue both stability and justice, assuming that soldiers can successfully undertake potentially conflicting roles.

POLITICAL FALLACIES

The victor is likely to *overestimate* the ease of transforming the defeated state's postwar political system, assuming that the loser's citizenry will be eager to participate in the new political process.

The victor is likely to *overestimate* the ease of transferring postwar power to local authorities, assuming that turning over the reins of government to the defeated society will be both speedy and seamless.

ECONOMIC FALLACIES

The victor is likely to *underestimate* the costs of postwar economic assistance to rebuild the defeated state, assuming that economic reconstruction will be smooth, fast, and inexpensive.

The victor is likely to *overestimate* the postwar benefits accruing to the victorious state, assuming that the winner will reap substantially greater gains than the loser.

SOCIAL FALLACIES

The victor is likely to *overestimate* the chances of the defeated state's postwar adoption of the victor's social values, assuming that the winner's values will become more attractive to the loser.

The victor is likely to *underestimate* the vanquished state's postwar social turmoil, assuming that unruly elements will readily move toward conformity to new social norms.

DIPLOMATIC FALLACIES

The victor is likely to *overestimate* the external legitimacy accorded to any postwar arrangement, assuming the outcome will provide a positive model admired by onlookers.

The victor is likely to *overestimate* its ability to transform positively domestic and international support for a postwar arrangement, assuming that onlookers' views are highly malleable.

post–Cold War security setting. It is notable but not surprising that these misperceptions reflect overconfidence on the part of the victor, not only because of the probable drift of selective attention, wishful thinking, and cognitive bolstering in the wartime context but also because tangible success—in terms of military triumph—typically leads to exaggerating one's capabilities. Following stellar combat performance, it would seem almost unpatriotic to question the postwar management capabilities of one's government, and for security policymakers both individual psychological processes and organizational bureaucratic incentives reinforce these tendencies. Across time and culture, there is a notable absence of restrained caution following success on the battlefield.

Victors are certainly not alone in possessing distorted views of postwar payoffs. In particular, defeated states often have the reverse misperceptions, one that if known could be helpful to winners achieving strategic victory: vanquished states tend to be reluctant to admit that the victor's postwar efforts are successful, overestimating the difficulties of postwar political transformation, underestimating the benefits from postwar economic reconstruction efforts, overestimating the likelihood and intensity of postwar social turmoil, and underestimating the external legitimacy of any postwar arrangement. Even international onlookers may be prone to perceptual distortion, skeptical that victory in warfare can create unambiguously positive regional or global effects.This study focuses on winners' misconceptions because they pose the most direct obstacles to achieving strategy victory, even though there is "greater understanding of the psychology of reactionary great powers content with the status quo [which have tended to be the military victors of late] than that of radical Third World states intent on overthrowing the global pecking order."[2] The patterns identified represent general distorting tendencies, which of course do not apply to every victorious leader in every postwar circumstance.

Ironically, the biggest negative impact of these misconceptions falls on the victors themselves. Although a defeated state society may bear some undesired consequences because the winner in battle has not prepared properly for managing the loser's postwar rehabilitation, it is the victor who sees its hopes dashed about attaining strategic victory and its triumphs on the battlefield yield little of value afterward. In painting an overly rosy postwar picture, victors have to weigh positive incentives, where an image of decisive victory can be the key to a leader's domestic political survival, against negative incentives, where such an image can prevent coping with complexities surrounding postwar payoffs.[3]

Informational Fallacies

The first informational fallacy by many victors is *overestimating the value of information technology* in war termination efforts, assuming its facilitation of postwar control of the defeated state. The victor's military forces can easily become hooked on technology as a panacea to all problems associated with strategic victory: in the twentieth century, "there has been continuous, rapid growth in the reach, lethality, speed, and information-gathering potential of armies," and these trends have increased the potential for technological addiction.[4] This addiction pertains not only to information technology but also more broadly to military developments such as smart weapons, stealth bombers, and night-vision goggles. A victor may overestimate its postwar ability to penetrate, manipulate, and disrupt opponents' information systems while at the same time underestimating its own information system vulnerability. Driving this exaggeration of advanced technology benefits are the underlying desires (1) to minimize collateral damage so as to assuage perceived public concerns and increase legitimacy; (2) to achieve force protection through increased reliance on safer forms of coercion; and (3) to attain a presumed "quantum leap" in cost-effectiveness.[5]

However, in reality advanced information technology faces inescapable postwar limitations:

> High-tech applications tend to be over-complex and, thus, susceptible to "Murphy's Law." High rates of mission capability are maintained only by Herculean maintenance efforts. Moreover, these systems, like all others, are vulnerable to counter-measures—but their high cost and long development cycles impede any quick adaptation to such counter-measures.[6]

Indeed, states extensively using information warfare may find themselves increasingly targets of the same kind of disruptive techniques: described by some as "the genie-in-the-bottle" syndrome, "once a cyber-attack has been unleashed, who's to say that in the interconnected world your carefully constructed virus won't spread to the networks of friendly or neutral nations?"[7] The diffusion of information warfare technologies—"the combination of low cost, widespread availability, and lack of controls makes the tools for waging digital warfare highly accessible"—makes it easy for virtually anyone to copy and apply them, from hacking into government websites or databases to launching disinformation campaigns.[8] So, rather than blind faith in the power of technology, "we would do better to develop experienced judgment and learn to become comfortable with uncertainty—with things that we cannot know beyond a reasonable doubt—than to delude ourselves that our technology will deliver all the knowledge we need to achieve victory."[9]

The second information fallacy involves the victor *overestimating its intelligence ability* to obtain an accurate postwar picture of the defeated society, assuming an ability to interpret correctly opportunities and obstacles. Part of the overconfidence of states involved in war is their tendency to neglect the substantial intelligence requirements.[10] A specific war termination intelligence challenge involves determining when insurgents are "war-weary," victims of war attrition, or so low on war-fighting resources that they might cease violent postwar resistance.

In contrast to positive expectations, however, the actual intelligence track record during the aftermath of recent wars has been less than spectacular. For example, in the 2003 Iraq War, intelligence did not "seem to have produced an accurate overall assessment of key problems in conflict termination and nation building, and it certainly did not effectively communicate such an assessment to senior policymakers"; although the administration did commission detailed reports about postwar problems and solutions, it largely ignored them.[11] Monitoring the rapidly transforming opportunities and dangers within a defeated society, frequently involving covert intervention and subversion, can pose quite an intelligence challenge.

Military Fallacies

One central military fallacy by many victors is *overestimating the postwar payoff of military power capabilities,* assuming that superiority in military force can guarantee compliance and deterrence. This distortion often associates with the aforementioned danger of feeling morally superior after victory. Those experiencing battlefield success often assume that using superior military power to destroy key enemy sites is sufficient for strategic victory.[12] Furthermore, the temptation to expand one's objectives following military triumph can, if unchecked, translate into a kind of "victory disease":

> The paradoxical logic of conflict, operating at all levels from high statecraft down to tactics, suggests that success can lure the victor down the road to eventual disadvantage and even destruction. At the level of statecraft, it is apparent that France in 1807 after the Treaties of Tilsit with Prussia and Russia, Germany in 1940, Japan early in 1942, and the United States in the 1990s all succumbed to a "victory disease" that disinclined their leaders to recognize the contexts and consequential terms of engagement that had yielded each of them such stunning successes.... Strategic success can fuel a political ambition for empire that exceeds the scale of mobilizable, or seizeable, resources, while it triggers the creation or augmentation of a hostile coalition.[13]

Under such circumstances, recognizing military power limits, including its inability to contain defeated society violence, seems highly unlikely.

This sense of superiority encompasses a couple of scenarios linked to the power ratio. The first wartime scenario occurs if a state with tangibly inferior military capabilities deludes itself into thinking that it is more powerful than its adversary, by exaggerating its own capacity and underestimating that of enemies, in which case its perceptions and behavior about victory could—regardless of the actual outcome—be way off the mark and undermine its own interests in the conflict. The second wartime scenario occurs if a state that enjoys tangible military superiority overestimates the sufficiency of this military advantage to produce quick and lasting strategic victory, in which case it will encounter disappointment but not as dismal a postwar predicament as with the first scenario. The American experience in the aftermath of the 2003 Iraq War demonstrates with crystal clarity that its overwhelming military superiority (badly underestimated by Saddam Hussein, given his conceit and inaccurate assessments by his sycophantic advisers) did give the United States a very quick military victory but at the same time (as of this writing) has not yet yielded strategic victory; thus, even the greatest military power in the world has faced a real humility lesson about the limits of what can be achieved with military superiority alone.

Overoptimism about the military power payoff can also lead to military planning that inappropriately calls for a quick, decisive end to the conflict. Many observers express caution to "those who see a quick offensive as the cure for their strategic difficulties."[14] Furthermore, blazing speed in winning on the modern battlefield may make management of postwar turmoil difficult; in particular, "the characteristics of the US style of warfare—speed, jointness, knowledge, and precision—are better suited for strike operations than for translating such operations into strategic successes."[15] This deficiency was evident during the early "shock and awe" stage of the 2003 Iraq War.

Some basic misguided assumptions support the certainty that military capabilities will ensure postwar payoffs. First, though hypothetically "both sides could avoid the costs and risks of war by negotiating a prewar bargain reflecting their relative power," in actuality when initiating war, states generally overestimate their ability to prevail in armed conflict.[16] Second, leaders of such states often exhibit an inadequate understanding of the power paradox in modern warfare, in which states tangibly superior in military power frequently do not ultimately emerge with larger gains:

> The idea of war is that battlefield success in the service of politics should translate into political achievements. Sometimes, however, military victory causes a state to lose at the bargaining table. Sometimes military victory causes both the victor and the vanquished to act in a manner that prevents settlement. And sometimes it happens that this failure to translate military gains into diplomatic ones is more pronounced because the military victory is dramatic and extensive.[17]

Third, particularly in the anarchic post–Cold War setting, a common disregard has existed for the highly transitory nature of both the power elements and coercive advantage in international relations, where security failures have often quickly followed security successes.

Thus, although generally "better armies still tend to win wars,"[18] in reality relying on military superiority to facilitate postwar payoffs in today's anarchic international security environment is a decidedly risky proposition. It is not surprising that advanced weapons systems reinforcing this trust in victory through technology, including precision-guided munitions, are not the best choice for managing many modern postwar instability predicaments.[19] For example, in postwar insurgency threats within densely packed urban settings, long-range target accuracy may lose its value: precision-guided munitions, "however useful against enemy armor in the open field, are next to useless in cities and in partisan warfare."[20] Superior military power seems particularly unlikely to translate into strategic victory during classic asymmetric warfare, in which a tangibly weaker state has far more zeal for its cause than a tangibly more powerful state, and thus "control over resources does not match actors' willingness to incur costs associated with the management of international conflicts or the risks associated with their potential escalation."[21] The Vietnam War experience should have taught the United States that "military superiority does not necessarily equal political victory," a lesson learned again during the 1993–1994 American military debacle in Somalia.[22]

A second major military fallacy involves *overestimating the postwar flexibility of armed forces to pursue both stability and justice,* assuming that soldiers can successfully undertake potentially conflicting roles. Western states generally accept that "armed forces must be able to adapt to differing modes of war, to become multifunctional," where "a military force may now be required to conduct intervention operations in conditions that correspond to neither classical warfare nor traditional peace-support operations."[23] Furthermore, in dealing with these dual challenges, members of the armed forces are caught in a soldier-warrior/soldier-diplomat trap, as within a defeated society they are expected to play multiple roles besides their traditional one of winning battles, including establishing and maintaining order, befriending civilians, protecting human rights, mediating disputes, and building civil society. Expectations seem boundless surrounding the versatility of military forces to cope with changing postwar challenges.

In reality, however, it may be impossible for soldiers to execute these multiple postwar functions with equal effectiveness. Despite the military "can-do" mentality, it is extremely difficult to be simultaneously adept at coercive and noncoercive means to address this wide range of postwar needs, as General Anthony Zinni colorfully outlines:

> What is the role of the military beyond killing people and breaking things? Right now, the military in Iraq has been stuck with this baby. In Somalia, it was stuck with that baby. In Vietnam, it was stuck with that baby. And it is going to continue to be that way. We have to ask ourselves now if there is something the military needs to change into that involves its movement into this area of the political, economic, and information management. If those wearing suits cannot come in and solve the problem—i.e., cannot bring the resources, expertise, and organization—and the military is going to continue to get stuck with it, you have two choices. Either the civilian officials must develop the capabilities demanded of them and learn how to partner with other agencies to get the job done, or the military finally needs to change into something else beyond the breaking and the killing.[24]

Even the most optimistic onlookers admit that "expecting the same forces to do both high-intensity warfighting and stability operations requires a grinding shift of mental gears for individual warfighters."[25] Soldiers just do not make ideal peacekeepers or counterinsurgency forces. Although international variation is significant, as some countries—such as British soldiers dealing with the violence in Northern Ireland—have achieved a measure of success in this regard, US forces have consistently encountered obstacles during post–Cold War foreign military interventions. In particular, "so long as soldiers see war-fighting as more heroic than war-prevention or war-ending, the constabulary function [where they are asked to play peace-keeping roles] of the military will take a poor second place."[26] Furthermore, inescapable tradeoffs tend to exist between humanitarian and security challenges in war-torn societies:[27] for example, in cases such as the 2001–2002 war on terrorism in Afghanistan, nongovernmental humanitarian organizations reported friction during warfare and its aftermath between their members and those of security-oriented state military forces—"the fact that the military personnel engaged in these [humanitarian] activities usually wore civilian clothing while carrying weapons blurred the necessary distinction between members of the military and humanitarian workers, potentially putting the latter at risk."[28]

Political Fallacies

Many victors *overestimate the ease of transforming the defeated state's postwar political system,* assuming that the loser's citizenry will be eager to participate in the new political process. In response to a question on *Meet the Press* three days before the start of the 2003 Iraq War about what would happen if the Iraqis resisted American occupation and a long, costly, and bloody stay ensued, Vice President Dick Cheney responded, "Well, I don't think it's likely to unfold that way…because I really do believe that we will be greeted as liberators."[29] Moreover, the United States proclaimed repeatedly in both the 2001–2002 war against terrorism in Afghanistan and the 2003 Iraq War that it assumes that the citizens of these states are yearning for political freedom, with the underlying assumption that the transition to democracy would be rapid after eliminating existing repressive regimes; for example, President George W. Bush stated, with reference to Iraq's postwar transfer of power to Prime Minister Allawi,

"Every conversation I've had with him has been one that recognizes, you know, human liberty, human rights; I mean, he's a man who is willing to risk his life for a democratic future for Iraq."[30]

In reality, after a war ends the defeated state's citizenry—including potential new leaders—may be hesitant about this participation:

> In many cases after a conflict, a country has neither a legitimate government in place nor even agreement on how to arrive at a process to determine what constitutes a legitimate government. Even if a government is in place and many of the country's citizens deem it legitimate, war and the attendant chaos often render its ability to deliver services to the population virtually nonexistent. At the same time, many citizens are hesitant to become overly involved in the political rebuilding process, having been conditioned by wartime realities to defer to individuals who exercised authority through the barrel of a gun.[31]

Postwar regime replacement is extremely difficult, with toppling an enemy leader a lot easier than putting in place in the vanquished state a new government "that could run a secure, viable country."[32] Tensions thus persist between contrasting modes stressing strong-armed coercion evident during a war and stressing self-reliance and voluntary participation after a war. Both Afghanistan and Iraq are struggling with these tensions in the wake of recent conflicts. Moreover, defeated citizens' unrealistically high demands on the new government can become a major hindrance. As Matthias Stiefel writes, "The advent of peace brings unrealistically high expectations by the people [related to immediate political transformation and economic prosperity], and this contrasts with the low capacity of the state to deliver; this is likely to lead to disillusionment which in turn diminishes the credibility of the state."[33]

A second closely related political fallacy is victors *overestimating the ease of transferring postwar power to local authorities,* assuming that turning over the reigns of government back to members of the defeated society will be both speedy and seamless. The underlying assumption here is that local authorities will possess the skills and legitimacy necessary to carry out these responsibilities. Victors tend to believe that if a few holes exist in local capabilities, relatively quick training will bring the most promising members of the defeated society up to speed. In the aftermath of the 2003 Iraq War, the United States believed that providing such training would make the transition to local rule seamless.

In reality, structural obstacles may make this transfer—particularly when the goal is transplanting democracy into a country with no prior experience with this form of government—a nearly insuperable challenge. There may be neither "a functioning electoral system" nor "the existence of credible, moderate local leaders who have genuine indigenous political support."[34] Indeed, after a war, the question of "when and how to conduct elections" is often "a thorny issue."[35] In terms of government security functions, locals may lack the skills to undertake effective policing and intelligence functions in the restrained and coordinated way the victor desires and, as in the aftermath of the 2003 Iraq War, become targets for insurgent violence. Even worse, pervasive political corruption, which is "endemic in virtually all post-conflict societies" (as well as in many authoritarian societies), clearly "jeopardizes the country's political stability and its prospects for peace." As one recent study reports, "Weak institutional structures, patterns of behavior exacerbated by war, a semi-lawless environment, and a shortage of well-paying jobs combine to create a hothouse environment that is ripe for corruption; the prospect of infusions of new money from the outside world during peacetime only heightens the challenge and the stakes."[36] Removing thugs from leadership may simply open the door to like-minded unsavory local replacements waiting to assume control, illustrated in the turmoil that resulted after power shifts in the Democratic Republic of Congo from 1997 to 2001 and in Liberia from 1997 to 2003.

Economic Fallacies

Victors often *underestimate the costs of postwar economic assistance*—money, material, and expertise—necessary to rebuild defeated states' shattered economies. The underlying assumption is that such economic reconstruction will be smooth, fast, and inexpensive. While a war is going on, participating states may distort information and even hide the true costs to build troop morale and to discourage domestic public criticism, but postwar distortions may be even greater.[37] In cases where the victor's domestic public is skeptical about entrance into a war in the first place, such as the 2003 Iraq War, such underestimation of postwar costs seems particularly likely.

In reality, the sheer magnitude of the price tag for economic assistance can be far higher than initially anticipated. For example, even during the 2003 Iraq War's major combat operations, it became clear that US "postwar costs, from peacekeeping and military occupation, to reconstruction of Iraq's battered infrastructure, to caring for US personnel wounded or made ill by their service in the war, [would be] likely to dwarf the short-term costs of the military campaign itself."[38] The higher costs associated with the peace-winning phase compared to the war-winning phase derive in part from the substantially greater time required after modern wars to achieve the rehabilitative postwar payoffs.

A second economic fallacy has many victors *overestimating the postwar benefits accruing to the victorious state,* assuming that the winner will reap substantially greater gains than the loser. Before a war is over, a state may prematurely relish the huge anticipated postwar payoffs, illustrated by high expectations before the 2003 Iraq War:

> Even at lower oil prices, Iraq should be able to earn more than $50 billion per year from oil exports within a few years—more than enough to pay for rebuilding that country without foreign aid. Lower oil prices will also jumpstart the world economy and raise US economic growth, which will increase federal revenues and help pay for the war. In the end, the economic benefits of the Iraq War are likely to greatly exceed the out-of-pocket costs.[39]

Indeed, it is still quite common for both political leaders and analysts to assume that after war, to the victor goes the spoils.[40]

However, in reality it is quite difficult today for a war victor to secure direct tangible economic benefits from the loser. Interfering with a one-way flow of benefits are a victor's economic dependence on vanquished states (possibly using defeated countries as markets or as sources of labor or raw materials) and its need to maintain positive relationships with economic partners. Moreover, corrupt local leaders endangering economic reconstruction and disaffected local groups sabotaging the vanquished state's economic assets can prevent postwar economic spoils from flowing to the victor.[41] Indeed, in today's interdependent global setting, winning a war may often be a losing financial proposition, as victory entails such large economic responsibilities to help the defeated state that expecting sizable net material benefits to flow back to the victor may well be futile. A classic example of the odd pattern here occurred in the aftermath of World War II: France and Great Britain were on the victorious side but afterward "never regained their former stature," whereas Germany and Japan were vanquished states yet afterward became "major powers in the world again."[42] Decades ago, a book (and subsequent movie) entitled *The Mouse That Roared* described a tiny fictional state initiating a war against the United States with the express purpose of losing so that this small country could reap the benefits of substantial economic reparations; the work was in many ways prophetic for modern victory's seemingly reverse economic payoff structure—where military winners can paradoxically end up being economic losers—in today's world.[43]

Social Fallacies

An important social fallacy among many victors is *overestimating the chances of the vanquished society's postwar adoption of the victor's social value system.* Victors often assume that after defeat, their social values (especially those surrounding civil society) will become more attractive to losers, internal animosities will vanish, and disaffected refugees will return peacefully. Particularly when industrialized states win over Third World states, the victor assumes that citizens of the defeated state will quickly see the tangible functional advantages of the modern values they introduce over the prewar traditional values.

In reality, Western states in particular have exhibited relative ignorance about how to transmit noncoercively their social values to countries that explicitly reject them, particularly if zealous religious or ideological beliefs predominate. Many defeated societies find that "painful and divisive memories of the conflict are difficult to set aside," and these memories "are often exacerbated by inappropriate policies that are insensitive to the impact they may have on relationships and thus on the promotion of peace or of conflict."[44] Moreover, "the resentment of the vanquished toward the victor, nurtured by the sacrifices it has suffered during the war, is exacerbated by the further sacrifices demanded of it" during the aftermath of warfare.[45] For example, many onlookers believe that "the US intention to push through the Western values and political systems in the Middle East region is bound to cause contradictions with those countries whose cultural backdrops and political systems are categorically different from those of the West and will stimulate the generation and development of extremist forces."[46] Moreover, preexisting social value differences—often sharply divisive for centuries and often linking to language and economic gaps—among different vanquished society ethnic, religious, or racial groups appear unlikely to disappear just because of a new political-military regime. Indeed, the postwar "vacuum of authority" could easily stimulate the intensification of both verbal barbs and hostile acts among these groups, as they jockey for position and influence while at the same time resenting the victor.[47] In the end, transforming the enduring social values among the defeated state population after warfare may be even more of a challenge than transforming their existing political or economic systems.

A second social fallacy has many victors *underestimating the vanquished state's postwar social turmoil,* assuming that unruly elements will readily move toward conformity to the new social order (which for many post–Cold War conflicts involves movement away from violence and toward civil discourse to resolve disputes). The underlying assumption is that dissident elements will recognize that continued fighting is futile once military defeat occurs in warfare. The German underestimation of resistance movements after its military victories over several European states during World War II illustrates this pattern.

In reality, managing such turmoil is very difficult after any type of major upheaval, and war is certainly no exception. External disruptive forces can play divisive roles in the defeated state in the aftermath of war, throwing their support behind a social faction that otherwise might have had to subordinate its interest to that of other groups; as disgruntled groups in the vanquished society seek and receive support from abroad, the chances of regional contagion of turmoil can escalate.[48] Because in recent years unruly elements within a defeated country assume that the occupying forces are temporary, they often see—often falsely—the initiation of violence as a way to hasten the departure of these unwanted occupying forces. During the late 1990s, Israel discovered this quandary when occupying southern Lebanon. As discussed earlier regarding morality, too much restraint or leniency by the victor in confronting unruly elements in the vanquished state can appear as a sign of weakness, and thus being perceived as overly sensitive about humanitarian concerns may sometimes actually worsen a victor's capacity to promote movement toward civil discourse: "unless comprehensive security needs are addressed up front, spoilers will find the weak areas and retain leverage to affect the political outcomes, vitiating the peace."[49] For example, it is widely recognized that Middle Eastern leaders interpret American restraint as weakness.[50]

Diplomatic Fallacies

A key diplomatic fallacy is victors *overestimating the external legitimacy of any postwar arrangement,* assuming the outcome will serve as a positive model admired by onlookers. Those most directly involved in war termination efforts may be the most optimistic. The Bosnian conflict illustrates this pattern, whereby after four years of war, signatories of the 1995 Dayton peace settlement had high expectations of internal compliance and external respect, despite the presence of "die-hard rejectionists in all three ethnic communities who have sought to thwart a single, multiethnic state."[51] Similarly, after ending major combat operations in the Iraq War in May 2003, US government officials appeared unrealistically "to hope that the threat of regime change may also dislodge hostile Syrian, Iranian, and North Korean regimes that support terrorism or are otherwise inimical to US security interests."[52]

In reality, tension frequently emerges between the conflicting prerequisites for international legitimacy and internal stability, as foreign observers inherently skeptical of a victor's claims about success sometimes place the preservation of defeated citizens' rights well above the need to establish internal order. Following the principles of attribution theory, such outside skeptics may view any postwar hiccups as intentional results of the victor's defective predispositions and policies rather than unintentional products of adverse situational events beyond the victor's control.[53] Moreover, the scarcity of overarching global security values makes international resentment and "outright hostility" likely to emerge in response to virtually any victory in war by a powerful state (particularly when a sizable power gap exists between winners and losers), no matter how the conflict ends and no matter what terms are imposed.[54] Onlookers seem most likely to view international coercion as legitimate when it confronts a universally opposed aggressor, an unlikely scenario in today's world.

A second diplomatic fallacy involves *overestimating the victor's ability to transform positively domestic and international support* for a postwar arrangement, assuming that onlookers' views are highly malleable. The underlying assumptions here are that the victor's propaganda can work well in this regard and that international observers will readily accept the perspective it presents on the postwar predicament. US optimism about its ability to garner international support for its 1965 Dominican Republic invasion and its 1983 Grenada invasion exemplifies this general pattern.

In reality, even if both sides' leaders are committed to such an arrangement, grumbling is likely to emerge among disaffected elements within the defeated country about unfairness, pointing to inadequate representation in postwar governance, for "war often leaves behind unresolved power struggles."[55] This residual dissatisfaction and power struggle are not readily susceptible to outside manipulation because disgruntled groups are already likely to be alienated from those involved in managing the aftermath of war. Moreover, in today's anarchic and interdependent global security environment, it seems quite difficult to manipulate the views of observing states about war outcomes: sympathy may exist, due to ethnic, religious, or ideological ties, to parts of the defeated state's population; and skepticism about the victor's reports about conditions within the defeated society remains high. The continued instability over recent decades in the West Bank in the Middle East, following the wars in 1967 and 1973 between the Arab states and Israel, illustrates this problem.

As a result, in modern times "fifty-four percent of peace agreements break down within five years of signature."[56] Though some scholars argue that just reaching an agreement is a monumental step, the track record of sustained effectiveness is bleak. Given the likelihood of substantial local disapproval, many postwar peace operations have to "use the threat of violence to compel opposing forces to seek accommodation or to abide by an existing truce or peace treaty."[57] Moreover, in attempting to maximize vanquished state compliance, the victor may find itself perceived as overly harsh by the defeated country, as was the case with Germany's perception of the outcome of World War I. Because many postwar agreements involve stern measures "to ensure that the enemy's defeat is irreversible," seeking "stability by eliminating an adversary's capacity to mount a future military challenge," the defeated country—which might have expected leniency or magnanimousness—could feel insulted or even betrayed, causing further opposition to the status quo after warfare.[58] The use of coercion may also cause international onlookers to become critical of the war outcome.

Concluding Thoughts

A victor's faulty overly positive postwar expectations, including exaggerating its abilities, its victory payoffs, and its ease of attaining these payoffs, pose a major obstacle to achieving strategic victory after military victory. The postwar predicament may be complex and quickly changing, and the passions following war may be fierce and promote emotional hyperbole, but to reap postwar payoffs, leaders must keep their heads and carefully assess existing opportunities and dangers. Although under such circumstances perceptual distortions are understandable, they prevent victors from thinking in a balanced way about how to manage successfully the challenges surrounding war termination. Strategic victory seems particularly susceptible to these misconceptions because it is a lot less tangible than military victory, and thus the ambiguity affords a greater opportunity for delusional thinking; the US Department of Defense's twenty-first-century strategic emphasis on future uncertainty and unpredictability fosters a high vulnerability to the entrance of preconceived bias.[59]

Understanding the tradeoffs associated with success in warfare is essential to achieving postwar payoffs. Often postwar exaggeration of the ease of technological control, intelligence gathering, power imposition, armed forces flexibility, regime transformation, local empowerment, cost-benefit assessment, civility implantation, and legitimacy acquisition can cause unnecessary and counterproductive postwar violence to occur. Overcoming the challenges to reaping postwar payoffs usually involves prioritizing competing objectives and priorities, and victors cannot undertake this prioritization effectively unless they have an accurate and comprehensive understanding—unprejudiced by their preferences—of the situation at hand.

During the heat of battle, misperceptions are harder to spot due to the rapid pace of events and the lack of time to scrutinize and second-guess decisions made. In the immediate aftermath of war, distorted images are much more obvious, yet optimistic biases persist. In light of the misconceptions surrounding strategic victory, one could conclude pessimistically that it is hopeless to expect victors in war to have a balanced understanding of postwar predicaments and, as a consequence, that leaders will continue blithely to hope for the best rather than more prudently to prepare for the worst. In contrast, however, this study assumes that—as subsequent chapters demonstrate—it is possible to *address* and *remedy* postwar perceptual distortions once they are identified. The consistency of overconfidence underlying these perceptual distortions suggests that, rather than simple awareness of them among policymakers combined with encouragement to try to avoid them, the solution may lie more in the direction of altering institutional design such that structural guarantees foster dispassionate debate, questioning of established ideas, and fresh analysis.[60] Recent difficulties in achieving strategic victory, compounded by the persistent gap between wartime expectations and actual postwar achievements, constitute a strong impetus to reexamine the realities surrounding war termination.

Notes

1. With regard to the first item, see Robert Jervis, *Perception and Misperception in International Politics* (Princeton, NJ: Princeton University Press, 1976), chapter 4. On the second item, see Robert Mandel, "Adversaries' Expectations and Desires about War Termination," in Stephen C. Cimbala, ed., *Strategic War Termination* (Westport, CT: Praeger, 1986), p. 177. The third point is discussed in Ralph K. White, *Nobody Wanted War: Misperception in Vietnam and Other Wars* (Garden City, NY: Doubleday, 1970), pp. 303–305.
2. Robert Mandel, "Psychological Approaches to International Relations," in Margaret G. Hermann, ed., *Political Psychology* (San Francisco: Jossey-Bass, 1986), p. 271.
3. Dominic Johnson and Dominic Tierney, *Failing to Win: Perceptions of Victory and Defeat in International Politics* (Cambridge, MA: Harvard University Press, forthcoming), chapter 1.
4. Stephen Biddle, "Land Warfare: Theory and Practice," in John Baylis, James Wirtz, Eliot Cohen, and Colin S. Gray, eds., *Strategy in the Contemporary World* (New York: Oxford University Press, 2002), p. 107.
5. Lutz Unterseher, "Interventionism Reconsidered: Reconciling Military Action with Political Stability," September 1999, http://www.ciaonet.org/wps/un101/index.html.
6. Ibid.
7. Joe Havely, "Why States Go to Cyber-War," February 16, 2000, http://news.bbc.co.uk/1/hi/sci/tech/642867.stm.
8. Gregory J. Rattray, *Strategic Warfare in Cyberspace* (Cambridge, MA: MIT Press, 2001), p. 141.
9. Antulio J. Echevarria II, *Globalization and the Nature of War* (Carlisle Barracks, PA: US Army War College Strategic Studies Institute, 2003), p. 16.
10. Dominic D. P. Johnson, *Overconfidence and War: The Havoc and Glory of Positive Illusions* (Cambridge, MA: Harvard University Press, 2004), pp. 4, 36.
11. Anthony H. Cordesman, *Iraq and Conflict Termination: The Road to Guerrilla War?* (Washington, DC: Center for Strategic and International Studies, 2003), p. 19; and James Fallows, "Blind into Baghdad," *Atlantic Monthly* 293 (January/February 2004), pp. 52–74.
12. Frederick W. Kagan, "War and Aftermath," *Policy Review* 120 (August-September 2003), pp. 3–27.

13. Colin S. Gray, *Modern Strategy* (New York: Oxford University Press, 1999), p. 99; and John W. Dower, *War Without Mercy: Race and Power in the Pacific War* (New York: Pantheon, 1987), pp. 260–261.

14. Gray, *Modern Strategy*, p. 99.

15. Antulio J. Echevarria II, *Toward an American Way of War* (Carlisle Barracks, PA: US Army War College Strategic Studies Institute, 2004), pp. 13–14, 16.

16. Johnson, *Overconfidence and War*, pp. 4, 36.

17. Zeev Maoz, *Paradoxes of War* (Boston: Unwin Hyman, 1990), p. 253.

18. Colin S. Gray, *Defining and Achieving Decisive Victory* (Carlisle Barracks, PA: US Army War College Strategic Studies Institute, 2002), pp. 21–23.

19. Robert Mandel, *Security, Strategy, and the Quest for Bloodless War* (Boulder, CO: Lynne Rienner, 2004).

20. Anatol Lieven, "Hubris and Nemesis: Kosovo and the Pattern of Western Military Ascendancy and Defeat," in Andrew J. Bacevich and Eliot A. Cohen, *War Over Kosovo* (New York: Columbia University Press, 2001), p. 120.

21. Andrew M. Mack, "Why Big Nations Lose Small Wars," *World Politics* 27 (January 1975), pp. 175–200; Ivan Arreguin-Toft, "How the Weak Win Wars: A Theory of Asymmetric Conflict," *International Security* 26 (Summer 2001), pp. 93–128; and Stuart Albert and Edward C. Luck, eds., *On the Endings of Wars* (Port Washington, NY: Kennikat Press, 1980), p. 243.

22. Carl Osgood, "Bush Administration's Strategic Policy Creates a Conundrum for US Military," *Executive Intelligence Review* 32 (May 20, 2005), http://www.larouchepub.com/other/2005/3220war_games.html.

23. Michael Evans, "From Kadesh to Kandahar: Military Theory and the Future of War," *Naval War College Review* 41 (Summer 2003), pp. 141, 143.

24. Anthony Zinni, "Forum 2003: Understanding What Victory Is," *Proceedings of the United States Naval Institute* 129 (October 2003), p. 32.

25. Wendela C. Moore, "Stability Operations: A Core Warfighting Capacity?" 2003, http://www.ndu.edu/library/n4/n03AMooreStability.pdf.

26. Adam Yarmolinsky, "Professional Military Perspectives on War Termination," in Albert and Luck, *On the Endings of Wars*, p. 126.

27. Matthias Stiefel, "Rebuilding after War: Lessons from WSP" (Geneva, Switzerland: War-Torn Societies Project, 1999), http://wsp.dataweb.ch/wsp_publication/rebu-05.htm.

28. James K. Bishop, "Combat Role Strains Relations between America's Military and Its NGOs," Summer 2003, http://www.humanitarian-review.org/ upload/pdf/BishopEnglishFinal.pdf.

29. Fallows, "Blind into Baghdad," p. 65.

30. "Transfer of Power in Iraq," *PBS Online News Hour,* June 28, 2004, http://www.pbs.org/newshour/bb/middle_east/jan-june04/sovereignty_628.html.

31. Center for Strategic and International Studies and Association of the United States Army, *Meeting the Challenges of Governance and Participation in Post-Conflict Settings* (Washington, DC: Center for Strategic and International Studies and Association of the United States Army, 2002), p. 1.

32. Richard N. Haass, "Regime Change and Its Limits," *Foreign Affairs* 84 (July/August 2005), p. 70.

33. Stiefel, "Rebuilding after War."

34. Minxin Pei, "Lessons of the Past," in Carnegie Endowment for International Peace, *From Victory to Success: Afterwar Policy in Iraq* (New York: Carnegie Endowment for International Peace, 2003), p. 53.

35. Phoebe Marr, "Occupational Hazards: Washington's Record in Iraq," *Foreign Affairs* 84 (July/August 2005), p. 181.

36. Center for Strategic and International Studies and Association of the United States Army, *Meeting the Challenges of Governance and Participation in Post-Conflict Settings*, p. 7.

37. Albert and Luck, *On the Endings of Wars*, p. 4.

38. William D. Hartung, *The Hidden Costs of War,* February 2003, http://www.fourthfreedom.org/pdf/Hartung_report.pdf.

39. Bruce Bartlett, "The 'Cost' of War: Iraq Oil Will Rebuild Iraq," March 26, 2003, http://www.nationalreview.com/nrof_bartlett/bartlett032603 .asp.

40. Allan C. Stam III, *Win, Lose, or Draw: Domestic Politics and the Crucible of War* (Ann Arbor: University of Michigan Press, 1996), p. 2.

41. Center for Strategic and International Studies and Association of the United States Army, *Meeting the Challenges of Governance and Participation in Post-Conflict Settings*, p. 7.

42. Richard Hobbs, *The Myth of Victory: What Is Victory in War?* (Boulder, CO: Westview Press, 1979), p. 475.

43. Leonard Wibberley, *The Mouse That Roared* (Boston: Little, Brown, 1955).

44. Stiefel, "Rebuilding after War."

45. Jay L. Kaplan, "Victor and Vanquished: Their Postwar Relations," in Albert and Luck, *On the Endings of Wars*, p. 78.

46. "Consequence of the Iraq War Is Worrying," *People's Daily Online,* March 2003, http://fpeng.peopledaily.com.cn/200303/25/eng20030325 _113943.shtml.

47. Anne Garrels, "Covering the War in Iraq," John F. Kennedy Library and Foundation, September 29, 2003, http://www.cs.umb.edu/jfklibrary/ forum_garrels.html.

48. Stiefel, "Rebuilding after War."

49. Center for Strategic and International Studies and Association of the United States Army, *Play to Win: Final Report of the Bi-Partisan Commission on Post-Conflict Reconstruction* (Washington, DC: Center for Strategic and International Studies and Association of the United States Army, 2003), p. 7.

50. Bernard Lewis, *The Shaping of the Modern Middle East* (New York: Oxford University Press, 1994).

51. Richard Holbrooke, "Rebuilding Nations," *Washington Post,* April 1, 2002, p. A15.

52. Thomas Carothers, "Why Dictators Aren't Dominoes," in *From Victory to Success: Afterwar Policy in Iraq* (New York: Carnegie Endowment for International Peace, 2003), p. 59.

53. Edward E. Jones and Richard Nisbett, "The Actor and the Observer: Divergent Perceptions of the Causes of Behavior," in Edward E. Jones et al., eds., *Attribution: Perceiving the Causes of Behavior* (Morristown, NJ: Silver Burdett, 1971).

54. Edward N. Luttwak, *On the Meaning of Victory: Essays on Strategy* (New York: Simon and Schuster, 1986), p. 289.

55. Stiefel, "Rebuilding after War."

56. Dan Smith, *The Penguin Atlas of War and Peace* (New York: Penguin Books, 2003), p. 106.

57. Kevin C. M. Benson and Christopher B. Thrash, "Declaring Victory: Planning Exit Strategies for Peace Operations," *Parameters* (August 1996), pp. 69–80.

58. Charles W. Kegley Jr. and Gregory A. Raymond, *How Nations Make Peace* (New York: St. Martin's Press, 1999), p. viii.

59. Fallows, "Blind into Baghdad," p. 53.

60. Comments from an anonymous manuscript reviewer, December 2005.

5

Victory in Recent Wars?

To illustrate the relationship between military victory and strategic victory, distinctive qualities of modern triumph, ongoing moral dilemmas, and common postwar misconceptions, this chapter reviews how recent major international conflicts have ended. Due to the conceptual focus of this volume, the case studies are quite brief, summarizing the origins and chronology of each conflict and analyzing the successes and failures involved in each postwar outcome to determine the extent to which strategic victory was achieved in each case. The selected cases—the 1991 Gulf War, 1999 Kosovo conflict, 2001–2002 war against terrorism in Afghanistan, and the 2003 Iraq War—are admittedly not representative of all recent warfare, but they do highlight the flavor of violent international confrontations in the post–Cold War setting. Because of the recency of these cases, some of the information may be unreliable, anecdotal, or still in flux. The emphasis within each case discussion is not on the idiosyncratic details but rather on elements that link to broader strategic security concerns.

Operation Desert Storm

Operation Desert Storm was a 43-day campaign initiated by the United States and its allies against Iraq between January 16 and February 28, 1991. Its primary stated goal was to liberate Kuwait, responding to Iraq's invasion in August 1990 and subsequent declaration of Kuwait as an Iraqi province. Coalition aircraft targeted strategic Iraqi military targets such as airports, command-and-control centers, missile launch sites, and radar stations, after which—during the last 100 hours of the war—the primary ground thrust occurred. The operation was completed in just over six weeks, with the coalition forces having defeated the Iraqi military and freed Kuwait.

Two key conditions contributed to the quick US-led military victory in the war. First, the United States possessed a vast technological advantage over Iraq, particularly in terms of advanced air power capabilities.[1] As Eliot Cohen writes, "The Gulf War showed air power off to great advantage but in extremely favorable circumstances—the United States brought to bear a force sized and trained to fight with the Soviet Union in a global war, obtained the backing of almost every major military and financial power, and chose the time and place at which combat would begin in a theater ideally suited to air operations."[2] Second, during the war Iraq manifested key deficiencies in leadership, number of troops, and soldier morale and training—"the enemy in the Gulf War was indeed 'perfect,'" as "it was mainly a deeply confused and remarkably ill-led rabble."[3] In light of these two highly propitious circumstances, the war probably did not present the kind of military test for the United States that would lead unruly observers to be deterred by the outcome.

However, policymakers associated with Operation Desert Storm did not appear to plan far beyond military victory. Indeed, "for all the effort President Bush and his advisors took in planning the liberation of Kuwait, they spent remarkably little time on ensuring a durable postwar settlement":

> In the period following the decision to announce a ceasefire, the United States did little to translate its tremendous battlefield advantage into leverage at the bargaining table. Rather, it squandered its influence and in the process reduced its chances of achieving a lasting peace. Nobody in a position of authority in Washington or Riyadh had given much thought to how to end the war; almost everything had to be improvised.[4]

Many analysts argue that "the United States chose to end the Gulf War prematurely," as "coalition forces stopped short of achieving a decisive victory," leading to "robbing the coalition of the opportunity to translate a lopsided battlefield victory into a durable postwar settlement."[5] As a result, controversy surrounds the evaluation of the outcome of the 1991 Gulf War. It is certainly possible to argue that the military victory was decisive and created an effective postwar sanctions regime that prevented the reestablishment of WMD (weapons of mass destruction) programs, and that the outcome contained Saddam Hussein internationally to some degree and caused Iraq to serve as a counterbalance against Iran. However, despite Operation Desert Storm's superficial success, a closer analysis indicates the limits of military victory's ability to achieve long-term political changes, with many observers—admittedly with the benefit of hindsight—finding the Gulf War's political outcome to be "disappointing."[6] Within Iraq, the war "failed to bring about the demise of the vicious regime which had caused the problem in the first place, and it helped to trigger two civil wars and directly caused a breakdown in sanitation facilities in Iraq."[7] Indeed, after the war, Saddam Hussein escalated his barbaric activities toward the people of Iraq:

> The winners of the war were congratulating themselves for having reestablished the principle that was meant to deter aggression: invade a neighboring state, and you will pay a price. But now the loser of the war was taking advantage of an awkward corollary: stay on your own territory, wrap yourself in the cloak of sovereignty, and you can do anything you want. Having been punished for violating the sanctity of borders, Saddam found protection behind that same principle as he butchered his own citizens.[8]

Thus, although Kuwait was free, the condition of the people in the defeated state in many ways deteriorated.

Considering the broader regional impact outside of Iraq, among the stated objectives of the war was "to promote the security and stability of the Persian Gulf," and in many observers' minds this was not achieved.[9] It is unfortunate that "having been crushed on the battlefield but spared total defeat, Saddam not only remained the scourge of his own people but seemed to be reemerging as a menace to his neighbors and to world peace as well.[10] Furthermore, though "there were hopes that the outcome of the Gulf conflict would result in a revolutionary change to the prevailing order in the Middle East," with successful state transitions to stable democracy, "in the aftermath of war, there has been little evidence that the principal actors in the Middle East have risen to this challenge."[11] Moreover, the victory was touted as "a triumph for democracy," but the Arab countries involved in the coalition were decidedly not democratic.[12] In a global sense, then, after the war "President Bush had little to show his constituents by way of a more orderly world."[13]

Although the United States never stated leadership decapitation as a goal of the war, for many observers the absence of positive postwar change within Iraq and the region as a whole was due to the continued rule of Saddam Hussein in Iraq. Hussein stayed in power and continued to be defiant of the United States and the international community for over twelve years afterward. Indeed, so long as Saddam Hussein ran Iraq, "there was a keen sense of unfinished business."[14]

Thus, although the 1991 Gulf War may have been more unambiguously a "just war" than the other cases discussed here and was very successful in expelling Iraq from Kuwait, doubts still surround whether the United States accomplished strategic victory in that war. Legitimacy in war efforts does not always translate into long-term success, and decisive military victory does not always lead to deterring one's adversaries from engaging in future disruptive behavior.

Operation Allied Force

On March 24, 1999, the North Atlantic Treaty Organization (NATO) initiated Operation Allied Force as a means to compel Serbian leader Slobodan Milosevic to cease ethnic cleansing and human rights violations in Kosovo, primarily against ethnic Kosovar Albanians, and to pull Serbian forces out of the disputed province. Fourteen nations waged the attack entirely by air, severely damaging Serbian infrastructure before ultimately ending Milosevic's rule. Like Operation Desert Storm, the war was remarkably one-sided from a military capabilities standpoint, as the United States defense budget alone was fifteen times the size of Serbia's entire gross national product.[15]

It is difficult to describe the outcome of this war as a swift and decisive military victory. Although utilizing a greater percentage of "smart" weapons than in any other conflict before it, the campaign's success required a surprisingly sustained effort over seventy-eight days:

> While we can marvel over the demonstrated capabilities of B-2s, JDAMs, laser-guided munitions, and Global Positioning System–assisted bombing techniques, looking at Allied Force objectively, it still looks like a win, but a rather ugly one. For starters, we got that "W" by applying a greater portion of the Air Force's total airframes during this operation than we did in the Korean War, during any period in the Vietnam War, or in Desert Storm. It took the air forces of 13 contributing NATO countries to

> batter Yugoslavia to the point that Milosevic agreed to withdraw his forces from Kosovo and permit the introduction of a UN peacekeeping force, including Russian troops, into the strife-torn province.[16]

Despite the precision of NATO air attacks, the estimated 5,000 to 10,000 casualties included hundreds of unintended injuries or deaths in Serbia, the displacement and massacre of large numbers of ethnic Albanian Kosovars, and people hurt through an embarrassing accidental demolition of a wing of the Chinese Embassy in Belgrade, all indicating some significant holes in intelligence and communication. The reliance on air power was partially due to an unwillingness to commit any ground troops, signaling to foes tentativeness about the effort. The unconventional nature of the warfare, involving nonstate military targets without clear demarcation from civilian installations, certainly complicated matters. Indeed, Serb units intentionally operated in the midst of civilian refugees and near prohibited targets; utilized extensive camouflage, concealment, and deception to fool NATO; and employed medium-altitude anti-aircraft missiles that forced NATO planes to fly at high altitudes, all making it difficult to identify definitively critical vulnerability points on the ground.[17]

The underwhelming reaction by the American public to the aftermath of the Kosovo conflict was perhaps symptomatic of this less-than-stellar political outcome:

> When NATO's war over Kosovo ended last June with the saving appearance of victory and not a single American life lost, there was, curiously, no sense of triumph among Americans: no jubilation, no parades, no boost in the polls for Bill Clinton. Was this because of general indifference to events in the Balkans—or widespread suspicion that the victory was hollow?[18]

The US government's ability to demonstrate dramatic and positive postwar change in Kosovo was decidedly limited. Furthermore, the United States and NATO may have been victims of their own over-optimism: "Operation Allied Force in 1999 proceeded on the illusory assumption that a three- or four-day demonstration of air power would persuade Slobodan Milosevic to submit to NATO's will."[19]

Despite the military victory, specifically the removal of Milosevic and the reduction of aggression in the region, the political payoff from the war was decidedly modest. Specifically, the alliance "went to war, by its own account, to protect the precarious political stability of the countries of the Balkans; the result, however, was precisely the opposite."[20] The aftermath of the Kosovo conflict was marked by "its inability to halt the reverse ethnic cleansing of Kosovo"; after the war, "estimates vary widely, but as many as 125,000 of the roughly 200,000 Serbs who lived in Kosovo before the NATO bombing have fled or been driven out," and gypsies, Turks, and Muslim Slavs "have also been the subject of widespread and indiscriminate attacks."[21] In the aftermath of war, the political question at its heart—the proper principle for determining sovereignty—"remained unsettled." As a result, "this made the war, as a deliberate act of policy, a perfect failure" because "the humanitarian goal NATO sought—the prevention of suffering—was not achieved by the bombing," and "the political goal the air campaign made possible and the Albanian Kosovars favored—independence—NATO not only did not seek but actively opposed."[22] Most generally, despite the removal of Milosevic, the people of the Balkans did not see their lives tangibly improve, and Kosovo today is decidedly not characterized by peace, democracy, stability, or prosperity.

Operation Enduring Freedom

Operation Enduring Freedom began on October 7, 2001, four weeks after the September 11 terrorist attacks on the World Trade Center and the Pentagon in the United States. The explicit goal was to defeat in Afghanistan the Taliban and Al-Qaida forces, identified as the perpetrators of the violence. Approximately 60,000 US soldiers were involved in the war effort at the peak of the conflict. A coalition of Afghan Northern Alliance fighters, air sorties by US planes, Western special operations forces and intelligence operatives, and a small contingent of Western ground forces participated in the action. Although most of the bombing had ended by late 2001, when the new government regime in Afghanistan was inaugurated, sporadic bombing continued through mid-January 2002, and violence has persisted long afterward.

Parallel to the military outcome in the 1991 Gulf War, the US military victory against the Taliban did not exactly inspire awe and fear among potentially disruptive observers. Many analysts assert that the reported stunning military successes were misleading (for example, "US airpower has been essentially unopposed") because the Taliban lacked the know-how to undertake deception or camouflage and the technology to implement electronic jammers and air defense systems.[23] Moreover, when facing a more difficult foe—the Al-Qaida terrorists, whose unbridled passion for their cause and apparent unwillingness to accept defeat made victory against them a real challenge—US military success has been a lot less decisive.

Indeed, this campaign highlighted key limitations of military victory against a hard-to-identify target. Despite "the adulation of Operation Enduring Freedom (OEF) as a 'finely-tuned' or 'bulls-eye' war, the campaign failed to set a new standard for precision in one important respect—the rate of civilians killed per bomb dropped; in fact, this rate was far higher in the Afghanistan conflict—perhaps four times higher—than in the 1999 Balkans war."[24] In part, this pattern reflected the incredibly high difficulty of distinguishing between civilians and the informally clad terrorist combatants.

Furthermore, in terms of reaping the political stability fruits of victory in Afghanistan, the war did not achieve strategic victory. Whereas the United States was thinking "that the same men who caused Afghanistan so much misery in the past will somehow lead it to democracy and stability in the future," the evidence "suggests that the opposite is happening," as "key warlords have returned to power" and "opportunities have been lost, goodwill squandered, and lessons of history ignored."[25] The rapid military victory of the Alliance and the collapse of the Taliban "released centrifugal tendencies throughout Afghanistan, giving warlordism, banditry, and opium production a new lease on life."[26] Indeed, the export of illicit drugs from Afghanistan to the rest of the world has dramatically escalated after the war. Perversely, "Operation Enduring Freedom's severing of [Al-Qaida's] symbiotic relationship with the Taliban and destruction of its training bases in Afghanistan have provoked even more decentralised modes of operation that are even more difficult to detect and target."[27] Perhaps most important, the war effort has so far (by the end of 2005) failed to achieve a key goal of capturing or killing Al-Qaida leader Osama bin Laden.

Thus, the long-term prospects do not appear to be unambiguously bright. Specific concerns have emerged about insufficient spending on postwar reconstruction and an inability to constitute a solid international peacekeeping force, along with continuing worry about violence and the pace of progress toward democracy.[28] Sadly, "there are increasing signs that the damage being done in Afghanistan will not be easily remedied" in the future, what with "its flourishing drug trade, widespread insecurity, sluggish disarmament, and insufficient international aid."[29] Within the country, "Hamid Karzai's government has won international aid and recognition but controls little of the countryside," and "US troops still hunt Taliban or [Al-Qaida] remnants and absorb occasional casualties" years after the war began.[30] Unfortunately, "the main victims of all this have been ordinary Afghans," and the Afghan public "has grown disappointed and disillusioned with the international community, which it increasingly blames for failing to deliver the lofty promises that preceded the US attack on the Taliban."[31] In the end, it is difficult to demonstrate convincingly that the overall conditions in the country or the region have dramatically improved as a result of the war.

Operation Iraqi Freedom

On March 20, 2003, US and British troops invaded Iraq to begin the second Gulf War. Despite US claims that its coalition included forty-nine nations, the only other countries to provide fighting forces were Australia and Poland (on land) and Denmark and Spain (at sea). The invasion reached a speedy conclusion, with Baghdad controlled on April 9, followed by the collapse of the Iraqi regime signified by the fall of Saddam Hussein's stronghold, Tikrit, on April 15. On May 1, 2003, President George W. Bush declared that major combat operations were over, and most analysts therefore concluded that military victory occurred by that date. Later on, in December 2003, the United States captured Saddam Hussein himself. The international community was divided on the legitimacy of this invasion, and the United States has received heavy criticism for the war from Belgium, Russia, France, China, Germany, and the Arab League.

The stated justification for the invasion included allegations that the Iraqi government produced weapons of mass destruction, had ties to the Al-Qaida terrorist group, and engaged in human rights violations, and as a result the primary initial goal was to rid the country of these arms and free the Iraqi people from the oppressive Saddam Hussein regime. White House Press Secretary Ari Fleischer specifically stated that the focus was on changing the Hussein regime and finding and destroying the chemical and biological weapons presumed to be in Iraq: "The definition of victory is those two factors."[32] In the aftermath of the war, however, the thrust changed considerably, focusing simply on bringing democracy and freedom to the Iraqi people.

The US military strategy in Operation Iraqi Freedom was designed to be quick and surgically effective against designated targets, with minimum loss of life. The underlying assumption was that precision weapons could wreak havoc unimpeded, aided by night missions, nullifying the capacity of the enemy to fight back. A key underlying component of the initial phase of this military strategy was dubbed "shock and awe," attempting to reduce the enemy's will to fight through a display of overwhelming force through superior technology.

Unfortunately, close scrutiny makes the US military victory against Iraq less than impressive. Despite the speed of the war, decent protection of the oil refineries, and American casualty counts before the end of major combat operations in May 2003 far lower—only 154—than those in the Gulf War, significant collateral damage to Iraqi people and property occurred during that time:

> As the battles dragged on week after week, it became evident that the unrelenting mathematics of war had reached a tipping point. American and British forces had used such a high number of smart bombs that the normal miss rate of the Joint Direct Attack Munitions (JDAMs) and Tomahawk cruise missiles had produced an inordinate number of civilian casualties.
>
> The most ominous sign, clearly documented on Al-Jazeera, but not on US news networks, was the daily growing number of women and children with missing limbs.... Doctors in Baghdad were so overwhelmed with casualties that they had neither the time, anesthetics nor antibiotics to repair complex injuries.[33]

Moreover, since May 2003, the postwar body count has dwarfed that during the war, with a total of well over 2,000 Americans killed in action by the end of 2005. The United States seems to have forfeited in the process the normal consequence of military victory that body bags cease to come home in large numbers after a war is won.

Misconceptions at the outset of the Iraq War created problems in attaining strategic victory following the end of major combat operations:

> Overoptimism in the planning of the war—about how many troops were needed and what they were likely to face after a military victory—spawned several failures of the occupation phase. [Secretary of Defense Donald] Rumsfeld's doctrine of using small, highly maneuverable forces plus overwhelming aerial bombardment proved successful in achieving quick military victories (both in

> Afghanistan and in Iraq), but it contained a hidden overoptimism about what these same forces would face the day after victory. In the planning phase, officials played down potential postwar problems partially in order to garner support for launching the war.[34]

The United States specifically underestimated the postwar violence in Iraq by opposition groups, the vulnerability of US supply lines, the potency of local guerrilla-style resistance, and the overall costs of reconstructing Iraq.[35] This overoptimism persisted even after major military operations ended: in May 2004, "General Richard Myers, chair of the Joint Chiefs of Staff, stated, 'I think we are on the verge of success here.'"[36] To many observers, "Iraq proves again, hard on the heels of Afghanistan, that the United States chronically underestimates the difficulties of nonmilitary aspects of foreign interventions and wildly inflates nonmilitary goals without committing the resources required to achieve them."[37] Moreover, misinformation concerning the presence of weapons of mass destruction in Iraq and the Iraqi regime's direct link to Al-Qaida terrorists has significantly eroded the international credibility of the United States.

A clear deficiency was evident in the Iraq War planning in concentrating on winning the war rather than on winning the peace. A Joint Chiefs of Staff report issued shortly after the war ended revealed that Operation Iraqi Freedom placed too much emphasis on military operations to defeat the Iraqi military and too little on political transition planning.[38] It has become clear in retrospect that "the US occupation of Iraq is a debacle not because the government did no planning but because a vast amount of expert planning was willfully ignored by the people in charge."[39] The US emphasis on military rather than political priorities, however misguided, was in some ways to be expected:

> Translating a military triumph into a political success—that is, a peace better than that of the pre-war situation—is an inherently difficult enterprise, especially for a country that has historically viewed war as a suspension of politics and military victory as an end in and of itself; this view was reflected in Operation Iraqi Freedom's virtually exclusive focus on the first half of the regime-change challenge—toppling the old regime—at the expense of the second and far more difficult challenge—creating a new political order amenable to US interests.[40]

In the end, it would be difficult to imagine a postwar predicament that more starkly contrasted the disjuncture between speedy military victory and agonizingly slow accomplishment of long-term informational, political, economic, social, and diplomatic objectives.

Within the postwar field operations themselves, US forces have felt torn between competing demands—on the one hand, promoting freedom and open civil society within Iraq; and on the other hand, maintaining order and deterring acts of violence. The inherent conflict between these mission tasks has become so severe that ultimately "America's ability to win the peace is in doubt":

> US forces are struggling to balance the doctrinal principles of security and legitimacy. Furthermore, they are doing it without a strong doctrinal foundation that prescribes important post-war practices. Consequently, victory appears distant, despite President Bush's declaration of the end of major combat operations in Iraq. Coalition forces continue to encounter resistance. This, however, is not surprising. Undeniably, US efforts are handicapped. Winning the peace in Iraq has been elusive because of a failure to win Iraqi hearts and minds, friction between security and legitimacy, and a failure of doctrine to underscore important post-war practices.[41]

Existing guidance to soldiers in terms of standard operating procedures for dealing with these mission tensions appears to be inadequate. Sensing increasing risk, US soldiers have been forced to operate with increased caution (for example, not removing helmets or leaving vehicles) and with growing suspicion of Iraqi citizens, in turn increasing local disenchantment with US soldiers and decreasing the kinds of positive interactions between sides necessary for strategic victory.

Due to these problems, with the violence continuing at the time of this writing, it would be difficult to classify the Iraq War outcome as a strategic victory. In many ways, the United States appears to have completely squandered "a decisive, potentially historic military victory":

> Mistakes were made at virtually every turn, and as the principal nation promoting the conflict and managing its aftermath, the United States bears the chief blame. In the weeks leading up to and following the war, the Bush administration depicted a liberated Iraq welcoming our invading troops as liberators, quickly stabilizing the political order, regaining economic vitality, and making the momentous transition to freedom—a transition that would, in turn, set off pressures for democratic change throughout the Middle East. But from the moment the war ended, Iraq fell into a deepening

> quagmire of chaos, criminality, insurgency, and terrorism, which, even in the months following the January 2005 elections, showed no prospect of ending anytime soon. During the period of occupational rule, Iraq became a black hole of instability and a justification for neighboring regimes that insisted their societies were not culturally suited or politically ready for democracy.[42]

In the immediate aftermath of the war, "US troops stood by helplessly, outnumbered and unprepared, as much of Iraq's remaining physical, economic, and institutional infrastructure was systematically looted and sabotaged."[43] After over two and a half years since the war was initiated, "Washington has made little progress in defeating the insurgency or providing security for Iraqis, even as it has overextended the US Army and eroded support for the war among the American public."[44] The harsh lessons for the United States in the aftermath of the fall of Baghdad include

> that occupying the country is much more difficult than conquering it; that a breakdown in public order can jeopardize every other goal; that the ambition of patiently nurturing a new democracy is at odds with the desire to turn control over to the Iraqis quickly and get US troops out; that the Sunni center of the country is the main security problem; [and] that with each passing day Americans risk being seen less as liberators and more as occupiers, and targets.[45]

The original American aspiration that the Iraq War "would set in motion a chain of events that would eventually democratize the entire region"[46] has not yet shown any signs of coming to pass.

As in the war against terrorism in Afghanistan, the long-term prospects for the United States in Iraq do not appear bright. Many analysts now believe that "the ongoing war in Iraq is not one that the United States can win" in the future; "as a result of its initial miscalculations, misdirected planning, and inadequate preparation, Washington has lost the Iraqi people's confidence and consent, and it is unlikely to win them back."[47] Due to "the continued attacks on the US military, other coalition forces, Iraqi recruits and police, and civilians (including UN staff), plus the soaring costs and controversial progress toward democracy,"[48] many observers have now lost hope for future strategic victory. The insistence by the US government that everything is going reasonably well, along with the refusal to recognize policies that are not working, has served to reduce these onlookers' expectations of significant improvement in the predicament. In June 2005, President Bush announced that the United States would leave Iraq when the Iraqis were ready to govern themselves; if the United States cannot leave without a well-functioning governance structure in place in Iraq, then the roadblock is that "decent governance is not possible without some minimal level of security," which so far Americans have been unable to provide to the Iraqi people.[49] Ironically, then, dissident elements within Iraq who want Americans to leave may be inadvertently doing everything possible to prevent their departure.

Concluding Thoughts

A few noteworthy patterns emerge from these four cases. Two of the cases (Allied Force and Enduring Freedom) involved more challenging subnational nonstate targets, and two (Desert Storm and Iraqi Freedom) involved a state's formal military forces as the target. Gathering intelligence and distinguishing between civilians and combatants appeared to be easier in Desert Storm than in either Allied Force or Enduring Freedom, given the more conventional nature of the warfare. Although the condition of weaponry was much more primitive in Desert Storm than in the later campaigns, the greater simplicity in targeting may have somewhat compensated for this deficiency; Iraqi Freedom, in comparison, came closest to experiencing the best of both worlds. Complications involving the multiple ethnicities of most of the cases, combined with the special difficulties in identifying key vulnerability points in Allied Force, compounded problems in achieving strategic victory. The genuinely unified intense resolve of the ideologically motivated target terrorists in Afghanistan seems to have provided more of a military challenge than the possibly artificially grafted sense of regime loyalty present in Iraq or Serbia, but the pattern of postwar violence within defeated states was quite sustained in all four wars.

Although each case involved unquestioned military victory by the United States and its allies, who possessed overwhelming advantages in military force, and each achieved an immediate goal (freeing people in Kuwait, Serbia, Afghanistan, and Iraq from an oppressive regime), in many ways each constitutes a vivid illustration of the pitfalls of pursuing strategic victory. Indeed, the general result has been decidedly disappointing long-term political consequences, to such a degree that—for some observers—it calls the value of these wars into serious question. Virtually all were followed by the emergence of regional instability (without the spread of peaceful democratic values), the presence of continued violence, the escalation of suffering for defeated states' citizenry, and some significant international resentment; and none of the cases unambiguously achieved dramatic positive postwar changes fitting all of the war objectives.

Several clear explanations emerge from the cases for the failure of military victory to be followed by strategic victory. First, in each instance the victor inappropriately placed *far too much emphasis on the war-winning phase* at the expense of the peace-winning phase of the conflict, with a notable absence of concerted planning for achieving postwar political payoffs—influenced by domestic political constraints—after military success on the battlefield. Second, in each case the victor exhibited *significant overconfidence about its ability to attain its postwar objectives* swiftly and painlessly, due in part to its overestimation of the postwar utility of superior technology in pursuing this end and its underestimation of postwar resistance and impediments to popular support and political stability within the defeated state. Third, the victor *exaggerated the magnitude of the postwar payoffs* in these cases, reducing the possibility of realistically achieving them. Fourth, once it became clear that obstacles stood in the way of accomplishing long-term goals, victors were *not adept in reacting to this recognition with different and more effective postwar management policies.* Fifth, the *objectives of each war were not generally well-defined,* well-defended, and explicitly limited in nature; in the worst case—the 2003 Iraq War—goals appeared to transform significantly as the conflict progressed. Due to this imprecision, in coping with the postwar dangers victors often found themselves torn between disengaging too early and staying for too long.

The recent string of strategic victory failures underscores that existing war termination policies are decidedly ripe for change. Avoiding current postwar management deficiencies, including the vicious cycle of continued counterproductive international violence, appears crucial.

> Army Col. Robert Killebrew (ret.), speaking at an April 11 [2005] conference at the American Enterprise Institute on the future of the Army, declared: "It is my contention that we no longer know how to fight and win wars. We have become very good at campaign planning. We are an excellent battle force; but in terms of linking the battles to strategic victory, tying it up in a bow with an outcome that totally satisfies our commitment and then moving on, I don't think we as a defense establishment anymore understand how to do

> that." Killebrew gave four reasons for this situation: There is nobody left in the defense establishment who remembers how we won World War II; during the Cold War, we deliberately limited our conflicts in order to avoid antagonizing our superpower rivals; the Defense Department has long had an infatuation with technology in order to limit liability in any conflict; and the military reform of the 1980s was incomplete.[50]

Though perhaps overly harsh, this stinging critique viscerally reflects the frustration of many American and other Western defense planners about the difficulties, illustrated in this chapter's cases, of securing strategic victory payoffs in today's anarchic global security environment. It is not that standards for victory have risen in recent years, but rather that the massive expectations now placed on the military are truly difficult to achieve in an international setting decidedly inhospitable to such mission accomplishment.

The unfortunate consequence of this pattern is that the cases do not in and of themselves provide very helpful clues about what is necessary to turn military victory into strategic victory. One might well ask why this book does not contain a recent case study of success in achieving postwar strategic victory in order to help provide guideposts to improve future conflict termination management. The difficulty here is that when examining the entire post–Cold War record of conflict outcomes, no such case exists. Indeed, many observers conclude that "excepting the demise of the Soviet Union, one could make the case that the United States has not achieved a strategic victory since World War II."[51] It is certainly possible to explore back before 1989 to find potential candidates for postwar strategic success: two interesting examples are the Allies' involvement in World War II, due to the tangible threat from Germany and Japan, clear goals, and huge commitment; and the British management of the Malayan Emergency between 1948 and 1960, in which there was an emphasis on promoting personal security and decent living standards to win "hearts and minds" of local citizens and reduce support for the insurgents. However; both cases are controversial, as the British engaged in some ruthless violence to repress the insurgency, and the Allies' motives and goals changed quite a bit as World War II progressed; and because these cases are quite dated, their relevance is decidedly limited in providing insight about how to attain strategic victory in today's post–Cold War global security environment.

Nonetheless, probing reflection on this chapter's cases offers a ray of hope, as they provide significant indications of specific areas where strategic victory might have been possible had winners on the battlefield placed more priority on this second phase of victory and handled the aftermath of warfare quite differently. In other words, despite the existence of major obstacles, if winners of military confrontations improved the ways in which they conclude wars, there appears to be no intrinsic reason why strategic victory cannot occur in today's global security environment. Just as taking courses from really bad teachers can sometimes provide inspiration about how to teach well, so attentively studying recent deficiencies in postwar management can help—perhaps even more than studying successes—decisionmakers figure out what not to do to have the greatest potential to achieve postwar payoffs. Although obviously having the benefit of hindsight makes it relatively easy to see what could have been done differently, the aspiration here is to translate this awareness of past mistakes into more effective forward planning about the termination of future wars. The next chapter builds on this possibility by suggesting more generally when strategic victory is most likely.

Notes

1. William J. Perry, "Desert Storm and Deterrence," *Foreign Affairs* 70 (Fall 1991), pp. 66–82.
2. Eliot A. Cohen, "A Revolution in Warfare," *Foreign Affairs* 75 (March/April 1996), pp. 30–40.
3. John Mueller, "The Perfect Enemy: Assessing the Gulf War," *Security Studies* 5 (Autumn 1995), p. 106; and Jeffrey Record, *Hollow Victory* (Washington, DC: Brassey's, 1993), pp. 6, 135.
4. Thomas G. Mahnken, "A Squandered Opportunity? The Decision to End the Gulf War," in Andrew J. Bacevich and Ephraim Inbar, eds., *The Gulf War of 1991 Reconsidered* (Portland, OR: Frank Cass, 2003), pp. 121, 136.
5. Ibid., p. 121.
6. Stephen Biddle, "Victory Misunderstood: What the Gulf War Tells Us about the Future of Conflict," *International Security* 21 (Fall 1996), p. 141.
7. John Mueller, "The Perfect Enemy: Assessing the Gulf War," *Security Studies* 5 (Autumn 1995), p. 117.
8. Strobe Talbott, "Post-Victory Blues," *Foreign Affairs* 71 (1991/1992), p. 63.
9. Mahnken, "A Squandered Opportunity?" p. 125.
10. Talbott, "Post-Victory Blues," p. 67.
11. Roland Dannreuther, *The Gulf Conflict: A Political and Strategic*

Analysis (London: International Institute for Strategic Studies Adelphi Paper #264, Winter 1991/1992), p. 81.

12. "Lessons of the Persian Gulf War," http://www.freedomrings.net/html/writings/essays/Lessons_of_the_Persian_Gulf_War.htm.

13. Lawrence Freedman and Efraim Karsh, *The Gulf Conflict 1990–1991: Diplomacy and War in the New World Order* (Princeton, NJ: Princeton University Press. 1993), p. 440.

14. Ibid., p. 427.

15. Andrew J. Bacevich and Eliot A. Cohen, "Strange Little War," in Andrew J. Bacevich and Eliot A. Cohen, eds., *War Over Kosovo* (New York: Columbia University Press, 2001), p. ix.

16. Earl H. Tilford Jr., "Operation Allied Force and the Role of Air Power" *Parameters* 29 (Winter 1999-2000), pp. 24–38.

17. William M. Arkin, "Operation Allied Force: 'The Most Precise Application of Air Power in History,'" in Bacevich and Cohen, *War Over Kosovo*, pp. 14–15.

18. "The Joyless Victory," *Wilson Quarterly* 23 (Autumn 1999), p. 79.

19. Andrew J. Bacevich, "'Splendid Little War': America's Persian Gulf Adventure Ten Years On," in Bacevich and Inbar, *The Gulf War of 1991 Reconsidered*, p. 154.

20. Brian Bond, *The Pursuit of Victory: From Napoleon to Saddam Hussein* (New York: Oxford University Press, 1996), p. 3.

21. David Rohde, "Kosovo Seething," *Foreign Affairs* 79 (May/June 2000), p. 70.

22. Michael Mandelbaum, "A Perfect Failure," *Foreign Affairs* 78 (September/October 1999), p. 5.

23. Thomas E. Ricks, "Bull's-Eye War: Pinpoint Bombing Shifts Role of GI Joe," *Washington Post,* December 2, 2001, p. A1. Fred Kaplan, "New Warfare: High-Tech US Arsenal Proves Its Worth," *Boston Globe,* December 9, 2001, p. A34.

24. Carl Conetta, "Operation Enduring Freedom: Why a Higher Rate of Civilian Bombing Casualties?" (Cambridge, MA: Commonwealth Institute, Project on Defense Alternatives *Briefing Report* #11, January 18, 2002; revised January 24, 2002), http://www.comw.org/pda/0201oef.html.

25. Kathy Gannon, "Afghanistan Unbound," *Foreign Affairs* 83 (May/June 2004), p. 36.

26. Carl Conetta, "Strange Victory: A Critical Appraisal of Operation Enduring Freedom and the Afghanistan War" (Cambridge, MA: Commonwealth Institute Project on Defense Alternatives Research Monograph #6, January 30, 2002), p. 18, http://www.comw.org/pda/0201strangevic.pdf.

27. Jeffrey Record, "The Limits and Temptations of America's Conventional Military Primacy," *Survival* 47 (Spring 2005), p. 36.

28. Dominic D. P. Johnson, *Overconfidence and War: The Havoc and Glory of Positive Illusions* (Cambridge, MA: Harvard University Press, 2004), p. 265.

29. Kathy Gannon, "Afghanistan Unbound," *Foreign Affairs* 83 (May/June 2004), pp. 41, 44.

30. Richard Whittle and David McLemore, "When Will Victory Be Achieved? Answer Isn't Easy to Come By," *Dallas Morning News,* April 6, 2003.

31. Gannon, "Afghanistan Unbound," p. 41.

32. Ibid.

33. Jim Wilson, "Smart Weapons under Fire," *Popular Mechanics* 180 (July 2003), pp. 42–43.

34. Johnson, *Overconfidence and War*, p. 201.

35. Ibid., p. 206–207.

36. Andrew F. Krepinevich Jr., "How to Win in Iraq," *Foreign Affairs* 84 (September/October 2005), p. 88.

37. Jessica Tuchman Mathews, "Now for the Hard Part," in Carnegie Endowment for International Peace, *From Victory to Success: Afterwar Policy in Iraq* (New York: Carnegie Endowment for International Peace, 2003), p. 51.

38. Rowan Scarborough, "US Rushed Post-Saddam Planning," *Washington Times*, September 3, 2003.

39. James Fallows, "Blind into Baghdad," *Atlantic Monthly* 293 (January/February 2004), p. 53.

40. Record, "The Limits and Temptations of America's Conventional Military Primacy," p. 42.

41. Justin Gage, William Martin, Tim Mitchell, and Pat Wingate, "Winning the Peace in Iraq: Confronting America's Informational and Doctrinal Handicaps" (Norfolk, VA: Joint Forces Staff College, September 5, 2003), p. 1.

42. Larry Diamond, *Squandered Victory: The American Occupation and the Bungled Effort to Bring Democracy to Iraq* (New York: Henry Holt, 2005), p. 279.

43. Larry Diamond, "What Went Wrong in Iraq," *Foreign Affairs* 83 (September/October 2004), p. 36.

44. Krepinevich Jr., "How to Win in Iraq," p. 87.

45. Fallows, "Blind into Baghdad," p. 54.

46. Christopher Preble, "After Victory: Toward a New Military Posture in the Persian Gulf," *Policy Analysis* 477 (June 10, 2003), p. 12.

47. James Dobbins, "Iraq: Winning the Unwinnable War," *Foreign Affairs* 84 (January/February 2005), p. 16.

48. Johnson, *Overconfidence and War*, p. 204.

49. Diamond, "What Went Wrong in Iraq," p. 42.

50. Carl Osgood, "Bush Administration's Strategic Policy Creates a Conundrum for US Military," *Executive Intelligence Review* 32 (May 20, 2005), http://www.larouchepub.com/other/2005/3220war_games.html.

51. Vincent J. Goulding Jr., "From Chancellorsville to Kosovo: Forgetting the Art of War," *Parameters* (Summer 2000), pp. 4–18.

6

Victory Challenges in Contemporary Warfare

In light of the case study findings discussed in Chapter 5, some general patterns emerge about the compatibility of strategic victory with contemporary warfare. This chapter begins by discussing state-level and system-level impediments to modern strategic victory, pertaining to Western states' character and existing global "rules of the game." It then turns more pragmatically to the identification of the conditions under which states seem most likely to achieve strategic victory in modern warfare, with the underlying understanding that different kinds of predicaments and "different sorts of political objectives lend themselves to different sorts of victory conditions."[1]

Western States' Limitations in Reaping Victory Payoffs

A general mismatch exists between the state-level pursuit of victory by the West and the security threats it faces within today's anarchic global security environment. Maintaining information control is increasingly difficult in today's porous and vulnerable international setting, as relatively easy means are available to deflect accurate intelligence gathering and to penetrate, manipulate, or scramble vital information systems. Moreover, ever-vigilant media and communications technologies spread information about undesired outcomes instantly to citizens worldwide without a government pursuing victory having a chance beforehand to try to explain how such incidents fit into the gradually developing big picture. Attaining postwar military deterrence is a major challenge, for the restraint and finite staying power associated with today's limited triumphs do not teach lasting punitive lessons to defeated states for the future or to other unruly states observing the aftermath of war. Aiming to achieve postwar political self-determination, economic reconstruction, and social justice goals may be noble, but given that the sources of international disruption tend to be either fiercely independent warlords or anti-Western forces resistant to these purposes and unappreciative of efforts to accomplish them, pursuing these ends may be a recipe for failure. Finally, reaping postwar diplomatic respect from one's own citizenry, allies, international organizations, and other outside observers may be problematic due not only to the inability to achieve unambiguous postwar aims but also because of the very different lenses these onlookers use to judge overall success.

The restraint by the West in its notion of victory, clearly eschewing the total war mindset from earlier eras, is incongruous with today's threats and can play directly into the hands of transnational terrorist groups and rogue states who are far less constrained in the pursuit of their objectives. In a sense, the West may be too civilized—in terms of values emphasizing freedom and human rights, the sanctity of human life, and acceptance of the self-determination of peoples—to defeat decisively its adversaries, who understand all too well the limits on what will come their way before, during, and after war. In confronting the current sources of violent international disruption, in many ways the West appears to be unprepared:

> For historical and cultural reasons, the armed forces of Western countries have been disinclined to prepare for military action that was considered uncivilized. As a consequence, policymakers, the military, and the public are psychologically ill-prepared for this war [the war on terror]. They have been used to concepts such as limited collateral damage, proportionality of response, and the absence of body bags. The current situation, however, calls for a willingness to abandon these ideas, at least partially, a sacrifice that may be difficult for some individuals and nations to make.[2]

Since 1945, domestic reluctance to countenance brutality has often caused democratic states to lose small wars against militarily inferior opponents.[3] Although some data also show that democracies are more likely than other forms of government to win military victories in wars, these states clearly have great difficulty reaping the strategic victory payoffs from their battlefield successes.[4] Unruly forces attempting to disrupt the international status quo thus benefit from both an asymmetry in their own sacrifice—the willingness to fight, kill, and die in combat—and an asymmetry in ruthlessness toward the enemy—the willingness to abandon or ignore the civilized rules in order to win a war or reap the postwar payoffs. In such cases, modern victory notions can unintentionally serve in the long run to encourage further belligerent behavior by such global disruptive forces.

Contributing to this problem is Western states' pattern of not always employing the most sophisticated notions of strategic victory in these confrontations. Many in the West still conceive of postwar triumph in rather simplistic ways, relating to one's own casualty aversion or a foe's leadership decapitation. The first perspective sees wars or foreign interventions resulting in sizable casualties as failures and ones involving few deaths as successes. The second perspective, in contrast, contends that victory occurs at the moment when the enemy leader is removed from power: for example, in this view the 2003 Iraq War would have boiled down simply to capturing Saddam Hussein, and the war against terrorism in Afghanistan would have boiled down simply to capturing or killing Osama bin Laden.

These common but misguided and oversimplified views of victory are dysfunctional because they ignore the multifaceted requirements needed to reap postwar payoffs from military triumphs. Specifically, the first perspective ignores that casualty counts bear no relationship to whether vital interests are at stake or fundamental goals are achieved, and the second perspective ignores that disruptive forces spearheaded by unruly leaders do not disappear when these political figures are gone because their elimination can lead to sympathy for their cause through martyrdom, the emergence of equally reprehensible replacements, or the eruption of violent chaos in new directions within their former strongholds.[5] If strategic victory involves genuine accomplishment of the short-term and long-term national, regional, and global goals for which the war was fought, then both leaders and the public in the militarily victorious state should see through the fog of cosmetic triumph, avoid simplistic signals of success, and understand the complexities involved in order to increase the probability through meaningful scrutiny that crucial positive postwar payoffs actually occur. However, it is interesting to note that if a war winner's domestic public did indeed possess the more simplistic yardsticks for strategic victory, in many cases the result could make success a lot easier for a government to accomplish and demonstrate; thus in a perverse way positive incentives could exist for an administration actively to encourage simpleminded metrics for victory in order to reap high levels of approval for its postwar effort.

In many ways the nature of Western states' victories in modern limited warfare can make it too easy for defeated parties to start up violent conflicts afterward. Generally, "maintaining peace is easier after very long and costly wars," at least in part because "the high cost of fighting gives states an incentive to avoid another war."[6] In the relatively low-cost wars common in the post–Cold War era, such an incentive does not exist for either side, and indeed in the aftermath of conflicts defeated parties and their internal and international sympathizers are usually left in pretty decent shape to regroup and launch another salvo when victors become distracted with other matters.

These severe deficiencies associated with victory in modern warfare might well cause some to wonder why Western states do not revert to the more decisive approach of premodern total war to cope with today's international threats. To achieve strategic victory against these threats, Western states might well ponder conducting unrelenting, ruthless, even savage campaigns to obliterate them. However, such an approach is not politically feasible—due to domestic political pressures, existing domestic and international law, diplomatic positions taken by other states, and the news media coverage—despite its potential to yield short-term payoffs. In contrast to earlier eras, the recent rejection of this primitive approach has been close to universal among Western states: "Since the end of the Cold War, challenges to the acceptability of armed force have continued and even escalated, particularly in open political systems," where policymakers find it hard to use force due to the media spotlight on wartime body bags coming home (the media ban on covering coffins coming home from Iraq during and after the 2003 Iraq War represents an only partially successful attempt to manage interpretations of success and failure). As a result, "leaders have responded by searching for modes of warfare that minimize friendly military and civilian casualties," but "such modes of warfare are inherently less decisive."[7] Western states would just not generally tolerate the level of coercion needed for total war to be effective, especially in missions classified as humanitarian that simply "do not allow for the use of overwhelming force to attain quick, decisive victories."[8]

Thus, to be consistent with its own stated enlightened democratic values, the West is forced to be civilized (or, at the very least, to appear to be civilized) about its mode for defeating dangerous opponents that themselves may be utterly uncivilized and barbaric. As a result, any move Western states make against perceived threats is highly vulnerable to immediate criticism from multiple directions over issues such as violating human rights, desecrating a holy book, abusing detainees, harming innocent civilians, or reflecting inadequate intelligence. For example, during the Tet Offensive in the Vietnam War, the international media focused heavily on US "atrocities" and only much later covered the gruesome mass executions by the Viet Cong. In response to the reality that Western states are held both internally and externally to higher standards to an extent that can become self-defeating, Western states have little in their arsenal to avoid a postwar image of hypocrisy or duplicity in the eyes of foreign or domestic skeptics.

Global Rules of the Game Obstructing Strategic Victory

Aside from these problems with Western states, the system-level international "rules of the game" have obstructed strategic victory.[9] The weaknesses they evidence have served to inhibit the unambiguous achievement of war outcomes with regard to information control, military deterrence, political self-determination, economic reconstruction, social justice, and diplomatic respect. Briefly reviewing the quagmire surrounding these rules helps to highlight the security challenges surrounding modern victory.

The notion of rules of the game in international relations has a long-standing history reflecting what is implicitly or explicitly permissible in interaction patterns on the conflict-cooperation continuum.[10] Although it may seem odd to be talking about rules of the game within a global setting characterized by chaotic anarchy, even on the most disorderly setting a functional set of rules—including those as crude as "might makes right"—exists that the players implicitly recognize. Global rules of the game apply specifically to both the ways by which victors win wars and the postwar obligations winners have to the losers.

With the old Cold War rules largely gone, there appears to be little understanding of—or compliance to—a new set of rules. Some have even argued that recent international system "changes are so thoroughgoing as to render obsolete the rules and procedures by which politics are conducted."[11] In the absence of a uniform and universal rule-set that is consistently voiced and followed, each player is free to behave largely according to its own idiosyncratic premises and to interpret the legitimacy and durability of war motives and outcomes as they see fit. A common image is that more powerful states play by the rules, since they set them, whereas others are more likely to ignore and violate them; but the reality is that nobody consistently plays by a coherent global set of rules, including the great powers.

The West generally assumes its rules are universal, and either projects in a misleading way this rule-set onto others (interpreting others' behavior in terms of its own rules) or attempts to impose directly its rule-set onto others and induce compliance. Indeed, the recent pattern of wars initiated by Western states seems predicated on the assumption that the people within the attacked enemy states all embrace Western ideals about postwar outcomes. The results here are often resentment, misunderstanding, and largely ineffective international initiatives, including strategic victory. In contrast to many past systems, core powers do not seem to be able to set by themselves the rules of the game, at least in part due to their lack of widespread legitimacy in the global arena. Western leaders operate as if a mix of military coercion, economic dependence, legal prohibition, and moral outrage will suffice to quell violations of their idea of the rules of the game.

With major powers still clinging to a largely outmoded set of rules, weaker states are able to ignore them, and nonstate groups can subvert them. The increasing popularity of moral relativism, with its premium placed on nonjudgmental multicultural patterns of diversity, can cause any discussion of establishing a more coherent set of rules of the game—especially by the West—to run the risk of comparison to the most virulent forms of cultural imperialism; to establish more universal rules in this way of thinking seems to be the equivalent of an antidemocratic squashing of each global player's ability to experience independent empowerment through defining its own mode of behavior. Because of this risk, Western states are forced to cope globally with multiple competing notions of what values are worth promoting, what rules should predominate, and what forms of war and victory are legitimate. In this setting, it is tough to reap the political fruits of military victory.

For disenfranchised states, the very notion of rules of the game in today's world is reminiscent of an era where they sacrificed autonomy in their foreign policy for what they perceived to be a quite arbitrary externally imposed world order. Moreover, for many disadvantaged states and groups that seem permanently unable to be upwardly mobile in the global hierarchy, violating the rules of the game may be a primary means for escaping from a stifling and humiliating status quo, a system whose premises they feel powerless to influence.[12] In a similar way, thwarting the desires and efforts of victors in war can serve to give those within vanquished states some sense of empowerment. Those who do not want to play by the rules, including rogue states and terrorist groups, know that in today's international system it is extremely difficult for major powers—including past victors in military confrontations—to exert effective pressure on them over the long haul to change their behavior, and indeed a significant component of these noncompliant parties' status appears to derive from their ability to thwart in flagrant ways the major powers' rules of the game and to get away with it without suffering devastating consequences. Thus in some ways it is actually useful for these unruly parties to have the West continue to portray its rules as universal so that their defiant power can be ever more visible.

Compounding these external impediments are sharp internal divisions within global public opinion, important in this context because compliance to international rules of the game may be heavily affected by domestic policy processes.[13] More specifically, the citizenry of these states is split between (1) those who want to eliminate the violations to the rules by unruly disruptive forces, and (2) those who want to preserve the right to reject externally imposed rules or who profit from disruptive rule-defying behavior. The inherent ambiguities surrounding the motives and outcomes of war amplify this public opinion split and serve to impede meaningful understanding, let alone widespread acceptance, of what victory really means. It appears highly unlikely that public opinion consensus on these issues will emerge in the foreseeable future due to a combination of mutual distrust, pessimism about the possibility of common values, and inattention to the severity and immediacy of the broad security dangers posed in part by the ambiguity of victory.

When Can Strategic Victory Follow Military Victory?

Despite this combination of state-level Western frailties and system-level rules-of-the-game deficiencies in the contemporary world, it is still possible under certain conditions for strategic victory to follow military victory. Military victory is necessary but clearly not sufficient for strategic victory, and in the aftermath of war political and military leaders are likely to encounter difficulties while they simultaneously attempt to manage relevant informational, military, political, economic, social, and diplomatic elements. Given the vacuum of specific guidance in this regard, this section examines when these ends would be most realistically attainable in today's global security environment.

It appears that three clusters of conditions affect the likelihood of strategic victory: the initiator preparation for postwar management, the susceptibility of the target postwar influence, and the ratio of initiator-target postwar resolve. The conditions involved are not fixed or immutable, as each represents a modifiable area where war participants can, if attentive, improve their chances for success. Figure 6.1 summarizes the circumstances conducive to strategic victory.

Initiator Preparation for Postwar Management

Looking first at the preparation of initiators for postwar management, it is quite surprising how many times wars have been initiated without focused strategic thinking about how to manage the aftermath of conflict. Strategic victory is most likely to occur if the victor in combat has previously thought about and devised explicit plans whereby the transition to postwar political self-determination, economic

Figure 6.1 When Can Strategic Victory Follow Military Victory?

INITIATOR PREPARATION FOR POSTWAR MANAGEMENT
Imposition of security and order
Familiarity with the defeated state
Training of locals to take over the reins of power
Willingness to make long-term resource commitment

TARGET SUSCEPTIBILITY TO POSTWAR INFLUENCE
Monitoring of dissident subversive groups
Suppression of volatile ethnic, religious, or nationalistic divides
Funneling of support toward sympathizers and away from insurgents
Demonstration to defeated population of value in protection from threat

RATIO OF INITIATOR-TARGET POSTWAR RESOLVE
Possession of equal or greater power and will than disruptive forces
Maintenance of positive support from domestic public and allies for postwar effort
Determination to stay in the combat zone until postwar payoffs are achieved
Resiliency in the face of adverse internal and external reactions

reconstruction, and social justice can occur quickly and smoothly and reinforce the interests of the victor in the region. For this planning to ameliorate postwar management problems, it is essential that top policymakers take such planning seriously in their direction of the military campaign and its aftermath. To ease this transition, a military victor needs to have focused in its advance planning on the strategic victory elements of information control, with great intelligence on enemies and security for its own information systems; and diplomatic respect, with a firm yet cooperative international image that generates internal and external support.

When and how is this initiator-focused advanced planning most likely to be present and effective? First, a victor in combat needs to have figured out how to impose quickly a postwar system of security and order, for without such security no postwar payoffs are possible. To facilitate this imposition of security, it would help to have identified in advance discrete command-and-control systems, weapons systems, and battle tactics that work best against unruly elements to maintain order. To isolate when this identification is most possible, tuned intelligence needs to reveal the optimal security approach in this context.

Second, the victor in combat needs to develop familiarity with the defeated state's traditional culture, prewar political system, and economic transaction patterns. To aid in this familiarity, those on the winner's side involved in the postwar transition need to have received extensive education and training about the enemy prior to the commencement of combat. For this kind of education and training to be possible, war initiation cannot be spur-of-the-moment and instead requires extensive advanced warning, allowing time for soldiers and statesmen to acquire and perfect needed skills.

Third, the military victor needs to have begun as soon as possible training the defeated state's locals to take over the political administration (including police functions), manage the economy, and move the society in the direction of civil discourse. To expedite this local reliance, even before the end of major combat, victors need to be screening and indoctrinating potential recruits from the indigenous population in the defeated state; otherwise, opportunists, corrupt individuals, and all-around troublemakers may enter the mix. Rather than dismantling the local security forces, such as the disbanding of the Iraqi army after the fighting ceased in the 2003 Iraq War, victors need simply to remove the dangerous leadership elements from army and police units. To accomplish this recruitment and indoctrination effectively, the victor must be willing to be quite patient, as some postwar turmoil is inevitable (though not nearly that of the widespread looting and violence following the 2003 Iraq War), and some locals will drop out, be killed by those opposed to the new regime, or prove incapable of managing the essential but complex postwar tasks.

Fourth, the victor in combat needs to be willing to devote a lot of resources—skilled personnel as well as money—for a long period of time within the defeated state in order to make the positive transformation become a reality. For example, some argue that for the United States to achieve its payoffs after the 2003 Iraq War "will require at least a decade of commitment and hundreds of billions of dollars."[14] Financial support from the victor's allies would always be helpful in this regard. To assist in this resource acquisition, leaders on the winner's side need to have a realistic idea of the number and type of people needed, the amount of money needed, and the specific purposes for which the money and personnel would be used; these leaders also need to be able to communicate these needs effectively to the appropriate domestic legislative body in order to have a good chance of receiving necessary support. To get this realistic idea, there needs to be a careful dispassionate analysis of costs in similar recent wars or interventions, insulated from the usual political incentives to distort these estimates.

Target Susceptibility to Postwar Influence

Turning next to the susceptibility of targets to postwar influence, even the most prepared, powerful, and committed initiator can find itself stymied in its attempt to achieve strategic victory if it has not focused adequately on identifying and exploiting enemy weaknesses in the aftermath of war. Strategic victory is most likely to occur if the victor in combat has within the defeated state located, deterred, and contained disruptive violent postwar insurgencies that might interfere with its stable and peaceful transition to postwar political self-determination, economic reconstruction, and social justice. To minimize the potential for this disruption, the victor should have investigated critical control nodes for insurgent movements. To use these control nodes to weaken antagonistic forces, the victor needs to engage in not only offensive military operations but also widespread penetration and manipulation of enemy information systems using information from sympathetic local citizens. As a means of reinforcing the success of this mission, the victor should have used diplomatic efforts to sway the hearts and minds of domestic and international public opinion against these disruptive insurgencies.

When and how are these target-focused prerequisites for strategic victory most likely to be present? First, the victor in combat needs to have quickly imposed a monitoring system for tracking the postwar movements of suspected enemy sympathizers and insurgents within the defeated society, with the express goal of neutralizing them. In the current interpenetrated global setting, advanced technology will be necessary to aid in this effort; however, sometimes even with the most sophisticated technology it is difficult to be certain who constitutes a threat. So to facilitate this monitoring, it would help to foster cooperation (using economic incentives where necessary) from the defeated state citizenry both in identifying and rooting out disruptive elements. To take advantage of this monitoring assistance from locals, intelligence needs to have carefully discriminated between dissident and subversive elements and friendly and supportive elements within the society. The victor would also need to have generated understanding among locals about the inevitable existence of intrusive checkpoints and inspections necessary to implement this monitoring.

Second, the victor in combat needs to attempt to suppress—or allow expression in a controlled manner—any volatile ethnic, religious, or nationalistic divides within the defeated state that have the potential to trigger violently disruptive postwar passions. Such passionate splits could exist among antagonistic groups within the defeated state or between the victorious state and the vanquished state. It is generally accepted that after a war, stable "peace is more difficult between enemies with a history of conflict" or "when one or both sides feel that their existence is threatened" (as is likely when high levels of emotion are involved).[15] To aid in this suppression, the victor needs to be fair-handed and respectful in its treatment of the various groups, avoiding any hint of favoritism, and make sure that it gives each one ample opportunity to participate in postwar political, economic, and social decisionmaking. For this kind of even-handed treatment to be possible, the victor needs to communicate frequently and openly with the different groups, as well as to encourage them to communicate more with each other, finding out in the process their desires and frustrations as well as ways to reduce existing antagonisms.

Third, the victor in combat needs to undertake tangible moves to reduce the viability and support for any groups still sympathetic to the defeated state's now-ousted political regime, and expand the support base for any existing indigenous movements working toward the victor's goals. To accomplish this shift in support, increasing economic and military assistance toward supporters and decreasing its availability to opposition groups may be a useful tool. To foster legitimacy for such shifts in support, it may be necessary on occasion to fan the flames of any existing internal or external antagonism toward supporters of the ousted regime. However, being able to distinguish between friend and foe quickly and unambiguously—a task that is usually harder after war than during war—is a prerequisite for such an approach. For success, a military victor needs to find ways to overcome the kinds of postwar difficulties evident in recent wars in Afghanistan and Iraq, where the inability to distinguish easily between supporters and opponents, as well as between innocent civilians and enemy combatants, has caused—much to the delight of violent subversive groups—the United States in its postwar efforts to have accidentally killed or militarily and economically assisted many of the "wrong people."

Fourth, the victor in combat needs to convince the defeated state's citizenry that the presence of its troops is necessary at least temporarily to manage these threats (insurgents, enemy sympathizers, and violent factions of divided ethnic, religious, or nationalistic groups). Postwar stability appears to be more likely when the defeated society perceives an internal or external threat and sees the victors as providing necessary protection against this threat.[16] To foster this image of protection against threat, the victor may utilize psychological operations to emphasize the gravity of the sources of instability and the value of the occupying forces in keeping citizens shielded from disruptive effects. In a sense, the locals need to realize that the war is not really over until stability is achieved. For this kind of image building to be successful, the defeated state citizenry must perceive a greater danger from insurgents, enemy sympathizers, and violent ethnic, religious, or nationalistic factions than they do from the victor's occupation forces themselves; because of this, a victor needs to minimize its postwar collateral damage in the vanquished state.

Ratio of Initiator-Target Postwar Resolve

Underlying all of these clusters of conditions conducive to strategic victory is the assumption that in the aftermath of war, the military victor needs to manifest substantial political will, with managing the postwar predicament an unambiguously top priority. Strategic victory is most likely if the victor in combat possesses and demonstrates greater will—in addition to greater power capabilities—to win the peace than that of the violent subversive elements within the defeated society to disrupt the peace. Although in today's anarchic international setting raw power advantage alone does not produce strategic victory, its value can rise significantly when combined with determined national will.[17] However, the capacity and will to manage the political, economic, and social aftermath of war is quite different from the capacity and will to fight and win a military victory in armed combat.

To maximize the chances of positive postwar payoffs, such postwar will—which links directly to the clarity of the national interests and the significance of the payoffs at stake in the conflict—needs to be demonstrably unwavering and clearly communicated to any existing enemies. To maintain this credible image of commitment, the victor in combat needs to exploit diplomatic channels fully to assure continued postwar support from its domestic population and political allies; postwar occupation by a United Nations or multilateral coalition can be means of increasing the likelihood of this support and moving in the direction of international consensus ideal for legitimizing postwar efforts. To have this diplomacy work, the victor needs to make sure that all of its postwar statements and actions are absolutely consistent in conveying the same message of unswerving commitment at home and abroad.

Western states today typically face enemies with vastly inferior coercive capabilities but superior determination and commitment to fight to the end—and to engage in endless violent disruptions of postwar stability—no matter what sacrifice is required. Having adversaries with passionate resolve for their causes or disregard for the value of their own lives, as opposed to conscripts who fight for pay or duty, poses obstacles to demonstrating postwar will: in many of today's intense religious and ideological struggles, targets seem to possess an advantage in zeal for their cause (asymmetric will) and appear willing to keep fighting while enduring unspeakable suffering against overwhelming odds. Having highly irrational or unpredictable targets generally makes matters worse; for reasons related to both cognitive and emotional issues, such adversaries may overestimate their own resilience in the face of significant losses or, alternatively, underestimate the opponent's will to continue the attack, making outright obliteration appear to be the only way to settle a conflict. So to translate military victory into strategic victory against such opponents, a victor in combat must find ways to match or exceed the commitment of such intractable foes to prevail in the long run; though clearly a tall order, any state unwilling or unable to do so would be unwise to enter such confrontations in the first place.

One key manifestation of a victor's national will is its staying power in the aftermath of war. A lofty ideal would be for onlookers to see this will as so resolute that they believe that the victor will absolutely not leave until its postwar payoffs are fully achieved. Clear evidence exists that for military occupations to be successful, they must be sustained over considerable time, preferably using massive manpower available immediately after military victory; yet doing so may elicit nationalistic reactions within the occupied population that may impede success.[18]

Because of this potential backfire effect, for strategic victory the military victory needs to be sufficiently resilient so that it can handle adverse reactions during what might prove to be an extended stay in the defeated country. To have a high chance of success, the victor must be willing—in the face of domestic and international skepticism—to stay in the combat zone for as long as its adversaries wreak substantial violent havoc there and local forces are unable to manage the turmoil. To enhance this resiliency, a victor needs not only to possess and articulate clearly and convincingly the core national interests at stake but also to persevere in increasing the pool of local citizens sympathetic to the victor's presence and antagonistic to those causing the turmoil.

Concluding Thoughts

Winners on the battlefield cannot apply a blanket formula for how to achieve strategic victory in the current international security environment. Working on a disadvantageous playing field—with internal state-level restraint and external system-wide norms mismatched to existing dangers—seems for the West to be an enduring component of post–Cold War conflict, and so those pursuing victory need to be adept and flexible enough to overcome these shortcomings. Confronting the kinds of determined and ruthless opponents it has faced in recent years, the West cannot be expected to abandon its restrained moral precepts—or deviate far from the civilized tenets of democracy—in its violent confrontations with ruthless enemies.

Moreover, it would be senseless for the West to sit back and hope that a more coherent set of global rules of the game would magically emerge in such a way that enlightened, just principles of global interaction would eliminate disruptive behavior by unsavory foes. Instead, for Western states to succeed in such a context, leaders need to recognize these dual handicaps, accept them, and find ways to circumvent and overcome them.

The identified conditions promoting strategic victory are in many ways avenues for the West to do just that. It appears that carefully maximizing preparation for postwar management, target susceptibility to postwar influence, and ratio of initiator-target postwar resolve provides the greatest potential for attaining postwar payoffs. Facilitating these conditions in the aftermath of warfare is by no means easy, and success is not guaranteed even if they are facilitated; however, making a concerted effort to realize these conditions seems vital for postwar success.

Although there is nothing novel or startling about the identified conditions, what has kept military victors from realizing them seems to be skewed priorities that concentrate on military victory, overconfidence that postwar payoffs will automatically fall into place, or fatalistic acceptance that the postwar challenges cannot be dramatically transformed. There is little doubt that the conditions conducive to strategic victory necessitate both sustained effort and significant sacrifice on the part of the military victor, not resting on its laurels after winning on the battlefield. Victors today may inappropriately assume that no amount of preparation for the postwar predicament is likely to improve their ability to manage the challenges involved, that no means exist to increase significantly an enemy's susceptibility to outside influence, and that no avenue exists to match the resolve of today's zealous ideologically motivated foes. In reality, however, there are indeed realistic and concrete steps that can be taken to realize these propitious conditions.

Notes

1. Monica Duffy Toft, "End of Victory? Civil War Termination in Historical Perspective" (paper presented at the annual national meeting of the International Studies Association, Honolulu, March 2005), p. 6.
2. Rob de Wijk, "The Limits of Military Power," *Washington Quarterly* 25 (Winter 2002), p. 80.
3. Gil Merom, *How Democracies Lose Small Wars: State, Society, and*

the Failures of France in Algeria, Israel in Lebanon, and the United States in Vietnam (New York: Cambridge University Press, 2003).

4. Dan Reiter and Allan C. Stam III, "Democracy, War Initiation, and Victory," *American Political Science Review* 92 (June 1998), pp. 377–389; and Allan C. Stam III, *Win, Lose, or Draw: Domestic Politics and the Crucible of War* (Ann Arbor: University of Michigan Press, 1996), p. 176.

5. "The Elusive Character of Victory," *Economist* 361 (November 24, 2001), p. 11.

6. Virginia Page Fortna, *Peace Time: Cease-Fire Agreements and the Durability of Peace* (Princeton, NJ: Princeton University Press, 2004), p. 211.

7. Steven Metz, *Armed Conflict in the Twenty-first Century: The Information Revolution and Post-Modern Warfare* (Carlisle Barracks, PA: US Army War College Strategic Studies Institute, 2000), p. 16.

8. Karl W. Eikenberry, "Take No Casualties," *Parameters* (Summer 1996), p. 112.

9. This section draws heavily from Robert Mandel, *Deadly Transfers and the Global Playground* (Westport, CT: Praeger, 1999), chapter 11.

10. Zeev Maoz, *Paradoxes of War* (Boston: Unwin Hyman, 1990), p. 9. See also Stephen Krasner, ed., *International Regimes* (Ithaca, NY: Cornell University Press, 1983).

11. William J. Olson, "The New World Disorder: Governability and Development," in Max G. Manwaring, ed., *Gray Area Phenomena: Confronting the New World Disorder* (Boulder, CO: Westview Press, 1993), p. 9.

12. Maoz, *Paradoxes of War*, p. 327.

13. Andrew P. Cortell and James W. Davis Jr., "How Do International Institutions Matter? The Domestic Impact of International Rules and Norms," *International Studies Quarterly* 40 (December 1996), pp. 451–478.

14. Andrew F. Krepinevich Jr., "How to Win in Iraq," *Foreign Affairs* 84 (September/October 2005), p. 104.

15. Fortna, *Peace Time*, p. 211.

16. David M. Edelstein, "Occupational Hazards: Why Military Occupations Succeed or Fail," *International Security* 29 (Summer 2004), pp. 61–65, 80–81.

17. Fortna, *Peace Time*, p. 211.

18. Edelstein, "Occupational Hazards," pp. 50–51.

7

Special Victory Challenges in Unconventional Wars

Much of this book's analysis of victory has focused on traditional warfare between states using conventional means to achieve success. However, both in today's world and in the future, unconventional wars involving unorthodox participants, weapons, and tactics deserve special attention due to their prospects for proliferation. This chapter begins by analyzing victory in three of today's most important unconventional challenges—weapons of mass destruction, terrorism, and low-intensity conflict. The chapter then examines victory in the context of three unconventional challenges likely to become more prominent in the future: (1) *changes in technology* that cause the outcome of warfare to become increasingly divorced from the performance of human soldiers on the battlefield; (2) *changes in armed forces* that cause governments involved in war to have less direct control over the course of the combat; and (3) *changes in threat* that cause the sources of disruption to be more difficult to identify, contain, and defeat.

Victory in Contemporary Unconventional Warfare

Wars involving weapons of mass destruction, terrorism, and low-intensity conflict differ sufficiently from conventional warfare in that they require special wrinkles in thinking about strategic victory. Though unconventional warfare has been with us for a considerable length of time, states have not yet figured out how to manage such unorthodox developments in violent conflict. Indeed, strategic victory appears to be considerably more difficult to achieve in unconventional than in conventional warfare.

The Challenge of Weapons of Mass Destruction

Weapons of mass destruction—defined as "weapons that are capable of a high order of destruction and/or of being used in such a manner as to destroy large numbers of people"—pose a simple yet fundamental question with regard to the achievement of postwar strategic victory: can there be such a triumph in a violent conflict that threatens to destroy most of humanity?[1] Bernard Brodie, a pioneer of nuclear confrontation theory, argued incisively decades ago that the development of atomic bombs changed the fundamental national security aim from winning war to averting war.[2] Many analysts still agree that

> terms such as "victory" or "win" lose their meaning when used in conjunction with the term "nuclear." One wins by accomplishing one's goals, which is also how one defines victory. One has difficulty imagining how any nation might accomplish a set of goals through an exchange of nuclear explosions.[3]

Indeed, "the traditional belief in the possibility of 'victory' in warfare has been most seriously undermined by the existence of nuclear weapons in control of more than one power," and considering past patterns, "the meaning of 'victory' in a war between nuclear powers was hard to imagine from the outset, and became even harder as both sides developed sophisticated delivery systems and defences."[4]

Although chemical and biological weapons do not possess the same immediate large scope of impact as a nuclear bomb, they do exhibit volatile uncontainability—in which they kill humans but leave man-made structures intact—and thus can create a parallel sense of fear: terror induction is a key strategic aim surrounding their usage, with such intimidation used "to speed up, solidify, and optimize the path to victory.... The unique sense of terror associated with this type of munitions" is "in some ways more acute than the terror connected to nuclear weapons."[5] Victory in a war where both sides use chemical or biological weapons may thus be as unsatisfying as winning a nuclear confrontation. These issues are especially pertinent to today's international security environment because "in the twenty-first century, weapons of mass destruction (WMD) remain the preferred weapons of the weak."[6] More specifically, "ever since the Gulf War, it has been clear that local powers and movements perceive weapons of mass destruction as a potential counter to US conventional capabilities and a way of striking decisively at the US."[7]

A probing examination of nuclear weapons (both atomic and thermonuclear), as well as weapons of mass destruction more generally, reveals a general tradeoff between victory and survival:

> From the beginning of history, political organizations going to war against each other could hope to preserve themselves by defeating the enemy and gaining a victory; now, assuming only that the vanquished side retained a handful of deliverable weapons ready for use, the link between victory and self-preservation had been cut. On the contrary, at least the possibility had now to be taken into account that the greater the triumph gained over an opponent who was in possession of nuclear weapons, the greater the danger to the survival of the victor.[8]

If both sides in a war have access to these armaments—as is increasingly likely with the diffusion of weapons technologies—then, due to the large-scale ensuing destruction, even a military victory would cause the winner to experience a hollow strategic victory.[9] Indeed, it appears to be foolish to assume that any large-scale nuclear exchange would now be limited in any meaningful sense, especially given the likelihood of heightened emotions and loss of control.[10]

However, this position is not universally endorsed. For example, Colin Gray argues that "recognition that war at any level can be won or lost, and that the distinction between winning and losing would not be trivial, is essential for intelligent defense planning"; that "victory or defeat in nuclear war is possible, and such a war may have to be waged to that point"; and that "nuclear war is unlikely to be an essentially meaningless, terminal event."[11] From this angle, "in some inherently unstable situations, if the adversary were to strike first with weapons of mass destruction, he might achieve victory, at least temporarily."[12]

Nonetheless, this study contends that though one side may sometimes be able to win a temporary military victory in a confrontation involving weapons of mass destruction, it is inconceivable for a strategic victory to be the result of such an encounter. Put succinctly, after such a war, the winner would experience losses that "far outweigh any political advantage derived from victory."[13] Furthermore, "since countries with survivable nuclear forces can devastate any attacker, the probable costs of aggression outweigh any possible gains."[14] As illustrated in Stanley Kubrick's movie *Dr. Strangelove*, it would be incredibly difficult to modify the meaning of strategic victory so as to fit the ensuing cataclysmic devastation in a two-sided WMD confrontation.

Thus, strategic victory for weapons of mass destruction could mean preventing the proliferation of these weapons, associated technologies, or related delivery systems into the hands of potentially hostile entities, requiring that those states and nonstate groups currently seeking WMDs be convinced that having them would confer no advantages and even might prove to be expensive liabilities. The political and psychological desired end states include discrediting the legitimacy of using weapons of mass destruction, transforming the political and economic conditions that gave rise to use of such weapons, providing concrete disincentives for such weapons usage, and fostering global norms and laws prohibiting such usage. Moreover, reducing the availability of WMDs could decrease the frequency of the type of highly complex and ambiguous limited war stimulated by the presence of nuclear weapons (especially during the Cold War), making strategic victory in conventional conflicts more probable. Progress in these directions has been painfully slow.

The Challenge of Terrorism

Of all the threats where victory has become confusing, terrorism—defined here as "the sustained use, or threat of use, of violence by a small group for political purposes"—is at the top of the list.[15] Due to the involvement of nonstate players, most of the traditional metrics for strategic victory, including political self-determination, economic reconstruction, and social justice, fall by the wayside: there is no government to reform, economy to rebuild, or society to transform. The US war on terrorism "is not war as traditionally understood, in the sense of organized military forces and recognizable political entities fighting for the control of territory," and "there is no enemy capital to occupy, and no precisely outlined goal or end-point."[16] Terrorists have no single physical location that can be identified, and they are dispersed, diffuse, loosely interconnected, dynamically varying, highly adaptive, innovative, opportunistic, and resourceful. Although the military dimension of the threat may be far less central than in interstate wars, the political, ideological, and diplomatic threat from terrorism—whose primary mode is, after all, inculcating fear in target populations—seems truly ominous.

Little consensus exists today about the meaning of victory over terrorism. Even US Secretary of Defense Donald Rumsfeld admitted in October 2003 that "today, we lack metrics to know if we are winning or losing the global war on terror."[17] It is specifically difficult to define minimally acceptable thresholds for successful outcomes, as some analysts talk about reducing or minimizing the terrorist threat whereas others aim for completely eliminating the terrorist threat. Both approaches contain difficulties: on the one hand, simply reducing the terrorist threat could still leave one's country vulnerable to a surprise terrorist attack, and as a result it may actually be crucial to eliminate this threat, signaling foes that you really mean business and that you have both the capability and will to commit whatever resources are necessary to stop terrorism in its tracks; on the other hand, if countries were to state their victory conditions in this absolute way, then in today's global security environment they may never be able to declare victory and may always be perceived as failures. Thus states waging war against terrorism may possess incentives to be as vague as possible—or as explicit as possible about cosmetic, easy-to-attain goals—about what constitutes victory.

Nonetheless, three components of military victory over terrorism—protecting the targets of terror, stopping the initiators of terror, and preventing support for terror—rise to the surface and are summarized in Figure 7.1. These components emphasize physical security for potential victims, coercive restraint of terrorists, and tangible elimination or containment of sources of support. Though not by any means attempting to encompass all possible counterterrorist strategies or to indicate the meaning of strategic victory over terrorism, these components suggest how at least military victory could be gauged.

Protecting the targets of terror in many ways represents the ultimate desired end from the war on terrorism. One approach to this goal emphasizes potential terror victims' broad feelings of safety and stability, frequently underscored by the US government in its global war on terror:

> "Victory" in the war on terrorism, President Bush has declared, will be a state of mind rather than a single event. There will be no surrender ceremony on a battleship's deck, US officials caution. "The president has said that the definition of victory is when freedom conquers fear and the world is safe," White House Press Secretary Ari Fleischer said.[18]

Figure 7.1 Military Victory in the War on Terrorism

PROTECTING TARGETS OF TERROR

Pursuing Ultimate Ends of Victory

Feeling of safety and stability
Absence of terrrorist atttacks

STOPPING INITIATORS OF TERROR

Pursuing Direct Means for Victory

Military destruction of powerful terrorist cells
Incarceration or execution of terrorist leaders

PREVENTING SUPPORT FOR TERROR

Pursuing Indirect Means for Victory

Diminution of hostility fueling terrorism
Elimination of efforts facilitating terrorism

Similarly, President George W. Bush's 2002 State of the Union message stated that beyond killing and capturing terrorists, the war on terrorism is about building "a just and peaceful world."[19] More generally, "the ultimate aim and measure of success is the establishment of a self-sustaining stability—one that does not leak terrorism."[20] A second more tangible approach to this goal involves the absence of terrorist attacks—for example, it is possible to define US victory against terrorism in terms of the United States not having been subject to a second major terrorist attack since September 11, 2001, or more broadly to look at the number of recent worldwide terrorist attacks.[21]

Stopping the initiators of terror represents the most important direct means to achieve the desired end from the war on terrorism. One approach emphasizes the military destruction of the most powerful terrorist cells in the world, including the closing of terrorist training camps.[22] Success in the war against terrorism may be a function of destroying specifically the organization that conducted the September 11 attacks, or of more broadly interfering with worldwide terrorist attacks.[23] Indeed, a common inclination exists to count the number of terrorists apprehended, the number of foiled terrorist attacks, or the net decline in membership of active terrorist organizations as ways of judging victory.[24] A second approach stresses decapitation—the incarceration or execution of terrorist leaders. For example, in May 2003 US Deputy Secretary of Defense Paul Wolfowitz said that "the defeat of Saddam Hussein is a victory in the war on terrorism," and for many such victory entails simply the end of Osama bin Laden.[25]

Preventing support for terror represents a crucial indirect means to achieve the desired end from the war on terrorism. One approach involves decreasing the sense of hostility fueling terrorism. Some analysts specifically argue that there needs to be reduced intensity of anti-Western antagonism—"hostile to freedom, democracy, and other US interests"—in the Muslim world:

> To achieve the destruction of the terror machine and to prevent its reconstruction, we must convince Afghans, Pakistanis, and most Muslim Middle Easterners that we are not their enemy; that we are prepared to live with governments produced by democratic elections, even if they are Islamic governments; and that we will use the full resources of our country to achieve a rapid, comprehensive, and just peace between Israel and the Palestinians.[26]

Indeed, it has become clear that the ongoing Israeli-Palestinian conflict helps "fuel the sense of grievance that terrorists feed on" when recruiting supporters.[27] Moving beyond the Muslim world, terrorists are more generally driven "by their opposition to what they see as foreign domination," and the West clearly needs to undertake steps to mitigate this perception.[28] To some extent, dealing directly with the root causes behind terrorist grievances may be essential here.

A second approach emphasizes eliminating outside efforts facilitating terrorism. The US Defense Department's National Defense Strategy states that "as in the Cold War, victory will come only when the ideological motivation for the terrorists' activities has been discredited and no longer has the power to motivate streams of individuals to risk and sacrifice their lives"; more specifically, "victory on battlefields alone will not suffice," for "to win the global war on terrorism, the United States will help to create and lead a broad international effort to deny terrorist extremist networks what they require to operate and survive."[29] Victory over terrorism may involve the use of both negative and positive incentives to prevent support for terrorists: (1) cowing or replacing regimes that encourage or aid in the promotion of terrorism, including freezing their funds, specifically deterring other states from serving as "Talibanesque" sponsors of terrorism; and (2) rewarding regimes that deny physical refuge and deny funding, supplies, and weapons to terrorist groups.[30]

All three victory components place considerable emphasis on military intelligence and military deterrence, even though many argue that "there is no purely military cure for terrorism, at least for democracies."[31] This focus raises an important question about whether it is reasonable to expect victory against terrorists to prevent their future disruptive behavior. Deterring terrorists is much harder than deterring states because terrorists possess extremist ideologies and zealous passion for their cause and do not have assets that can easily be held at risk, or threatened, in retribution for harm.[32] Many analysts believe that "only a decisive American victory in the present conflict with terrorism will create the conditions in which such a resolution could become imminent," but—as noted earlier—modern war rarely produces such victory.[33] The special difficulties in identifying terrorists further hinder decisive victory: in addition to being a mix of civilians and soldiers, often no reliable way exists of identifying who is friend or foe, or even ascertaining where key terrorists might be located. Thus despite being a worthy focus, deterring terrorism is a decidedly uphill battle.

In contrast to military victory, strategic victory over terrorism (like that for wars involving weapons of mass destruction) emphasizes more political and psychological desired end states. These include discrediting the legitimacy of terrorism among populations that had previously supported it or acquiesced to it, transforming the political/economic conditions that gave rise to terrorism into ones that do not support terrorism, achieving regional stability in an area previously wracked by terrorism, providing concrete disincentives for terrorist disruption, restraining the contagion of terrorist violence, reducing mass fear of terrorism, and creating a global strategic environment utterly inhospitable to terrorism. Because military victory over terrorism has proven to be so difficult, states currently fighting terrorism have not come close to attaining these goals.

The Challenge of Low-Intensity Conflict

Lastly, low-intensity conflict—recently more often called "irregular warfare"—poses a different set of problems for the concept of victory. To begin with, ambiguity exists about the meaning of low-intensity conflict. This category of warfare first received the "low-intensity conflict" label during the 1970s, describing foreign military interventions committing relatively limited military resources to cope with insurgencies.[34] The US Joint Chiefs of Staff provided in 1986 a detailed explanation of low-intensity conflict:

> Low-intensity conflict [LIC] is a limited politico-military struggle to achieve political, social, economic, or psychological objectives. It is often protracted and ranges from diplomatic, economic, and psychosocial pressures through terrorism and insurgency. Low-intensity conflict is generally confined to a geographic area and is often characterized by constraints on the weaponry, tactics, and level of violence. LIC involves the actual or contemplated use of military means up to just below the threshold of battle between regular armed forces.[35]

For many analysts today, low-intensity conflict "refers to the range of activities and operations on the lower end of the conflict spectrum involving the use of military or a variety of semimilitary forces (both combat and noncombat) on the part of the intervening power to influence and compel the adversary to accept a particular political-military condition."[36] Low-intensity conflict may often just be a by-product of traditional warfare: "In more cases than not, the aftermath of conventional conflict is going to be low-intensity conflict and armed nation building that will last months or years after a conventional struggle is over."[37] The key is that this conflict form is below the level of major theater war in scale and scope.

Low-intensity conflict usually has more limited objectives than conventional war. In many cases, the ultimate measure of success is simply political stability. The emphasis is less on changing a country's regime and more on influencing lower-level players. Whereas in traditional wars the enemy usually possesses large conventional military forces—tanks, combat aircraft, naval vessels, ground forces—that must be defeated, in low-intensity conflict very little of this is present; the fighting is clandestine, and the opponent generally has small arms, is hard to identify, and is absolutely committed to its cause in a personal way, including being willing to martyr itself. Because the context so greatly emphasizes the political over the military components of conflict, a war winner's objectives would have the same focus, expressing "victory" as achieving a predetermined political-military situation, such as "the insurgency threat seeking to overthrow the friendly regime is suppressed and political stability has been restored to the nation." Thus "the objective of LIC does not end at the military level alone but transcends to political, social, economic and even psychological levels."[38] The aims pursued by a state intervening in low-intensity conflict are also limited in the sense that it is not seeking decisive victory over an enemy, but rather the establishment of a more favorable political/military/civil order or the correction of some sort of serious power imbalance.

Partially due to these definitional ambiguities, low-intensity conflict makes it hard to achieve victory in modern warfare:

> The experience of LICs fought since World War II shows that many governments were ill-prepared to handle them.... Even if the opponents in such LICs were eventually defeated, the amount of damage, casualties, suffering and political objectives created by the opponents made such victories by the governing powers meaningless. Hence, true victory by the governing regime, if we are to follow the definition strictly, is often difficult to achieve; if not impossible.[39]

The reasons it is difficult to achieve victory in low-intensity conflict include the unsuitability of conventional military forces for this task; limited commitment by the intervening state; difficulties in eliminating external support for the insurgent group; divisive societal problems caused by maldistribution of wealth, poverty, corruption, repression, and collapse of social structure; long-standing mutual hostility among the sides; inadequate adaptability by the intervening state to the changing predicament; and insufficient stamina by the intervening state for protracted conflict.[40] In low-intensity conflicts, "a 'fluid' battle area, not bound by conventional considerations and enmeshed in the political-social fabric of the political system, creates difficulties for the intervening power that may be insurmountable in terms of 'conquest' or 'victory.'"[41]

Low-intensity conflict often particularly negates the advantages of advanced technology and superiority in military force:

> Low-intensity conflict makes it much harder to utilize most technical advantages in combat—because low-intensity wars are largely fought against people, not things. Low-intensity wars are also highly political. The battle for public opinion is as much a condition of victory as killing the enemy. The outcome of such a battle will be highly dependent on the specific political conditions under which it is fought.[42]

Many argue that "low-intensity conflicts cannot be won or even contained by military power alone"; when nonstate forces are involved in these conflicts, traditional military forces of states like Israel, Britain, Russia, and the United States may become "all but useless."[43] So military success on the battlefield means less here than in conventional warfare:

> Lasting victory in LIC comes more from achieving political success rather than military or economic success. Unlike conventional wars where defeating the opposing military forces would usually secure victory for the state, the mere capture or destruction of such LIC forces would not totally remove their influence on the populace due to the existence of sympathisers. New groups would simply spring up to continue the fight since the root cause of LIC has not been resolved. The political aspects in LIC therefore take paramount importance over the military and other aspects.[44]

With low-intensity conflict often involving asymmetric warfare between foes of differing motivation levels, for an intervening state "this mismatch in the level of commitment makes a clear-cut victory hard to achieve."[45]

Because of the inherently political nature of successful low-intensity conflict outcomes, when dealing with elusive and transitory adversaries lasting victory is also more difficult to recognize:

> From the many internal wars that have been waged, it is clear that it is not easy to completely remove such insurgency or guerrilla movements once they have established themselves. But is victory in LIC merely the termination of such groups, or should governments concentrate on ending the causes fought by these groups? Often the coups, revolts and revolutions may be prevented and defeated, but the causes for which these are fought are seldom completely defeated. In such situations, victory may end up having only a temporal effect and hence [be] ineffective.[46]

Indeed, low-intensity conflict often remains unresolved for a substantial period of time.[47] Attempts to define precisely military victory in low-intensity conflict, such as "'victory' in low-intensity conflicts can be considered achieved in situations where the threatened government is able to conquer or pacify the illegitimate arms-organised group or limit the conflict to a manageable proportion at a domestically 'acceptable' cost," are usually controversial due to ambiguities about what level of cost is tolerable.[48] Thus many low-intensity conflicts turn into protracted wars of attrition, preventing the identification of a decisive winner or loser in terms of long-term elimination of existing frustrations or transformation of disruptive elements within the area of turmoil.

Low-intensity conflict's subjective political aims and nondefinitive outcomes frequently deflate even the best efforts by an intervening party to establish order and resolve disputes. Although in theory strategic victory in low-intensity conflict would mean achieving political and psychological desired end states parallel to those discussed for strategic victory in the war on terrorism, in practice postwar payoffs from low-intensity conflict seem decidedly low, involving simply an escape from the predicament without too many losses, too much international animosity, or too great a downturn in the situation.

Victory in Future Unconventional Warfare

Future warfare involving changes in technology, armed forces, and threat may make victory even more elusive than in today's unconventional confrontations. Although robotized armies, private mercenaries, and clandestine diffuse insurgency movements are all present to some degree today, in the future they are likely to become a lot more widespread. While not undergoing radical discontinuous change, future warfare may very well present new challenges—and require new thinking—to achieve victory:

> The merging of modes of armed conflict suggests an era of warfare quite different from that of the recent past. Fighting in the future may involve conventional armies, guerrilla bands, independent and state-directed terrorist groups, specialized antiterrorist units, and private militias. Terrorist attacks might evolve into classic guerrilla warfare and then escalate to conventional conflict. Alternatively, fighting could be conducted on several levels at once. The possibility of continuous, sporadic, armed conflict, its engagements blurred together in time and space, waged on several levels by a large array of national and subnational forces, means that the reality of war in the first decade of the twenty-first century is likely to transcend a neat division into distinct categories, symmetry and asymmetry.[49]

The transformation of future conflict may render irrelevant traditional strategies for military success devised for yesterday's conventional warfare. Moreover, from an intelligence perspective, while generally the operational signatures of conventional military forces are well known, the newer unconventional threats have vastly different signatures, or no signatures, necessitating an entirely different intelligence strategy on our part and requiring, in turn, a drastic reorientation of intelligence.

The Challenge of Change in Technology

Extrapolating ongoing battle technology trends into the future, it appears that warfare will move even further than it has today from traditional human-to-human combat on the battlefield. Without doubt, despite its limits for strategic victory, technology will play an increasingly pivotal role in the way wars are fought and won:

> On the wartime battlefield of the future, wartime leaders will know more, faster, than ever before. But like those who have already fought, those whose battles are yet to come will still have to decide which information to rely on and which to discard. As the availability of information grows, so do the chances that actors will see the world through different lenses. Thus, the study of how nations fight will increasingly become the study of how nations use information in war.[50]

Although "states are often wrong in their assessment of how technology will actually work in war," because the possession of technology can lead to expectations of quick and decisive victories and inflation of political objectives and the victory payoffs, technology "appears to be a strong predictor of state objectives in war."[51] In the future, access to and use of vital information and technology may be far more crucial to strategic victory than possession of larger or better-trained armed forces.

However, having technology dominate future warfare makes it difficult to determine when the enemy is truly defeated. One obstacle here revolves around the growing speed of technological diffusion, which often prevents a state with superior technology from emerging victorious after a war; given ongoing trends concerning porous state boundaries, covert arms transfers, and the proprietary technology piracy, in the future virtually anyone may be able to get his or her hands on the latest weaponry. A second obstacle deals with the inherent ambiguity surrounding technological confrontations: as one military analyst quips, "When you're launching a computer attack against somebody, how do you know you've got them and haven't hurt yourself?"[52] A third obstacle focuses on potential backfire effects from technological disruption: if one's technological interference leaves "the enemy command with no means to fight, it is then nonetheless unable to communicate its desire for surrender or truce to its troops."[53]

With the changing nature of fighting forces and targets, some current strategies for military victory may become tangential, with human casualty counts degrading even further as an indicator of who is winning. Potentially also headed for the scrap heap is today's concept of attrition in warfare, through which it has been possible to predict with relative precision from intelligence when the enemy's back is broken: according to this traditional approach, one could wear down enemies to the point where they are not able to launch any further resistance, and then they accept militarily defeat and order their troops to withdraw, stop fighting, and lay down their arms. If future technological advances reduce the pivotal role of soldiers in fighting and winning wars, it might be more difficult to determine whether the enemy's back is broken, or even for the enemy to execute a withdrawal from battle. Ultimately, the first side to capitulate may be the one that can no longer protect or gain access to vital war-fighting technologies.

More specifically, perhaps the most important future change in war-related technology may be the move toward largely mechanized warfare involving the use of robotic soldiers and unmanned vehicles. This development reduces the need to emphasize force protection of soldiers' lives in peril. Due to concerns about human casualties, in the future, aside from self-defense, it may be that "only such conflict as can take place without soldiers is likely to be tolerated…and robotic weapons will be used increasingly."[54] Ironically, "the spread of chemical, biological, and nuclear arms in the world is also likely to promote robotization by creating battlefields just too toxic for human soldiers."[55]

The use of robotic soldiers and unmanned combat vehicles as a means of securing victory has four justifications. First, such mechanized means of combat provide distinct advantages in terms of quick application of potent firepower to virtually any designated target. Second, robots can reduce costs compared to human soldiers, whose costs include not only months of training but also substantial retirement benefits: "the median cost of a soldier is about $4 million today and growing," according to a Pentagon study, and "robot soldiers cost a tenth of that or less."[56] Third, using machines instead of people to fight wars reduces the likelihood that moral or public opinion pressures would constrain or twist the war effort in directions not optimal for achieving victory. Fourth, reliance on such technology reduces or eliminates the role that human frailty plays on the battlefield:

> "They don't get hungry," said Gordon Johnson of the Joint Forces Command at the Pentagon. "They're not afraid. They don't forget their orders. They don't care if the guy next to them has just been shot. Will they do a better job than humans? Yes."[57]

Wars "still fought by flesh-and-blood human beings, who have to suffer mutilation and often death in pursuit of victory," introduce the possibility that "their feelings, desires, and attitudes—sometimes the attitudes instilled to make them more effective warriors—can get them in the way of neat endings to war."[58]

Many possible uses exist for robots in warfare, despite the tendency of extensive mechanization to create major challenges dealing with control, breakdown, and repair:

> Once science fiction, today the robots and the attack laser are fact. They are part of a massive research effort in labs across the US that will give the US military the ability to dominate the battlefield of the 21st century.... Critics say that the US already has the most powerful armed forces in the world and will retain that position far into the future. But the US military believes technologically superior weapons will reduce casualties and deter future wars if an enemy believes it has no hope of defeating such a formidable force.... On the future battlefield, robots will be king. The US Air Force envisions unmanned aircraft that can be launched from submarines, ships or runways, and has already awarded Lockheed Martin a $120 million US contract to start work on such a project. An unmanned aircraft can fly faster and higher at half the price of manned fighters. The US Navy envisions using robot crabs to scurry across beaches, defusing mines. The US Army wants to use robots for battlefield reconnaissance. In October, the Marines will test a robot mortar called Dragon Fire; once the device's sensors detect an enemy formation the mortar begins firing. The Marines are also considering using the robot mortar in conjunction with drone planes that could locate an enemy.[59]

Future combat could thus differ dramatically from the past:

> Within 20 years, squadrons of unmanned planes will swarm enemy sites like killer bees, launching missiles and avoiding detection with sophisticated jamming devices.

> Self-programmed submarines will...detect and disarm mines. Robotic mules the size of pickups will haul ammunition, medical supplies and food.
>
> Drone ambulances will load wounded soldiers and cart them to hospitals. Crablike robots will crawl into buildings to sniff out chemical stashes.
>
> The transition to mechanized weaponry is key to the military's transformation from heavy ground forces to smaller human units fortified with robotic weapons. The goal: to limit casualties.[60]

A key challenge in mechanization's value for strategic victory is that developers have so far been better at conceiving new ideas for automation than at identifying specific practical scenarios in which they could be beneficial in the field integrated with traditional combat tactics.

Rather than being part of an unrealistic pipe dream, defense policymakers are already taking concrete steps in the direction of automating military forces. For example, the unmanned aircraft Predator proved to be vital in the war against terrorism in Afghanistan in 2001–2002 to find and track targets.[61] In 2005 an armed bomb-disposal robot, capable of firing 1,000 rounds a minute, was sent to Baghdad to help with the war in Iraq.[62] On July 8, 2003, the US House of Representatives approved by a vote of 399 to 19 a whopping $369.1 billion Pentagon spending bill for 2004 that specifically earmarked $1.7 billion for the US Army's Future Combat Systems, a network of ground-based and air-based robots, sensors, light armored vehicles, and guns.[63] Indeed, even by 2005 the emphasis on Future Combat Systems—"a joint (across all the military services) networked (connected via advanced communications) system of systems"[64]—has become enormous: "The Pentagon predicts that robots will be a major fighting force in the American military in less than a decade, hunting and killing enemies in combat; robots are a crucial part of the Army's attempt to rebuild itself as a 21st-century fighting force, and a $127 billion project called Future Combat Systems is the biggest military contract in American history."[65]

The future plan is clearly to have robots gradually enter the mix of fighting forces in warfare:

> For the really tight spots, we are developing robots to replace soldiers. Already robots guard some installations and can be used to enter dangerous buildings or approach suspected bombs. Soon, no doubt, they will be able to take a share of the real fighting, demon-

> strating an ability to identify and engage resisting targets on a smoke-obscured battlefield under remote direction.[66]

Initially, "they will be remote-controlled," but "as the technology develops" and "their intelligence grows, so will their autonomy."[67]

However, worries persist about robotic assaults increasing questionable activities during and after combat. Robots designed to achieve military victory could easily serve more nefarious purposes:

> When flying robots weighing less than a gram can act as spies collecting accurate, digital, and up-to-date information are feasible—as they will be soon—then organizations won't need a full-fledged network of human spies to gather data. Those same robots in slightly different configurations could easily kill a selected individual or group, perhaps by putting strychnine in their coffee or cyanide in their corn flakes.[68]

Others are concerned simply about ineffectiveness—shifting tasks from humans to robots has long been met with limited success because "robots cannot reproduce the complexity of the human brain," as "they react poorly to unexpected circumstances, which is what war is all about."[69] Outside of cognitive limitations, robots would have difficulty distinguishing between morally acceptable and unacceptable actions during and after war. Still others worry that mechanization of warfare may eventually remove humans from the decisionmaking loop, leading to the chaos depicted in the 1983 film *War Games*. However, even the harshest critics admit that this mechanization seems inevitable.

The Challenge of Change in Armed Forces

Projecting ongoing military recruitment trends, it appears that in the future combatants in warfare increasingly will not be government troops. Instead, private military company personnel and mercenaries are likely to replace traditional professional members of state armed forces.[70] In order to circumvent a state's intolerance of its own casualties, "one scheme would be to follow the Ghurka model, recruiting troops in some suitable region abroad" and having them serve as private mercenaries for the commissioning government in wars overseas.[71]

There are multifaceted roots to the future explosion of private soldiers used in warfare. First, from a broad systemic level, a unique post–Cold War confluence of systemic global supply and demand trends makes future growth of private security providers virtually inevitable:

> But why did these companies emerge at this time in history? The answer, briefly, is that the conjunction of market forces was just right early on in the decade. On the demand side, there was a marked increase in the number of domestic conflicts around the world: the collapse of both the Soviet Union and Yugoslavia resulted in civil wars; in Africa, the economic stresses of the 1980s manifested themselves in the intensification of civil wars in Sudan, Angola, Sierra Leone, Rwanda and the former Zaire.... If demand for non-indigenous military expertise increased, so supply conditions favoured the privatization of war-fighting. First, the end of the Cold War and a number of related conflicts had a marked effect on the world's military forces. The end of East-West rivalry led to large-scale downsizing of military establishments all over the world; very quickly, many early-retired officers and soldiers with considerable military expertise and combat training found themselves on the market. Second, the collapse of the Soviet Union had a marked impact on one important aspect of supply: technologically sophisticated military equipment, such as helicopter gunships, that a private actor could never have acquired during the Cold War was now available for hire.[72]

Second, from a narrower nation-state level, strong Western governments are becoming reluctant to intervene with their own government forces to achieve stability in distant parts of the world where core national interests are not at stake, with an increasingly unclear basis for legitimate coercive action due to the uncertain payoff, the high risks of involvement, and murkiness about which side to assist. Private military companies offer such countries another option (potentially also substituting for mandatory conscription), which has the advantage of plausible deniability for undesired outcomes. Moreover, because Western leaders "have become quite terrified of taking casualties" through warfare, private military forces have begun to look awfully attractive:

> An American ambassador in Europe told dinner guests a couple of years ago that his country could no longer emotionally, psychologically or politically accept body bags coming home in double figures. By the start of the Kosovo war, just 15 months ago, that number had been reduced to zero. So we tried to fight a war from 15,000 feet. That taught us the limits of stand-alone air power. We

> couldn't stop or slow the pogroms, so we creamed the capital city of the guilty nation until after 74 days a fat Russian stepped in, slapped down his protégé Slobodan Milosevic, and procured a chaotic form of peace. We managed to kill 14 times more Serb civilians than uniformed soldiers and zero secret-police killers. But we avoided casualties and called it a victory. The utter horror of taking casualties has not extended to Britain and France, but is subscribed to by the rest of Europe. As for any kind of involvement in a lethal hellhole in Central or South America, Africa or Asia, simply on humanitarian grounds—forget it. We might use our own troops to extricate our own citizens, or even to protect a massive national economic or strategic facility, but that is about it. We watch the charnel house of Sierra Leone with horror but impunity. Then into the frame, to politically correct cries of "Yuck," steps the professional mercenary.[73]

The idea of victory without casualties in a "bloodless war" can be extremely appealing to democracies with narrow national interests.

Third, from a public opinion standpoint, greater public exposure to incidents of "terrorism, kidnapping, random acts of violence, urban unrest, increasing general crime, corporate crime, and weakened and poorly resourced and trained state law enforcement agencies" has fueled perceptions of insecurity and openness to privatized military solutions.[74]

Private sources of military force, whether highly unstructured and informal like modern mercenary groups or highly formal and structured like today's major private military companies (such as Virginia-based Military Professional Resources Incorporated), have some special practical advantages in dealing with ruthless opponents. Mercenaries feel free to engage in a wide variety of extra-legal types of force, including covert assassination, kidnapping, or sabotage, and in recent times have been less scrupulous about the exercise of restraint during war, including respect for human rights and protection of innocent civilians in war zones. Speed and flexibility are trademarks of private military action, avoiding layers of bureaucracy to get approval for a mission or months of preparation to ensure minimal collateral damage during missions.

Although private armed forces have been around for centuries, recent examples illustrate their huge future proliferation possibilities. In Bosnia and Afghanistan, "large indigenous friendly ground forces served as surrogates, thus holding down US casualties and their perceived potential domestic political consequences."[75] The role of private military companies later received a significant, if little noted, boost, albeit not directly a part of war-fighting strategy, in November 2002 when the Virginia-based contractor DynCorp received a new assignment from the State Department's Diplomatic Security Service to help protect Afghan president Hamid Karzai.[76] From 1994 to 2002, the Pentagon entered into more than 3,000 contracts with private military firms, serving to "provide the logistics for every major American military deployment."[77] During the 2003 Iraq War and its aftermath, the use of private contractors has been so extensive for so many purposes that they have constituted a sizable chunk of those captured or killed.

In the future, private armies could even be used to combat transnational terrorism.[78] Counterterrorist action is an area where Western states have been particularly unsuccessful, in terms of both destroying targets and protecting noncombatants from harm. Mercenaries often have linkages to arms dealers who sell weapons to terrorists, providing an intelligence opportunity; and private military forces are not subject to the restrained means handcuffing Western government soldiers in actual combat against terrorists. Thus private military forces may prove to be most effective in counterterrorist action when a state government is concerned about force protection among its own government soldiers yet feels it needs to employ intense coercion exceeding normal bounds against one or more terrorist groups.

As with the use of robot technology, the introduction of private military can muddy moral questions surrounding war termination and can make it less clear when war is over. The rights of mercenaries captured in battle are unclear under the Geneva Conventions, as are the limitations imposed on their wartime operations. If an enemy's government troops are defeated, then it can renew its struggle using private forces. However, private military forces may not be able to handle the tasks of postcombat mop-up as well as government soldiers. Ultimately, the first side to capitulate may be the one that can no longer afford monetarily to hire any more private soldiers to fight for its cause.

Moreover, the use of private soldiers during wartime raises some potential control issues. For example, "relying on a proxy army can have its drawbacks, especially in a place such as Afghanistan, where ethnic and tribal rivalries run deep and the United States might not be able to control its surrogates."[79] Private armies may also lack the most sophisticated war-fighting military technologies. Third World countries may perceive Western reliance on private soldiers for foreign military action as a signal of even less commitment than the use of government troops conveys today. Furthermore, when a government chooses to outsource to private security providers, it may bear little public accountability for undesired consequences, deaths of citizens, or moral dilemmas surrounding the legitimacy of a foreign military action.[80]

The Challenge of Change in Threat

Finally, projecting trends in ongoing sources of threat, it appears that in the future enemies will be even harder to monitor, predict, and contain than they are today. Specifically, we are likely to witness increasingly ideologically driven actions associated with more clandestine insurgency-oriented threats. This pattern fits nicely with one predicted in the early 1990s by Alvin and Heidi Toffler: "the 'de-massification' of threats in the world," where "a single giant threat of war…is replaced by a multitude of 'niche threats.'"[81] In the future, "war will not be waged by armies but by groups we today call terrorists, guerrillas, bandits, and robbers," and "their organizations are likely to be constructed on charismatic lines rather than institutional ones, and to be motivated less by 'professionalism' than by fanatical, ideologically-based, loyalties."[82] From the experience of violent conflicts after the Cold War, "a key lesson hostile movements have learned is to mutate, disperse, and fragment" because "limited actions that provoke disproportionate fear and 'terror' force the US and its allies into costly, drastic, and sometimes provocative responses."[83] This orientation means that zealous commitment to rigid beliefs may become more common among adversaries and may increase both the probability and duration of war. Emotional, seemingly irrational foes, who at least on the surface do not follow traditional Western cost-benefit analysis in deciding when to start and stop fighting, may become even more commonplace than they are today.

Compromise and negotiated settlement may become rare, as both sides in a conflict press indefatigably for victory. This evolving threat pattern may involve enemies being more intransigent and desired outcomes being harder both to achieve and to stabilize. Ultimately, the first side to capitulate may be the one that literally has nobody left able to fight for its cause.

In the future, this evolving nature of the threat may expand the notion of irregular warfare beyond its previous bounds. Future wars will be marked by differences in religion, culture, or ethnic identity more than in the past, with fierce struggles for power and control, creating the specter of more intractable conflict needing new kinds of strategies for strategic victory.[84] Furthermore, the further spread of cyberterrorism through computers, the Internet, and complex information systems may globally empower these unruly forces.[85]

The changing nature of the threat seems likely to make enemies more difficult to defeat and thus victory more elusive. As foes move underground and become more covert, dispersed, and decentralized, target identification and battle planning becomes a huge challenge. It may become virtually impossible to launch a successful major military assault against such targets:

> How do you "massively retaliate" against a terrorist gang or narco-warlord, or even a tiny state, that has no important infrastructure or command center to attack? Or a team of "info-terrorists" arriving in the United States to sabotage critical nodes in the country's highly vulnerable communication system and satellite links. Or, indeed, not arriving at all, but sitting at computer screens somewhere half a world away and penetrating the networks that process and carry satellite-derived data.[86]

The spread of this type of enemy further exposes Western states' high vulnerability to disruption.

For these future adversaries, ambiguity will be a real asset. More than anything else, "the problem will be sustaining the utility of military force in the absence of clarity, particularly when enemies discover that the use of protracted warfare in physically, ethically, legally, and politically complex environments offers protection against the terrible, swift sword of the American military."[87] Although advanced technology may seem like the solution to this problem, with, for example, precision armaments potentially discriminating among hard-to-hit targets during warfare, in many ways future changes in technology and changes in threat can become mutually reinforcing, as improved transportation and communication systems facilitate the dangerous clandestine dispersal of foes capable of significant internationally disruptive behavior.[88]

Disruptive elements outside of the state—well beyond the terrorism that exists today—will pose special victory problems, as increasingly "transnational and substate forces threaten not just states but entire societies and thus the fabric of international stability itself."[89] These forces' proclivities toward "protracted conflict, ethical, political, and legal ambiguity, and operating within population centers make them particularly virulent" and tough to vanquish.[90] Because "nonstate enemies will be the most adaptable and least encumbered by bureaucracy or international law and norms," those seeking victory against such foes would have to be equally adaptable in their creative countermeasures.[91] A truly nightmarish victory challenge would be "the possibility of continuous, sporadic, armed conflict, its engagements blurred together in time and space, waged on several levels by a large array of national and subnational forces."[92]

Concluding Thoughts

Unconventional warfare does not make victory easy. In today's world, in circumstances where weapons of mass destruction, terrorism, and low-intensity conflict are involved, a pressing need exists to reconsider and retune the strategies for pursuing strategic victory by taking carefully into account the special obstacles injected by these dangerous irregular conflicts, which bestow special advantages on weak, unruly, disruptive global forces. Figure 7.2 highlights the contrast between contemporary victory in unconventional and conventional warfare. Aside from the different meanings of military victory and strategic victory in this context, several key distinctions are evident: military superiority tends to play a more important role in conventional than in unconventional war; conventional warfare tends to be more symmetric (while still not being completely symmetric) than the highly asymmetric unconventional warfare; unruly disruptive forces tend to prefer unconventional to conventional conflict; and participants in conventional conflict tend to be more concerned about inflicting human casualties and property damage than are participants in unconventional conflict. All in all, strategic victory in unconventional conflict seems to have much more fluid bounds than conventional conflict.

Looking to the future, significant changes in international conflict may increase even further the complexity of strategic victory in unconventional warfare. Knowing emerging trends in how war-fighting techniques affect war outcomes can help to build adaptability and flexibility into the current strategies to achieve postwar payoffs. The increasing indirect involvement of government troops in future wars—especially in the context of clandestine and diffuse ideologically driven insurgency-oriented threats—poses a huge impediment to achieving strategic victory: in this predicament, those deciding to

Figure 7.2 Conventional vs. Unconventional Victory

	Conventional Warfare	Unconventional Warfare
Value of Military Superiority	High—	Low—
	Soldiers trained for threat	Soldiers untrained for threat
	Threat containable	Threat uncontainable
Ratio of Political Will	More symmetric	More asymmetric
	Both sides willing to sacrifice	One side possesses zealous resolve
	Both sides willing to compromise	One side unwilling to compromise
Appeal to Disruptive Elements	Low—	High—
	Defer to Western military powers	Counter to Western military powers
	Appeal to the strong	Appeal to the weak
Tolerance of Collateral Damage	Low—	High—
	Avoid killing innocent people	Willing to kill innocent people
	Avoid peripheral property damage	Willing to damage peripheral property
Meaning of Military Victory	Defeat enemy soldiers in combat	Protect potential victims
	Achieve battlefield goals	Stop potential perpetrators
	Halt foe's war-making potential	Prevent support for perpetrators
Meaning of Strategic Victory	Information control	Discredit legitimacy of action
	Military deterrence	Transform underlying causes
	Political self-determination	Achieve regional stability
	Economic reconstruction	Provide disincentives for disruption
	Social justice	Restrain contagious violence
	Diplomatic respect	Reduce mass sense of fear

fight the war, formulating the wartime strategies, and choosing when to stop fighting the war may lack complete control of those wreaking havoc and destruction against the enemy, creating the possibility that leaders will want peace but somehow will not be able to implement in a timely manner an end to the fighting. With each side knowing this possibility, as a war winds down each side's verbal statements may lack credibility, impeding effective signaling despite communication improvements. Without government representatives (national armed forces) at the core of the conflict, and with the possibility of private military forces on one side and covert insurgents on the other, these signaling and intelligence deficiencies increase the potential for misinterpretation of what one's adversary intends. If one then adds in the potential for plausible deniability for "accidents" or supposedly unintended destruction of a foe's assets, the future outlook for war termination looks really bleak.

Taking into account the dangers associated with both ongoing and emerging forms of unconventional warfare, the need for changes in the way military victors in warfare approach strategic victory—specifically proposed in the next chapter—has never been more evident. Just continuing with dogged adherence to standard ways of winning is decidedly not adequate to deal with this irregular conflict. Unless wars degrade into cosmetic incidents designed simply to signal onlookers that some effort—however futile—is occurring to confront dangers, hopes for global stability are likely to rest on single-minded pursuit of strategic victory using adaptable means to manage these truly persistent and pesky current and future threats.

Notes

1. The definition of weapons of mass destruction is from Joint Publication 1-02, *Department of Defense Dictionary of Military and Associated Terms* (Washington, DC: Government Printing Office, 1994), pp. 571–572.

2. Bernard Brodie, *The Absolute Weapon* (New York: Harcourt Brace, 1946), p. 76.

3. John M. Gates, *The US Army and Irregular Warfare* (unpublished manuscript), chapter xi.

4. Brian Bond, *The Pursuit of Victory: From Napoleon to Saddam Hussein* (New York: Oxford University Press, 1996), p. 174.

5. Robert Mandel, "Chemical Warfare: Act of Intimidation or Desperation?" *Armed Forces & Society* 19 (Winter 1993), pp. 190, 204.

6. Malcolm R. Davis and Colin S. Gray, "Weapons of Mass Destruction," in John Baylis, James Wirtz, Eliot Cohen, and Colin S. Gray, eds., *Strategy in the Contemporary World* (New York: Oxford University Press, 2002), p. 255.

7. Anthony H. Cordesman, *Lessons of Post–Cold War Conflict: Middle*

Eastern Lessons and Perspectives (Washington, DC: Center for Strategic and International Studies, 2004), p. iv.

8. Martin Van Creveld, "Through a Glass Darkly: Some Reflections on the Future of War" (unpublished paper, 2000).

9. Robert Jervis, *The Meaning of the Nuclear Revolution: Statecraft and the Prospect of Armageddon* (Ithaca, NY: Cornell University Press, 1989), pp. 4–8.

10. John Steinbrunner, "Nuclear Decapitation," *Foreign Policy* 45 (Winter 1981–1982), pp. 22–23.

11. Colin S. Gray and Keith Payne, "Victory Is Possible," *Foreign Policy* 39 (Summer 1980), pp. 14, 20, 26.

12. Barry R. Schneider, "Principles of War for the Battlefield of the Future," in Barry R. Schneider and Lawrence E. Grinter, eds., *Battlefield of the Future: A Twenty-first Century Warfare Issue* (Maxwell Air Force Base, AL: Air War College Studies in National Security #3, 1995).

13. Paul Kecskemeti, *Strategic Surrender: The Politics of Victory and Defeat* (Stanford, CA: Stanford University Press, 1958), p. 249.

14. Peter Liberman, *Does Conquest Pay? The Exploitation of Occupied Industrial Societies* (Princeton, NJ: Princeton University Press, 1996), p. 11.

15. James D. Kiras, "Terrorism and Irregular Warfare," in Baylis, Wirtz, Cohen, and Gray, *Strategy in the Contemporary World*, p. 211.

16. Dominic Johnson and Dominic Tierney, "Winning and Losing the War on Terror" (paper presented at the annual meeting of the International Studies Association, Honolulu, March 2005), p. 1.

17. Ibid., p. 2; and Donald Rumsfeld's memorandum, October 16, 2003, http://www.usatoday.com/news/washington/executive/rumsfeld-memo.htm.

18. Richard Whittle, "In New War, Victory Isn't Easy to Define," *Dallas Morning News,* September 22, 2001.

19. "Saddam's Defeat a Victory over Terrorism, Wolfowitz Says," http://japan.usembassy.gov/e/p/tp-20030603a9.html.

20. Carl Conetta, *Strange Victory: A Critical Appraisal of Operation Enduring Freedom and the Afghanistan War* (Cambridge, MA: Commonwealth Institute Project on Defense Alternatives Research Monograph #6, 2002), p. 33, http://www.comw.org/pda/0201strangevic.pdf.

21. Richard Gwyn, "Victory in War on Terrorism Can't Be Won by Military," *Toronto Star,* September 15, 2003, p. A8; and Johnson and Tierney, "Winning and Losing the War on Terror," pp. 1–2.

22. Paul W. Schroeder, "The Risks of Victory," *National Interest* (Winter 2001/2002), p. 32.

23. Peter D. Feaver, "To Maintain That Support, Show Us What Success Means," http://www.duke.edu/web/forums/feaver.html.

24. Johnson and Tierney, "Winning and Losing the War on Terror," p. 2.

25. "Saddam's Defeat a Victory over Terrorism, Wolfowitz Says," http://japan.usembassy.gov/e/p/tp-20030603a9.html; and Schroeder, "The Risks of Victory," p. 32.

26. Ian S. Lustick, "The Political Requirements of Victory," *Middle East Policy* 8 (December 2001), p. 15.
27. "Saddam's Defeat a Victory over Terrorism, Wolfowitz Says," http://japan.usembassy.gov/e/p/tp-20030603a9.html.
28. F. Gregory Gause III, "Can Democarcy Stop Terrorism?" *Foreign Affairs* 84 (September/October 2005), p. 65.
29. "National Defense Strategy of the United States of America: A Defense Strategy for the Twenty-first Century," March 2005, http://www.globalsecurity.org/military/library/policy/dod/nds-usa_mar2005_iib.htm.
30. Schroeder, "The Risks of Victory," p. 32; and Feaver, "To Maintain That Support, Show Us What Success Means."
31. C. J. Dick, *Conflict in a Changing World: Looking Two Decades Forward* (Surrey, UK: Conflict Studies Research Centre, 2002), p. 16.
32. "National Defense Strategy of the United States of America: A Defense Strategy for the Twenty-first Century," March 2005, http://www.globalsecurity.org/military/library/policy/dod/nds-usa_mar2005_iib.htm.
33. Conrad Black, "What Victory Means," *National Interest* (Winter 2001/2002), p. 158.
34. Loren B. Thompson, "Low-Intensity Conflict: An Overview," in Loren B. Thompson, ed., *Low-Intensity Conflicts* (Lexington, MA: Lexington Books, 1989), p. 2.
35. *Joint Low-Intensity Conflict Project Final Report* (Fort Monroe, VA: United States Army Training and Doctrine Command, 1986), p. 3.
36. Sam C. Sarkesian, "American Policy and Low-Intensity Conflict," in Sam C. Sarkesian and William C. Scully, eds., *US Policy and Low-Intensity Conflict* (New Brunswick, NJ: Transaction Books, 1981), p. 3.
37. Anthony H. Cordesman, *The "Post Conflict" Lessons of Iraq and Afghanistan* (Washington, DC: Center for Strategic and International Studies, 2004), pp. ii–iii.
38. Matthew Kee Yeow Chye, "Victory in Low-Intensity Conflicts," 2000, http://www.mindef.gov.sg/safti/pointer/back/journals/2000/Vol26_4/4.htm.
39. Ibid.
40. Ibid.
41. Sarkesian, "American Policy and Low-Intensity Conflict," p. 4.
42. Cordesman, *Lessions of Post–Cold War Conflict*, p. 17.
43. Michael T. Klare and Peter Kornbluh, "The New Interventionism: Low-Intensity Warfare in the 1980s and Beyond," in Michael T. Klare and Peter Kornbluh, eds., *Low-Intensity Warfare* (New York: Pantheon Books, 1987), p. 5; and Martin Van Creveld, *The Transformation of War* (New York: Free Press, 1991), pp. ix–x, 2, 29, 62, and 224–225.
44. Chye, "Victory in Low-Intensity Conflicts."
45. Ibid.
46. Ibid.
47. James D. Kiras, "Terrorism and Irregular Warfare," in Baylis, Wirtz, Cohen, and Gray, *Strategy in the Contemporary World*, p. 213.

48. Hong Kian Wah, "Low-Intensity Conflict," 2000, http://www.mindef.gov.sg/safti/pointer/back/journals/2000/Vol26_3/7.htm.

49. Michael Evans, "From Kadesh to Kandahar: Military Theory and the Future of War," *Naval War College Review* 41 (Summer 2003), pp. 140–141.

50. Scott Sigmund Gartner, *Strategic Assessment in War* (New Haven, CT: Yale University Press, 1997), p. 177.

51. Monica Duffy Toft, "End of Victory? Civil War Termination in Historical Perspective" (paper presented at the annual national meeting of the International Studies Association, Honolulu, March 2005), pp. 11, 13.

52. CNN News, "Fierce Cyber War Predicted," http://www.cnn.com/2003/TECH/ptech/03/03/sprj.irq.info.war.ap/.

53. Karl Kuschner, "Legal and Practical Constraints on Information Warfare," http://www.airpower.maxwell.af.mil/airchronicles/cc/kuschner.html.

54. Edward N. Luttwak, "Where Are the Great Powers? At Home with the Kids," *Foreign Affairs* 73 (July/August 1994), p. 27.

55. Alvin Toffler and Heidi Toffler, *War and Anti-War* (New York: Warner Books, 1993), p. 126.

56. Tim Wiener, "A New Model Army Soldier Rolls Closer to the Battlefield," *New York Times,* February 16, 2005, p. C4; and Gregory M. Lamb, "Battle Bot: The Future of War?" *Christian Science Monitor,* January 27, 2005, p. 14.

57. Wiener, "A New Model Army Soldier," p. C1.

58. Adam Yarmolinsky, "Professional Military Perspectives on War Termination," in Albert and Luck, *On the Endings of Wars*, p. 121.

59. David Pugliese, "The Future of War," *Defence Associations National Network News* 5 (Summer 1998), http://www.sfu.ca/~dann/Backissues/nn5-2_3.htm.

60. Jon Swartz, "New Breed of Robots, Gizmos Take War to the Next Level," *USA Today,* May 12, 2003, p. 3B.

61. David A. Fulghum, "UAVs Whet the Appetite," *Aviation Week & Space Technology* 158 (March 3, 2003), p. 52.

62. Wiener, "A New Model Army Soldier," p. C4.

63. Dan Morgan, "House Approves $369 Billion for Defense Spending: Funds Lay Groundwork for Shift that Rumsfeld Is Seeking to Lighter, More Mobile Military Force," *Washington Post* (July 9, 2003), p. A4.

64. "Army Accelerates Selected FCS Capabilities," July 22, 2004, http://www4.army.mil/ocpa/read.php?story_id_key=6179.

65. Wiener, "A New Model Army Soldier," p. C1.

66. Harvey M. Sapolsky and Jeremy Shapiro, "Casualties, Technology, and America's Future Wars," *Parameters* (Summer 1996), pp. 119–127.

67. Wiener, "A New Model Army Soldier," p. C1.

68. Paul Musgrave, "Will Technology Be Used to Make War More Humane? Warfare and the Information Revolution," February 2003, http://www.paulmusgrave.net.

69. Swartz, "New Breed of Robots," p. 3B.

70. This section draws heavily from Robert Mandel, *Armies Without States: The Privatization of Security* (Boulder, CO: Lynne Rienner, 2002).

71. Luttwak, "Where Are the Great Powers?" p. 28.

72. Kim Richard Nossal, "Bulls to Bears: The Privatization of War in the 1990s," http://www.onwar.org/warandmoney/pdfs/nossal.pdf.

73. Frederick Forsyth, "Send in the Mercenaries," *Wall Street Journal,* May 15, 2000.

74. Alex Vines, "Mercenaries, Human Rights, and Legality," in Abdel-Fatau Musah and J. Kayode Fayemi, eds., *Mercenaries: An African Security Dilemma* (London: Pluto Press, 2000), p. 169.

75. Jeffrey Record, "Collapsed Countries, Casualty Dread, and the New American Way of War," *Parameters* (Summer 2002), p. 4.

76. David Isenberg, "Security for Sale in Afghanistan," *Asia Times Online*, January 4, 2003, http://www.atimes.com/atimes/Central_Asia/EA04Ag01.html.

77. P. W. Singer, "Have Guns, Will Travel," *New York Times,* July 21, 2003, p. 15A.

78. Robert Mandel, "Fighting Fire with Fire: Privatizing Counterterrorism," in Russell D. Howard and Reid L. Sawyer, eds., *Defeating Terrorism: Shaping the New Security Environment* (New York: McGraw-Hill, 2003).

79. Tom Bowman, "War Casualties Could Test Public's Resolve: Officials Fear Support Could Shrink as Troops Search for Bin Laden," *Baltimore Sun,* November 18, 2001, p. 19A.

80. David Shearer, *Private Armies and Military Intervention* (London: Oxford University Press, International Institute for Strategic Studies Adelphi Paper 316, 1998), pp. 69–72.

81. Toffler and Toffler, *War and Anti-War*, p. 104.

82. Van Creveld, *The Transformation of War*, p. 197.

83. Cordesman, *Lessons of Post–Cold War Conflict*, p. iv.

84. Kiras, "Terrorism and Irregular Warfare," pp. 226–227.

85. Ibid., p. 227.

86. Toffler and Toffler, *War and Anti-War*, p. 122.

87. Steven Metz and Raymond A. Millen, *Future War/Future Battlespace: The Strategic Role of American Landpower* (Carlisle Barracks, PA: US Army War College Strategic Studies Institute, 2003), p. 18.

88. Ibid., pp. 18–19.

89. Evans, "From Kadesh to Kandahar," p. 135.

90. Metz and Millen, *Future War/Future Battlespace,* p. viii.

91. Ibid., p. 27.

92. Evans, "From Kadesh to Kandahar," p. 140.

8

Conclusion: Managing Strategic Victory

"Victory in war does not depend entirely on numbers or courage; only skill and discipline will ensure it."

—*Flavius Vegetius,* A.D. *378*

What specific steps can states take to manage better the complexities of winning war and achieving strategic victory in the current international security setting? Indeed, "determining when [and how] to end a war is one of the greatest challenges that soldiers and statesmen face."[1] Because "each war produces widely held lessons concerning how the next war should be avoided or fought" and "the disorderly nature of the [war] ending process may create the strains on which future conflicts are based," meaningful "victory often goes to the side that learns—thus, learns to change—fastest."[2] This concluding chapter endeavors to accelerate this learning process by providing recommendations conducive to achieving stable and secure postwar strategic victory.

The policy advice noted within this study (linking directly to the discussion in Chapter 6 of when strategic victory is most attainable) includes five clusters of suggestions: rethink the entrance into and the exit from war, limit war involvement, integrate the means of pursuing victory, redirect postwar security resources, and guide the enemy's postwar actions. Figure 8.1 summarizes this policy advice. Though admittedly quite tentative and general, these recommendations provide at least some coherent direction for improving postwar success.

Figure 8.1 Victory Management Prescriptions

Rethink Entrance into and Exit from War
Intervene only in cases with large payoff prospects
Develop proper exit strategy before intervention

Limit War Involvement
Constrain war ends
Constrain war means

Integrate Means of Pursuing Victory
Stress human-intensive more than technology-intensive strategies
Assimilate military and political strategies

Redirect Postwar Security Resources
Reorient intelligence thrust
Refocus defense expenditures

Guide Enemy's Postwar Actions
Instill restraint in foes
Channel favorably locally determined changes

Rethink Entrance into and Exit from War

Intervene Only in Cases with Large Payoff Prospects

Perhaps the broadest implication of this study is that states should carefully rethink—taking into account both moral and pragmatic concerns—the circumstances justifying foreign military intervention within the current international setting. As a part of this calculation, taking into account domestic political reactions, national leaders should evaluate carefully the probable short-term payoffs associated with war-winning strategies versus the probable long-term payoffs associated with peace-winning strategies. This focus could help prepare a state contemplating war initiation for postwar management by giving it a clearer idea of the probability of accomplishing its absolutely minimal postwar bottom line, forcing its leadership to consider outcomes to differentiate—in a manner quite uncommon during warfare—between what it needs and what it wants.

Many current opportunities for foreign military intervention exhibit a quite low probability and magnitude of positive postwar payoffs. Warfare can certainly still serve vital purposes in today's world, but an international coercive effort needs a compelling and powerful impetus to be sound, equipped with an understanding that defeated societies' willingness and ability to undertake a positive postwar transition may be very much in doubt. Peripheral, transitory, or uncertain national interests, desires simply to signal dominance or superiority, or misguided assumptions about aspirations of the enemy state's people can all degrade the viability of the rationale for war.

As a result, states should limit war initiation to those cases where initiating military intervention is absolutely vital to achieve core objectives and where the probability, size, and centrality of the payoff are really worth the effort. Given the progressive nature of the elements of strategic victory, there specifically needs to be a high probability of medium-term transformation and rehabilitation of the target. Such careful consideration of postwar payoffs—including understanding in advance the limitations on what military victory today's wars can achieve—would almost certainly prevent some of them from being initiated, and at least change the timing and scope of others, possibly saving lives in the process. It is decidedly foolish to ignite violent global confrontations based on blindly optimistic bravado about attaining one's objectives rather than sober recognition of the sometimes insuperable obstacles that lie ahead.

The United States especially needs to resist always succumbing to the temptation to use its superior military power to intervene in real and perceived sources of instability around the world. In the aftermath of military success in one part of the world, US security policymakers need to avoid overestimating the payoff of superior military capabilities in other regions and to "continue to pursue the strategies that brought them victory in the utterly new and inappropriate circumstances that the victory has created."[3] Regardless of one's raw power advantage, rigorous and dispassionate assessments of postwar payoffs prior to military intervention seem essential, with decisionmakers carefully paying attention to the content of these assessments, because obstacles to strategic victory cannot be overcome by superior military capabilities. The best way for the US government to determine whether its citizens (including its soldiers) are willing to incur the costs to achieve these postwar payoffs is "by presenting them with a clear strategy for victory and a full understanding of the sacrifices required."[4]

Develop Proper Exit Strategy Before Intervention

In cases where a war involves one's troops being present on enemy soil, it has become fashionable to demand a linkage between the declaration of victory and the articulation of a specific and rapid exit strategy. In reality, however, in the aftermath of today's wars the persistence of insurgency activity and disruptive violence makes any thoughts of quick exit—or of precise and definitive advance notice of the timing of one's exit—troublesome. As Richard Holbrooke remarks, "Let us therefore talk no longer of exit strategies or firm timetables" but rather demonstrate commitment to stay "as long as necessary, until we have finished the job."[5] Moreover, a victor's open pronouncements about exit timing can sometimes lead to protraction of conflict, as clever foes seek to highlight the victor's inability to keep its word; Western states in particular often underestimate the extent to which enemies can detect and exploit transitions of authority where coordination is far from perfect. In light of these pitfalls, a poorly conceived or articulated exit strategy can easily turn military success into strategic failure.

Often external pressure causes an occupying state to announce or implement a postwar exit strategy long before it is warranted. Outside of domestic public opinion pressures, this "quick fix" is in part due "to the budgetary drain of complex contingency operations on programmed operations and maintenance" and to "the impact of multiple deployments, many of them both unpredicted and indeterminate in length, on service people and their families...[degrading] morale and retention."[6] Inherent in this premature exit strategy are often quite abbreviated notions of mission success, such as simply the removal of a particular leader from power. The impact of departure too soon can be deadly. As one military scholar writes, "The intervening force will go home sometime. If it leaves right after the end of hostilities, then the conflict will surely re-ignite. The initial military occupation should remain in place long enough to demobilize the combatants and to prevent establishment of a *de facto* national government."[7] During "protracted, asymmetric, ambiguous, and complex conflicts," a narrow-minded emphasis on a speedy exit from the combat zone seems doomed to failure, as the ability "to sustain efforts over many months and years is particularly crucial in these strategic battlespaces since they are the ones where rapid, decisive operations will seldom, if ever, lead to strategic victory."[8]

Furthermore, the optimal timing for the departure of the victor's occupying forces may occur significantly prior to the optimal timing for local security forces to provide order or for local citizens to take over the reigns of government: "as conditions change, the overall security situation no longer warrants the large presence of military forces prepared to engage in high-intensity combat with belligerents;

this, however, often occurs well before legitimate indigenous security institutions are organized, trained, and equipped to assume local security responsibilities."[9] If the victor exits too soon, then the result can "yield an incomplete victory and leave in place a foe that is weakened but unchastened"; if, however, the victor exits too late, then the result can "sap domestic and international support for military action while strengthening the adversary's resolve."[10] In the aftermath of the 2003 Iraq War, for example, most analysts—including those within the Bush administration—agree that "the surest way to snatch defeat from the jaws of an overwhelming military victory would be to overstay our welcome in Iraq."[11]Even so, it is certainly difficult to determine exactly what level of postwar objective fulfillment, Iraqi stability, local readiness for governance and security provision, and anti-American sentiment should trigger the exit of the troops.

Given the importance of proper disentangling from the arena of turmoil for not only military but also diplomatic and political ends, it is vital to establish early on a well-conceived exit strategy affecting the timing of military disengagement, but not allowing exit operations to become transparent or to be fully specified until stipulated victory conditions are achieved. Such a well-formulated exit strategy needs to have the flexibility to change within certain bounds in response to fluctuating war conditions, but not in a public setting where loss of face and a reputation for inconsistency can easily result. Thus the military victor in a war needs to maintain a combination of credibility (1) with its own domestic public that it will avoid an endless and costly quagmire and undertake a relatively swift exit, and (2) with its enemy that it has the resolve and capabilities to stay as long as it takes to achieve strategic victory. Maintaining credibility with these two audiences is a daunting, nearly zero-sum proposition, and it requires exceedingly delicate diplomacy and communication control to work properly.

Limit War Involvement

Constrain War Ends

A basic obstacle to achieving strategic victory lies in the expansive and largely unbounded statements about a conflict's overarching motives and purposes. Powerful states engaged in warfare may lose focus on what precisely they are trying to achieve. Having sharply delineated outcomes in warfare seems like a no-brainer but has frequently been missing in many post–Cold War international conflicts.

It is therefore important that war aims be explicitly constrained. Specifically, what is preferable is "limiting objectives and choosing options that signal a desire to negotiate and leave an opponent an honorable way out to help to stabilize war termination."[12] For overall effectiveness, separating which postwar stability objectives require the presence of the victor's military forces and which do not would be useful.[13] Limiting goals can also sometimes make their accomplishment more tangible and thus more detectable. Of course, limiting war aims "so minimally that it will be easy to meet them, declare victory, and go home" makes strategic victory hollow.[14]

Constraining the aims of warfare can be a daunting task. For example, "in wars that cannot be decided quickly because of the relatively balanced capabilities of the contenders...there is apparent from historical examples a very strong tendency on the part of the belligerents to vilify their adversaries in order to mobilize the mass public commitment of a moral crusade for the war effort."[15] The more a war initiator works up its domestic public into frenzy about a crusade against a fundamentally evil threat, the less willing the citizenry will be to accept anything other than total decisive victory.[16] Thus it is a real challenge to limit successfully one's aims in warfare while simultaneously successfully convincing one's domestic public, allies, and international onlookers that the war is one of necessity and that winning it is vital.

Perhaps the biggest danger threatening the limitation of war aims in pursuing strategic victory is the oft-cited problem of "mission creep," in which the original war aims keep expanding as time passes: "The root of mission creep is the intersection of imprecise political guidance with the military's traditional 'can do' attitude. The military officer, moreover, cannot stand inaction, especially when he or she sees a potential risk for the force. In the absence of action by other interagency players, we act."[17] At the same time states avoid mission creep during warfare, it is vital that leaders not feel straightjacketed in terms of their ability to make slight adjustments to objectives in response to changing circumstances.

Constrain War Means

The vices associated with unbounded overarching motives and purposes surrounding a conflict are parallel to the vices associated with unbounded strategy and tactics used during and after a war. For both moral and pragmatic reasons, the winner in battle needs to impose clear constraints on coercive techniques used to accomplish strategic victory, especially the postwar need to "recast its security assistance programs...in ways that do not abuse human rights."[18] These limitations are directly intertwined with the war winner's attempt to achieve the diplomatic respect element of strategic victory.

The biggest danger resulting from unconstrained strategy and tactics is stooping to the level of one's most unscrupulous opponents. Once a victor begins to engage in postwar excesses in the defeated society, such as torture or mistreatment of prisoners or citizens, destruction or looting of culturally important symbols, use of inhumane or unsanctioned weapons, or indiscriminate killing or injuring of innocent bystanders, it loses not only the moral high ground in the conflict but also internal and external legitimacy for any desired political, economic, or social changes. A temptation exists to mimic the tactics of one's enemies: "War being among the most imitative of all human activities, the very process of combating low-intensity conflict will cause both sides to become alike, unless it can be brought to a quick end."[19] The victor bears all the responsibility here, for a defeated country "plagued by internally or externally imposed conflict often lacks the mechanisms or institutions to provide for its own security, to uphold the rule of law, or to address human rights abuses."[20] Morally inexcusable excesses, even if unintentional or security-motivated, can—especially given the global spread of democratic values—cause withdrawal of international support for postwar efforts and, ultimately, mission failure.

If a defeated enemy senses incoherence in postwar operations, with evident chaos or hypocrisy, then the chances for strategic victory vanish. Trust is essential for a smooth postwar transition, and no apology by the perpetrators of excesses will be sufficient to eradicate the sense of betrayal. Moreover, outside sympathizers—particularly those linked to particular ethnic or religious groups within the defeated society—will underscore the unworthiness of the victor's behavior, and violent disruptive elements will flourish under these propitious conditions.

To enforce the constraints on strategy and tactics in the aftermath of war, the victor should implement tight command-and-control systems that minimize the chances of unwarranted actions by those fighting (including friendly fire, mistreatment of war prisoners, and unintended destruction of enemy targets). This would involve clear and centralized responsibility for postwar operations, maximizing the accountability for any problems that emerge. The victor should also invite international observers in to verify that constraints on actions are being followed. Any violations—especially by the victor's occupying armed forces—need to be quickly and openly punished. Essential to this process is consistent and transparent monitoring, as well as resistance by the victor to overestimating a war outcome's external legitimacy and the malleability of domestic and international support.

Integrate Means of Pursuing Victory

Stress Human-Intensive More Than Technology-Intensive Strategies

To achieve strategic victory, it also seems prudent for the military to rely more heavily on the human element than on high-tech warfare. Necessitating trained personnel for both security and humanitarian purposes, "manpower skills, not technology, are the key" to force transformation in the aftermath of war.[21]

> It is not enough to consider simply how to pound the enemy into submission with stand-off forces.... Control cannot be achieved by machines, still less by bombs. Only human beings interacting with human beings can achieve it. The only hope for success in the extension of politics that is war is to restore the human element to the transformation equation.[22]

Because "technology, as weaponry or as equipment in support of weaponry, does not determine the outbreak, course, and outcome of conflicts," victors need to avoid overestimating the role of technology in solving the problems of war termination.[23] Of course, a human emphasis means that their training needs to be extensive, including expertise on integrating the use of technology, in operating effectively during and after warfare.

This more labor-intensive approach may be more costly in the short run than capital-intensive technological fixes, but in the long run it has the potential to yield more sustained postwar benefits because working one-on-one with the people within the vanquished state can engender understanding and trust of what the victor is trying to accomplish and thus increases the chances for stable positive outcomes. Moreover, the human element appears to be even more important for strategic victory than for military victory because of the cultural sensitivity necessitated. In this conception, precision-trained people would be more essential than precision-guided munitions.

Decisive human control of war-winning and peace-winning technologies seems especially important. During warfare, even the most sophisticated smart bombs can hit the wrong target if not properly monitored and guided by human operatives, and the potential for robots or unmanned mechanized vehicles running amok is well documented. Similarly, during peace operations in the aftermath of warfare, technology designed to deter disruptive violence can easily malfunction or backfire.

This human-intensive approach appears to be most essential after a war in which communication between opposing sides, or between each government and its people, has become degraded or distorted. When dealing with the rise of covert, dispersed, and decentralized insurgency threats or the spread of transnational terrorism, the skill, intelligence, and training of human soldiers becomes crucial because the communication gap between the victor and the vanquished can be even wider than when dealing with traditional state-to-state confrontations.

Assimilate Military and Political Strategies

In the aftermath of warfare, it is increasingly important for states to integrate their military and political strategies rather than keeping the two quite separate and disconnected. This lesson is not a recent one: for example, "Lieutenant General Sir Gerald Templer, Britain's high commissioner and director of operations during the Malayan insurgency in the 1950s, observed that the political and military sides of counterinsurgency must be 'completely and utterly interrelated.'"[24] Nonetheless, the changing nature of modern warfare and contemporary international threat make a fresh outlook essential in this regard: "Military operations are now completely integrated with political, diplomatic, economic and cultural activities. Strategy is no longer simply a matter of defense. The problem is now, more than ever, to conceive military operations in a political framework."[25] Careful monitoring is vital to ensure that military coercion and political diplomacy are mutually reinforcing rather than mutually undercutting.

The ongoing challenge of transnational terrorism vividly illustrates this need to improve the postwar relationship between military and political initiatives. Any sound counterterrorist strategy would require absolutely tight political-military coordination:

> Effective action against terrorism depends on a unique synergy of military and non-military measures—the latter including diplomatic, humanitarian, development, peace-building, and law enforcement efforts. The synergy of the military and non-military aspects of response is that the latter serve to keep threat generation down to a level that military efforts can manage. In turn, military efforts serve to guarantee non-military measures and help maintain the conditions in which they might hope to succeed.[26]

The recent focus in the war on terrorism on military rather than non-military measures highlights critical deficiencies in this regard.

As part of this political-military integration, improved coordination between military and civilian efforts is essential, with a carefully defined and limited role for military personnel and increased unity in the civil-military thrust. To accomplish this improved coordination, military personnel need to broaden their orientation toward victory:

> We need to train our officers and leaders for a different kind of mission. We do not need people who are only good at killing and breaking; we need people that have the breadth of education, experience, and intellect to take on all the rest of these missions that they are going to be saddled with when the shooting stops or subsides....
>
> Our military men and women should never be put on a battlefield without a strategic plan, not only for fighting—our generals take care of that—but also for the aftermath and winning that war.[27]

Rather than viewing participation in politically charged postwar mop-up operations as peripheral to their mission and inconsistent with their skills, military personnel—through retraining—need to see this activity as just as integral to victory as fighting to win on the battlefield. One possible option in this regard would be to have multiple types of security forces available for postwar management, allowing for the availability of specialized police forces—without the stigma of undertaking second-rate activities—for mop-up operations.

As a component of this effort, better coordination needs to exist between the competing pressures of security and legitimacy in the aftermath of warfare. In addressing this issue, a victor needs to avoid overestimating the flexibility of the armed forces to pursue simultaneously both stability and justice. Within defeated states experiencing postwar turmoil, reconciling the protection of freedom and open society with the need to restrict violence is a major challenge, and new guidelines are essential to soldiers on the ground. Without such guidelines, neither mission thrust stands much of a chance of successful postwar completion.

Redirect Postwar Security Resources

Reorient Intelligence Thrust

Currently political-military intelligence during the latter stages of a war and its aftermath focuses primarily on threat identification rather than on other impediments to strategic victory, such as obstacles to political self-determination, economic reconstruction, or social justice within vanquished states. To attain strategic victory, the intelligence thrust should place more emphasis on the peace-winning phase, determining "the necessary and sufficient conditions that must exist for the conflict to terminate and the post-conflict efforts to succeed."[28] The requirements for strategic victory thus ought to influence more the intelligence focus, with a military victor specifically needing sound intelligence on obstacles to postwar stability.

Achieving strategic victory necessitates a transformed intelligence strategy, well beyond what has become entrenched after fifty years of the Cold War. Social, cultural, ethnic, religious, and political intelligence have become vastly more important and thus deserve considerably more attention. However, information gathering in these areas is much more difficult than traditional military intelligence, which focuses more simply on hardware and military unit size, composition, and performance. Such expanded intelligence could promote strategic victory conditions by increasing the situational awareness of those managing postwar threats.

In particular, because psychological operations have become so important in the aftermath of war to achieve strategic victory, there needs to be more intelligence support for this effort. For example, in order for psychological operations to have a significant effect on discouraging enemy troops from continuing to fight during a war, or on discouraging insurgents from continuing to engage in violence after a war, intelligence is needed to identify the specific leverage points that would be most effective for these purposes. During the 2001–2002 war on terrorism in Afghanistan, specialists in psychological operations, "armed with mobile broadcast stations, leaflets and loudspeakers," sought "to demoralize and strike fear in the Taliban while bucking up refugees and convincing Afghans that Osama bin Laden, not the United States, is their enemy."[29] During the 2003 Iraq War, "American cyber-warfare experts…made an e-mail assault against Iraq's political, military and economic leadership, urging them to break with the regime"; sent messages "to private cell phone numbers of specially selected officials"; and dropped more than eight million leaflets "warning Iraqi anti-aircraft missile operators that their bunkers will be destroyed if they track or fire at allied warplanes."[30] For success, such efforts obviously depend on highly accurate intelligence.

This need to reorient the postwar intelligence thrust is directly aimed at helping to attain the information control element of strategic victory. To accomplish this reorientation, a victor needs to avoid any tendency to overestimate its intelligence ability to gather accurate information about its adversary. Improved "strategic assessment represents a crucial element in a state's ability to adapt strategy to the changing wartime situation, which in turn plays a critical role in determining the outcome and costs of wars."[31] Without significantly transformed monitoring and assessment capabilities, the best-laid war termination plans can fall flat.

Refocus Defense Expenditures

Given the limits of military superiority alone to guarantee strategic victory, a substantial shift in defense expenditures is warranted in many Western states. In such a context, funding advanced war-fighting technologies that provide superior battlefield capabilities may not be as wise as funding expenditures—such as for training soldiers to assist the defeated state with needed political, economic, and social changes—that secure crucial postwar payoffs from military victory.

The composition of the defense program needs to change substantially, with greater resources allocated to special operations, counterinsurgency and proinsurgency, counterproliferation, linguists, information operations, and irregular warfare. The emphasis on military superiority and advanced war-fighting capabilities is likely to decline as irregular warfare becomes more pervasive, but—for strategic victory—policymakers in militarily victorious states cannot afford to wait for such an evolutionary development. Defense expenditures need alteration long before tangible changes in the nature of warfare force the issue.

Shifting defense expenditures for strategic victory will not be easy. First, many powerful vested interests support traditional technology-intensive investments. Second, differences of opinion within the security bureaucracy about how to define and achieve strategic victory inhibit these shifts. Third, it is much harder to demonstrate "bang-for-the-buck" for expenditures dealing with the peace-winning phase of victory than with the war-winning phase, and choosing which peace-winning option to fund will also be difficult. Fourth, as a result, public support for such a transition would—at least initially—be decidedly mixed. To overcome these roadblocks, institutional reforms conducive to the emergence of support for required expenditure shifts seem essential. Included among these reforms would be the kind of restructuring that would overcome the prevalent overconfidence among victors and would promote challenges to status quo assumptions in order to facilitate discovery of alternative optimal security resource allocation arrangements. Changes in the incentive structure, including special rewards for innovative ideas and for questioning ongoing expenditure patterns, would seem necessary to support these institutional reforms.

For the United States, there is considerable ongoing debate within the Pentagon about how to translate strategy into force structure, programs, and systems. Although the United States may always require military superiority in conventional warfare, reflected by its "32 percent real increase in defense expenditure" since 1998, it clearly needs better means of bringing the kind of violent international conflict it chooses to enter to a rapid, uncontested conclusion.[32] Like other Western states, it is still learning how to allocate resources that may not traditionally fall under a typical Defense Department mandate but may be as essential as troops and tanks to strategic victory.

Guide Enemy's Postwar Actions

Instill Restraint in Foes

After a war, instilling stabilizing restraint in foes seems important for strategic victory. Yet restraining global violence effectively seems elusive in the current anarchic security environment. This difficulty is perhaps best illustrated by the reality that "both Osama bin Laden and the Taliban could have predicted that the United States would respond to their attacks [on September 11, 2001], yet they acted anyway."[33]

Both positive and negative incentives (carrots and sticks) warrant application in this regard. For positive incentives, the rewards and benefits—including military, economic, and political assistance—granted to former adversaries need to be maximized if their postwar behavior is cooperative and compliant. To achieve long-term stability, this assistance should be augmented by the establishment of credible justice and reconciliation mechanisms within the vanquished state. The danger to be avoided is having the victor get trapped in long-term postwar assistance commitments that yield few, if any, tangible improvements in the vanquished state. For negative incentives, enhancing the vanquished state's fear of the victor is the key to a stable outcome. This effort is directly aimed at achieving the military deterrence element of strategic victory, preventing aggressive disruptive behavior from upsetting the status quo. Both capability and will are involved here—the victor needs to possess a sizable well-equipped military force and communicate sustained resolve, with the victor possessing at least as great resolve as the target. To cope with the challenge, "traditional concepts of deterrence and defense need to be supplemented by new doctrines of security preëmption, security prevention, and expeditionary warfare"; for example, "the new concept of US warfighting and deterrence...rests on a foundation of global and rapidly-deployable reconnaissance, attack, and defense capabilities," including "command, control, and communication capabilities which depend heavily on America's unique advantage in space-based and airborne assets."[34]

A key obstacle to instilling restraint in one's enemies after victory is the often unconvincing and nearly invisible nature of meaningful triumph in modern warfare. Considering the positive incentives, for a convincing display of granting assistance and instilling justice mechanisms, the war outcome must demonstrate to the people of the defeated society and to the outside world that the situation after the war has improved substantially from what it was prior to the conflict. Turning to the negative incentives, for a compelling display of both the will to use force and the size and skill of the military instruments involved, the victor must avoid the danger of conveying an image of weakness through too much restraint while at the same time be humane and discriminating enough so as not to inflame the local population. Particularly when a history of distrust, misunderstanding, or enmity exists between the two sides of a war, the punishment for unruly parties who attempt to take advantage of any perceived leniency should be swift and severe.

To attain this deterrent end, optimistic delusions about the benefits of military superiority need to be abandoned. The widespread underlying assumption that small limited triumphs in one part of the world—requiring relatively little expenditure or sacrifice compared to full-scale, all-out war—will cause other potentially unruly states to become more restrained in their belligerent international action makes little sense. One clear limitation of modern victory is that due to the anarchic global security environment, it generally lacks transparent transitivity as a global warning to those who would disrupt the status quo. In the aftermath of war, "military threats and bluster" rarely "oust defiant dictators" in other states.[35]

Favorably Channel Locally Determined Outcomes

Fostering postwar political, economic, and social improvements in a defeated state initially sounds universally beneficial. Yet a central dilemma lurks in the background: a victor focusing on these noble goals in a vanquished state renounces its right to determine the exact outcomes and instead must trust that the locals assuming power in the defeated state will *voluntarily* choose to follow its desires. This dilemma is embedded in the quest to achieve the political self-determination, economic reconstruction, and social justice elements of strategic victory.

As a result of this dilemma, victors in recent wars often have attempted to win over the "hearts and minds" of the vanquished people in order to increase the probability that favorable political, economic, and social outcomes will emerge from the defeated population's own postwar choices.[36] This emphasis makes a lot of sense and is certainly more promising than simply trying to kill all the disruptive insurgents in a vanquished society.[37] However, this delicate task, reflecting the target's susceptibility to postwar influence, is very difficult to accomplish. For example, the US government in the 2003 Iraq War has appeared to be "trapped by its own rhetoric" in this regard: "On the one hand, the president has repeatedly declared his commitment to democracy and to allowing the Iraqi people to govern themselves," but "on the other hand, others in the administration have said that they will not allow an Islamic government similar to that in Iran come to power."[38]

The challenge of favorably channeling locally determined postwar outcomes is partially a perceptual one. Though incorporating local populations into postwar governance structures can make citizens in the defeated state "more confident that they will indeed control their own futures," such inclusion can also cause the new government "to appear as a lackey of the occupying power."[39] For a victor to persuade not only local administrators that their decisions should be compatible with its desires but also internal and external onlookers that these decisions are completely isolated from its influence is a truly daunting proposition.

In order to overcome these roadblocks, victors must be willing to invest significant resource allocation—in terms of time, money, and people—for administration and policing, business venture start-ups, and civil society promotion within the defeated society. For the victor to be willing to allocate these resources, it cannot overestimate the ease of transferring power to local authorities and of transferring its social values to the defeated society. The best way for local leaders to see for themselves the virtues of the political, economic, and social structures desired by the victor is for the resources to be available that increase the chances that the initial small steps in this direction within the vanquished state will prove visibly successful. This cannot be a cheap rush job, as progress will inevitably be slow and costly.

Concluding Thoughts

Ideally, as civilization progresses, there would be no need to fight wars as the means to resolve international disputes. However, assuming continued violent international conflicts to cope with persistent security threats, those participating need to manage victory better to achieve both fulfillment of their own political aims and stability in the international system as a whole. Despite centuries of interstate bloodshed, lessons about dealing with the aftermath of war have progressed at a snail's pace, with cumulative learning about how to reap the postwar payoffs from victory still in its infancy.

This study has highlighted real challenges to achieving decisive strategic victory in warfare. Some of the obstacles have psychological roots in human nature, and others have institutional roots in the nature of security bureaucracy; regardless of the origins, however, these pervasive and persistent roadblocks make effective postwar management extremely difficult. The modern informational, military, political, economic, social, and diplomatic elements of strategic victory may be more enlightened than those associated with premodern warfare, but the chances of attaining them are low against the stubborn, unruly threats faced in today's world. In particular, dramatic visible short-run positive postwar changes in these foes—in the direction of political self-determination, economic reconstruction, and social justice—appear unlikely. Moreover, universal approval of strategic victory aims appears remote due to the differing interpretive lenses in today's global security environment. However, even though modern strategic victory entails large sacrifices and small and transitory victory payoffs, "if victory is often costly, defeat is always worse."[40]

In light of these challenges, a fatalistic tendency exists today among many onlookers to declare all wars as futile.[41] In this view, achieving military victory with lasting postwar payoffs would be utterly impossible in the current international security setting. Underlying this belief is the assumption that winning militarily on the battlefield does not work anymore as a means to achieve desired ends. Some analysts believe, for example, that military victory is "the least important factor" in winning against terrorism, because whereas "military power can protect and deter and punish," it "cannot alter ideological convictions."[42] The resulting prescription would be not to fine-tune management of strategic victory but rather to strive for the elimination of war itself.

Even among observers who do not see war as futile, a belief persists among some that the proportion of wars ending in victory ought to be decreased.[43] Such analysts assume that it is far preferable to have wars end through negotiated settlements than through the superior military force of one side crushing the other, followed by a one-sided imposition of terms by the victor on the vanquished. Supporting this line of reasoning is the argument that sustained peace is less likely after a decisive victory than after a simple cessation of hostilities—due to "the chastening such an experience makes possible"—with the underlying premise that such indecisive outcomes possess the greatest potential for mutual understanding and respect among contending parties.[44] This orientation looks beyond military victory for arrangements that would more successfully terminate international hostilities by incorporating the preferences and interests of all parties involved in the conflict. Underlying this approach is a certain degree of moral relativism, assuming that all sides in a war can justify their positions and deserve a say in the outcome, and that most wars in today's world are not classic black-and-white "good-versus-evil" confrontations.

Still others believe that because of the challenges outlined in the contemporary international security environment, aiming for strategic victory may be "out of reach" for twenty-first-century conflicts.[45] Such an approach argues that if a country faces a genuine imminent external threat, it might make sense for it to undertake foreign military intervention even if the chances for strategic victory are extremely low and the probability of resulting regional chaos are extremely high. Viewed from this perspective, strategic victory is today simply an impossible dream.

In contrast to these three avowedly anti-victory perspectives, this book accepts that—as long as wars are fought—circumstances exist where strategic victory is both desirable and feasible. Although achieving strategic victory is likely to be increasingly elusive, and "strategic victory is almost always more costly than simple military victory," pursuing this lofty goal will remain important in the future.[46] Defense policymakers will need to prioritize achieving strategic victory over other foreign security goals, or else international disruptions will simply reemerge time after time following military victories. Being satisfied with less than such triumph is likely to lead to frustrated aims and—ultimately—global insecurity: "alternatives to decisive victory are far less stable," and "the prospects for peace are dimmer when war ends in a military draw than when one side wins a decisive victory," illustrated by the instability following many recent wars with indeterminate outcomes.[47]

So military victory in war can indeed achieve progressive postwar objectives, but to accomplish them security policymakers and military commanders need a much more probing understanding than they have today about the complexities surrounding strategic victory. By considering the multifaceted interconnected elements of victory, states can improve their coordination of strategies to achieve them. By comprehending the differences between modern limited-war victory and premodern total victory, states can channel their postwar thrust to the attainment of constrained rehabilitative aims. By attending thoughtfully to the moral dilemmas surrounding victory, states can more carefully weigh the tradeoffs between principled action that generates long-term legitimacy and trust, and expedient action that creates short-term efficiency and effectiveness. By recognizing the common overoptimistic fallacies surrounding victory, states can commence the war termination process with a much more realistic plan about what problems to expect and how to deal with them. By reflecting on the conditions most conducive to strategic victory, states can foster a security environment where reaping postwar payoffs is realistically possible. By investigating the special challenges associated with unconventional warfare, states can tune their strategies better to cope with emerging threats that defy standard operating procedures. By realizing the drawbacks of restrained Western states confronting ruthless threats in a world devoid of universal enforceable rules of behavior, states can figure out new ways to succeed in this disadvantageous playing field. Finally, by being open to incorporating some different modes for managing war termination, states can more flexibly and coherently address and resolve whatever problems they face in assuring positive stable conflict outcomes.

A key overarching question is whether grand strategy can shift to accommodate the realistic limitations of modern military victory, while at the same time avoiding the pitfalls of enormous expectations. Although a full response to this question is beyond the purview of this volume, a possible first step involves the reframing of postwar objectives. For example, the United States could state the aims of military interventions as explicitly tied to the simple, old-school military goals that can easily be recognized and appreciated by everyone—voters, foreign observers, and domestic political opponents alike. Specifically, it is possible to suggest that policymakers should publicly emulate the metrics of premodern total war to improve the chances of short-term success, while actually pursuing the more subtle metrics of modern strategic victory, to make the positive outcome more enduring.[48] In this approach, pursuing the more subtle strategic victory ends, such as democracy, economic development, social justice, and diplomatic respect, would remain as underlying goals, but the government would choose not to publicize them as primary objectives. Then, when and if the victor achieved these intangible but critical objectives, they would appear as icing on the cake.

In the end, managing victory poses a major challenge for today's global leaders. Truly great ones will understand and flexibly and creatively pursue the appropriate meanings of strategic victory, taking into account both what is desirable and what is feasible, across a wide and varied range of international predicaments. The proposed policy recommendations, along with the guidelines about conditions conducive to strategic victory, certainly can help, but wise situational judgment is always critical. Armed with this study's insights, then, perhaps leaders mired in circumstances warranting warfare can find better ways to comprehend and cope with the obligations and opportunities surrounding victory.

Notes

1. Thomas G. Mahnken, "A Squandered Opportunity? The Decision to End the Gulf War," in Andrew J. Bacevich and Ephraim Inbar, eds., *The Gulf War of 1991 Reconsidered* (Portland, OR: Frank Cass, 2003), p. 121.

2. Stuart Albert and Edward C. Luck, eds., *On the Endings of Wars* (Port Washington, NY: Kennikat Press, 1980), p. 5; and Martin C. Libicki, *Illuminating Tomorrow's War* (Washington, DC: National Defense University Institute for National Strategic Studies, McNair Paper #61, 1999), p. 66.

3. James Kurth, "The American Way of Victory," *National Interest,* Summer 2000, http://www.ciaonet.org/olj/ni/ni_00kuj01.html.

4. Andrew F. Krepinevich Jr., "How to Win in Iraq," *Foreign Affairs* 84 (September/October 2005), p. 104.

5. Richard Holbrooke, "Rebuilding Nations," *Washington Post,* April 1, 2002, p. A15.

6. James M. Castle and Alfred C. Faber Jr., *Anarchy in the Streets: Restoring Public Security in Complex Contingencies* (Carlisle Barracks, PA: US Army War College Strategy Research Project, 1998), pp. 2–3.

7. Manfred K. Rotermund, *The Fog of Peace: Finding the End-State of Hostilities* (Carlisle Barracks, PA: US Army War College Strategic Studies Institute, 1999), p. 55.

8. Steven Metz and Raymond A. Millen, *Future War/Future Battlespace: The Strategic Role of American Landpower* (Carlisle Barracks, PA: US Army War College Strategic Studies Institute, 2003), p. 27.

9. Center for Strategic and International Studies and Association of the United States Army, *Play to Win: Final Report of the Bi-Partisan Commission on Post-Conflict Reconstruction* (Washington, DC: Center for Strategic and International Studies and Association of the United States Army, 2003), p. 13.

10. Mahnken, "A Squandered Opportunity?," p. 143.

11. Christopher Preble, "After Victory: Toward a New Military Posture in the Persian Gulf," *Policy Analysis* 477 (June 10, 2003), p. 11; Conrad C. Crane and W. Andrew Terrill, *Reconstructing Iraq: Insights, Challenges, and Missions for Military Forces in a Post-Conflict Scenario* (Carlisle Barracks, PA: US Army War College Strategic Studies Institute, 2003), p. vi; and Michael Eisenstadt and Eric Mathewson, eds., *US Policy in Post-Saddam Iraq: Lessons from the British Experience* (Washington, DC: Washington Institute for Near East Policy, 2003), p. 70.

12. Gordon A. Craig and Alexander L. George, *Force and Statecraft* (New York: Oxford University Press, 1983), pp. 206–207.

13. David J. Bame, "The Exit Strategy Myth and the End State Reality" (Washington, DC: unpublished US State Department paper, 2001), p. 46.

14. Johanna McGeary, "Did the American Mission Matter?" *Time,* February 19, 1996, p. 36.

15. Clark Claus Abt, "The Termination of General War" (PhD diss., Massachusetts Institute of Technology, 1965), p. 269.

16. Ibid., p. 270.

17. Kevin C. M. Benson and Christopher B. Thrash, "Declaring Victory: Planning Exit Strategies for Peace Operations," *Parameters* (August 1996), pp. 69–80.

18. Anthony H. Cordesman, *The "Post Conflict" Lessons of Iraq and Afghanistan* (Washington, DC: Center for Strategic and International Studies, 2004), p. 10.

19. Martin Van Creveld, *The Transformation of War* (New York: Free Press, 1991), p. 225.

20. Hans Binnendijk and Stuart Johnson, eds., *Transforming for Stabilization and Reconstruction Operations* (Washington, DC: National Defense University Center for Technology and National Security Policy, 2003), p. 89.

21. Cordesman, *The "Post Conflict" Lessons of Iraq and Afghanistan*, p. iv.

22. Frederick W. Kagan, "War and Aftermath," *Policy Review* 120 (August–September 2003), pp. 3–27.

23. Colin S. Gray, *Modern Strategy* (New York: Oxford University Press, 1999), p. 37.

24. Krepinevich, "How to Win in Iraq," p. 98.

25. Loup Francart and Jean-Jacques Patry, "Mastering Violence: An Option for Operational Military Strategy," *Naval War College Review* 53 (Summer 2000), p. 145.

26. Carl Conetta, *Strange Victory: A Critical Appraisal of Operation Enduring Freedom and the Afghanistan War* (Cambridge, MA: Commonwealth Institute Project on Defense Alternatives Research, 2002), p. 33, http://www.comw.org/pda/0201strangevic.pdf.

27. Anthony Zinni, "Forum 2003: Understanding What Victory Is," *Proceedings of the United States Naval Institute* 129 (October 2003), p. 33.

28. William Flavin, "Planning for Conflict Termination and Post-Conflict Success," *Parameters* 32 (Autumn 2003), p. 101. See also Cordesman, *The "Post Conflict" Lessons of Iraq and Afghanistan*, pp. v–vi.

29. Andrea Stone, "Soldiers Deploy on Mental Terrain," *USA Today*, October 3, 2001, p. 7A.

30. Thom Shanker and Eric Schmitt, "Firing Leaflets and Electrons, US Wages Information War," *New York Times*, February 24, 2003, p. A1.

31. Scott Sigmund Gartner, *Strategic Assessment in War* (New Haven, CT: Yale University Press, 1997), p. 163.

32. Carl Conetta, *The Pentagon's New Budget, New Strategy, and New War* (Cambridge, MA: Commonwealth Institute Project on Defense Alternatives Policy, 2002), http://www.comw.org/pda/0206newwar.html.

33. Jack Spencer, *Presidential Authority in the War on Terrorism: Iraq and Beyond* (Washington, DC: Heritage Foundation, 2002), http://www.heritage.org/Research/MiddleEast/bg1600.cfm.

34. Michael Evans, "From Kadesh to Kandahar: Military Theory and the Future of War," *Naval War College Review* 41 (Summer 2003), p. 139; and Conetta, *The Pentagon's New Budget*.

35. Thomas Carothers, "Why Dictators Aren't Dominoes," in Carnegie Endowment for International Peace, *From Victory to Success: Afterwar Policy in Iraq* (New York: Carnegie Endowment for International Peace, 2003), p. 59.

36. Justin Gage, William Martin, Tim Mitchell, and Pat Wingate, "Winning the Peace in Iraq: Confronting America's Informational and Doctrinal Handicaps" (Norfolk, VA: Joint Forces Staff College, September 5, 2003), p. 1.

37. Krepinevich, "How to Win in Iraq," pp. 88–89.

38. Preble, "After Victory," p. 9.

39. David M. Edelstein, "Occupational Hazards: Why Military Occupations Succeed or Fail," *International Security* 29 (Summer 2004), p. 67.

40. Brian Bond, *The Pursuit of Victory: From Napoleon to Saddam Hussein* (New York: Oxford University Press, 1996), p. 199

41. Russell F. Weigley, *The Age of Battles: The Quest for Decisive Warfare from Breitenfeld to Waterloo* (Bloomington: Indiana University Press, 1991), pp. xii–xiii.

42. Richard Gwyn, "Victory in War on Terrorism Can't Be Won by Military," *Toronto Star,* September 15, 2003, p. A8.

43. Lincoln P. Bloomfield, "Why Wars End: CASCON's Answers from History," *Millennium: Journal of International Studies* 26 (1997), pp. 709–726.

44. J. Glenn Gray, "Ending with Honor," in Albert and Luck, *On the Endings of Wars*, pp. 153–154.

45. Comments from an anonymous manuscript reviewer, December 2005.

46. Metz and Millen, *Future War/Future Battlespace*, p. 31.

47. Virginia Page Fortna, *Peace Time: Cease-Fire Agreements and the Durability of Peace* (Princeton, NJ: Princeton University Press, 2004), p. 211; and Monica Duffy Toft, "End of Victory? Civil War Termination in Historical Perspective" (paper presented at the annual national meeting of the International Studies Association, Honolulu, March 2005), pp. 2–3.

48. Comments from an anonymous manuscript reviewer, December 2005.

Selected Bibliography

Abt, Clark Claus. "The Termination of General War." PhD diss., Massachusetts Institute of Technology, 1965.

Albert, Stuart, and Edward C. Luck, eds. *On the Endings of Wars.* Port Washington, NY: Kennikat Press, 1980.

Alger, John I. *The Quest for Victory: The History of the Principles of War.* Westport, CT: Greenwood Press, 1982.

Arreguin-Toft, Ivan. "How the Weak Win Wars: A Theory of Asymmetric Conflict." *International Security* 26 (Summer 2001): 93–128.

Benson, Kevin C. M., and Christopher B. Thrash. "Declaring Victory: Planning Exit Strategies for Peace Operations." *Parameters* (August 1996): 69–80.

Biddle, Stephen D. *Military Power: Explaining Victory and Defeat in Modern Battle.* Princeton, NJ: Princeton University Press, 2004.

———. "Victory Misunderstood: What the Gulf War Tells Us About the Future of Conflict." *International Security* 21 (Fall 1996): 139–179.

Black, Conrad. "What Victory Means." *National Interest* (Winter 2001/2002): 155–164.

Bloomfield, Lincoln P. "Why Wars End: CASCON's Answers from History." *Millennium: Journal of International Studies* 26 (1997): 709–726.

Bond, Brian. *The Pursuit of Victory: From Napoleon to Saddam Hussein.* New York: Oxford University Press, 1996.

Calahan, H. C. *What Makes a War End?* New York: Vanguard Press, 1944.

Carnegie Endowment for International Peace. *From Victory to Success: Afterwar Policy in Iraq.* New York: Carnegie Endowment for International Peace, 2003.

Carroll, Berenice A. "How Wars End: An Analysis of Some Current Hypotheses." *Journal of Peace Research* 6 (December 1969): 295–320.

Castle, James M., and Alfred C. Faber Jr. *Anarchy in the Streets: Restoring Public Security in Complex Contingencies.* Carlisle Barracks, PA: US Army War College Strategy Research Project, 1998.

Center for Strategic and International Studies and Association of the United States Army. *Play to Win: Final Report of the Bi-Partisan Commission on Post-Conflict Reconstruction.* Washington, DC: Center for Strategic and International Studies and Association of the United States Army, 2003.

———. *Building Better Foundations: Security in Post-Conflict Reconstruction.* Washington, DC: Center for Strategic and International Studies and Association of the United States Army, 2002.

Cordesman, Anthony H. *The "Post Conflict" Lessons of Iraq and Afghanistan.* Washington, DC: Center for Strategic and International Studies, 2004.

Crane, Conrad C., and W. Andrew Terrill. *Reconstructing Iraq: Insights, Challenges, and Missions for Military Forces in a Post-Conflict Scenario.* Carlisle Barracks, PA: US Army War College Strategic Studies Institute, 2003.

Diamond, Larry. *Squandered Victory: The American Occupation and the Bungled Effort to Bring Democracy to Iraq.* New York: Henry Holt, 2005.

Edelstein, David M. "Occupational Hazards: Why Military Occupations Succeed or Fail." *International Security* 29 (Summer 2004): 49–91.

Evans, Michael. "From Kadesh to Kandahar: Military Theory and the Future of War." *Naval War College Review* 41 (Summer 2003): 132–150.

Flavin, William. "Planning for Conflict Termination and Post-Conflict Success." *Parameters* 32 (Autumn 2003): 95–112.

Fortna, Virginia Page. *Peace Time: Cease-Fire Agreements and the Durability of Peace.* Princeton, NJ: Princeton University Press, 2004.

Fox, William T. R. "The Causes of Peace and Conditions of War." *Annals of the American Academy of Political and Social Science* 392 (November 1970): 1–13.

Gartner, Scott Sigmund. *Strategic Assessment in War.* New Haven, CT: Yale University Press, 1997.

Gage, Justin, William Martin, Tim Mitchell, and Pat Wingate. "Winning the Peace in Iraq: Confronting America's Informational and Doctrinal Handicaps." Norfolk, VA: Joint Forces Staff College, September 5, 2003.

Goemans, H. E. *War and Punishment: The Causes of War Termination and the First World War.* Princeton, NJ: Princeton University Press, 2000.

Gray, Colin S. *Defining and Achieving Decisive Victory.* Carlisle Barracks, PA: US Army War College Strategic Studies Institute, 2002.

———. *Modern Strategy.* New York: Oxford University Press, 1999.

Gray, Colin S., and Keith Payne. "Victory Is Possible." *Foreign Policy* 39 (Summer 1980): 14–27.

Hanson, Victor Davis. *Why the West Has Won: Carnage and Culture from Solamis to Vietnam.* London: Faber and Faber, 2001.

Hobbs, Richard. *The Myth of Victory: What Is Victory in War?* Boulder, CO: Westview Press, 1979.

Howard, Michael. "When Are Wars Decisive?" *Survival* 41 (Spring 1999): 126–135.

Iasiello, Louis V. "*Jus Post Bellum*: The Moral Responsibilities of Victors in War." *Naval War College Review* 42 (Summer/Autumn 2004): 33–52.

Ikenberry, G. John. *After Victory: Institutions, Strategic Restraint, and the Rebuilding of Order after Major Wars*. Princeton, NJ: Princeton University Press, 2001.

Ikle, Fred Charles. *Every War Must End*. New York: Columbia University Press, 1991.

Johnson, Dominic D. P. *Overconfidence and War*. Cambridge, MA: Harvard University Press, 2004.

Johnson, Dominic D. P., and Dominic Tierney. *Failing to Win: Perceptions of Victory and Defeat in International Politics*. Cambridge, MA: Harvard University Press, forthcoming.

———. "Essence of Victory: Winning and Losing International Crises." *Security Studies* 13 (Winter 2003/2004): 350–381.

Johnson, James Turner. *Morality and Contemporary Warfare*. New Haven, CT: Yale University Press, 1999.

Kagan, Frederick W. "War and Aftermath." *Policy Review* 120 (August–September 2003): 3–27.

Kecskemeti, Paul. *Strategic Surrender: The Politics of Victory and Defeat*. Stanford, CA: Stanford University Press, 1958.

Krepinevich, Andrew F. Jr. "How to Win in Iraq." *Foreign Affairs* 84 (September/October 2005): 87–104.

Kurth, James. "The American Way of Victory." *National Interest* (Summer 2000): 5–16.

Liberman, Peter. *Does Conquest Pay? The Exploitation of Occupied Industrial Societies*. Princeton, NJ: Princeton University Press, 1996.

Liddell Hart, B. H. *Strategy*. New York: Penguin, 1991.

Lustick, Ian S. "The Political Requirements of Victory." *Middle East Policy* 8 (December 2001): 14–17.

Luttwak, Edward N. *On the Meaning of Victory: Essays on Strategy*. New York: Simon and Schuster, 1986.

Mack, Andrew M. "Why Big Nations Lose Small Wars." *World Politics* 27 (January 1975): 175–200.

Mandel, Robert. *Security, Strategy, and the Quest for Bloodless War*. Boulder, CO: Lynne Rienner, 2004.

———. *Armies Without States: The Privatization of Security*. Boulder, CO: Lynne Rienner, 2002.

———. "What Are We Protecting?" *Armed Forces & Society* 22 (Spring 1996): 335–355.

———. "Adversaries' Expectations and Desires About War Termination." In Stephen C. Cimbala, ed., *Strategic War Termination*. Westport, CT: Praeger, 1986.

Maoz, Zeev. *Paradoxes of War*. Boston: Unwin Hyman, 1990.

Merom, Gil. *How Democracies Lose Small Wars: State, Society, and the*

Failures of France in Algeria, Israel in Lebanon, and the United States in Vietnam. New York: Cambridge University Press, 2003.

Noonan, Michael P., and John Hillen. "The New Protracted Conflict: The Promise of Decisive Action." *Orbis* 46 (Spring 2002): 229–246.

O'Connor, Raymond G. "Victory in Modern War." *Journal of Peace Research* 6 (1969): 367–384.

Oren, Nissan. "Prudence in Victory." In Nissan Oren, ed., *Termination of Wars: Processes, Procedures, and Aftermaths.* Jerusalem: Magnes Press, 1982.

Pillar, Paul R. *Negotiating Peace: War Termination as a Bargaining Process.* Princeton, NJ: Princeton University Press, 1983.

Record, Jeffrey. *Dark Victory: America's Second War Against Iraq.* Annapolis, MD: Naval Institute Press, 2004.

———. "Exit Strategy Delusions." *Parameters* 31 (Winter 2001–2002): 21–27.

———. *Hollow Victory.* Washington, DC: Brassey's, 1993.

Reiter, Dan, and Allan C. Stam III. "Democracy, War Initiation, and Victory." *American Political Science Review* 92 (June 1998): 377–389.

Rotermund, Manfred K. *The Fog of Peace: Finding the End-State of Hostilities.* Carlisle Barracks, PA: US Army War College Strategic Studies Institute, 1999.

Schelling, Thomas C. *Arms and Influence.* New Haven, CT: Yale University Press, 1966.

Schroeder, Paul W. "The Risks of Victory." *National Interest* (Winter 2001/2002): 32.

Stam, Allan C. III. *Win, Lose, or Draw: Domestic Politics and the Crucible of War.* Ann Arbor: University of Michigan Press, 1996.

Taylor, A. J. P. *How Wars End.* London: Hamish Hamilton, 1985.

Toffler, Alvin, and Heidi Toffler. *War and Anti-War.* New York: Warner Books, 1993.

Van Creveld, Martin. *The Transformation of War.* New York: Free Press, 1991.

Von Clausewitz, Carl. *On War*. New York: Penguin Books, 1982.

Wang, Kevin, and James Lee Ray. "Beginners and Winners: The Fate of Initiators of Interstate Wars Involving Great Powers Since 1495." *International Studies Quarterly* 38 (March 1994): 139–154.

Weigley, Russell F. *The Age of Battles: The Quest for Decisive Warfare from Breitenfeld to Waterloo.* Bloomington: Indiana University Press, 1991.

Wright, Quincy. "How Hostilities Have Ended: Peace Treaties and Alternatives." *Annals of the American Academy of Political and Social Science* 392 (November 1970): 51–61.

Zinni, Anthony. "Forum 2003: Understanding What Victory Is." *Proceedings of the United States Naval Institute* 129 (October 2003): 32–33.

Index

About the Book

How has the concept of victory evolved as the nature of conflict itself has changed across time, circumstance, and culture? And to what end? Robert Mandel addresses these questions, considering the meanings, misperceptions, and challenges associated with military victory in the context of the nontraditional wars of recent decades.

Without an understanding of precisely what victory means, Mandel argues, the outcome can involve policy paralysis, loss of public support, escalating postwar violence, and ultimately, foreign policy failure. Grappling with the moral complexities of victory in limited war, he discusses issues of security, war crimes, self-determination, reconstruction, and social transformation. He also identifies common fallacies held by victors. Case studies of recent military actions, including the ongoing war in Iraq, inform a discussion of the usefulness of notions of victory in dealing with contemporary challenges.

Robert Mandel is chair and professor of international affairs at Lewis & Clark College. Among his many publications are *Armies Without States* and *Security, Strategy, and the Quest for Bloodless War.*